Inside The Scriptures

Simple Book by Book Bible Commentary
WITH BONUS APPENDICES on topics
every Christian must know!

H.S. Dean

Waldenhouse Publishers, inc.
Walden, Tennessee

Inside the Scriptures

Cover photograph by H. S. Dean
www.insidethescriptures.com
Published by Waldenhouse Publishers, Inc.
100 Clegg Street, Signal Mountain, Tennessee 37377 USA
423-886-2721   www.waldenhouse.com
ISBN: 978-1-947589-54-4
Library of Congress Control Number: 2022942817

Each book of the Bible is briefly introduced, the main events are highlighted, and the content is summarized. Topics are explained with chapter and verse references in the appendices, along with a commentary of every book in the Bible presented in a simple and easy-to-understand format. - Provided by publisher

REL006050   RELIGION / Biblical Commentary / General
REL006000   RELIGION / Biblical Studies / General
REL070000   RELIGION / Christianity / General
P 1

Table of Contents

Appendices Contents

Introduction ~ To Help You Understand God's Word

Nothing contained in this publication could ever replace God's word or the blessings you'll receive when studying the Bible for yourself. There's not a word in the Bible that could be stated any better here or anywhere else. So if you're able, read your Bible as often as you can by setting time aside in your busy schedule to do so. You'll receive blessings beyond measure.

Many of us are so busy with our careers, children and obligations that we struggle to find enough time to read the bible. God's word is so important and crucial to our everyday lives that everyone should have a quick and easy-to-understand book to reach for when a reading opportunity comes available. We all need to know how God wants us to live, and to feel the enrichment that comes from following a path leading us to Jesus and into eternal life. We pray that this book will help fulfill those needs. Naturally, everyone doesn't digest and absorb the same knowledge when reading the Bible, which is one reason there are hundreds of reported church denominations and branches in the U.S. with differences in their beliefs, and a reported thousands worldwide. The hope here is that every believer would pick up some revelation or inspiration from reading this book because it'll remind you of God's unfaltering love.

This publication contains the notes and summaries recorded after studying the King James Version of the Bible for several years. It's a believer's interpretation of God's word using only what is recorded in the Bible. We should never add to or take away from what the Bible says, so every effort has been made to strictly follow exactly what is written. It's non-denominational, open to any Christian and any reader. Read for yourself every chapter and verse referenced in this publication to know exactly what the Bible teaches. Absorbing God's word will always be a good thing.

This Christian writer is not a pastor or trained student of the Bible, but through much prayer for knowledge and understanding, this book strives to explain and interpret God's word so that anyone and everyone might understand both the Old Testament Jewish history and the earthly ministry of Jesus in the New Testament. The target audience for this publication might be anyone who has limited time to study God's word or has trouble interpreting the messages and teachings found in the scriptures. Someone who isn't able to attend church regularly might use this to worship from home, or someone teaching a bible study class might find this useful when drafting their presentations and class agendas.

When you read your Bible, you should pray first that God will open ears and open hearts so that you can fully understand more about our Lord and Savior. So begin your journey here, and learn how God wants us to live, to love, to worship, and most importantly how to believe in Him through faith. We want this document to be a blessing to you, but reading your Bible and praying to God will always bring more knowledge and blessings than anything else ever could.

~ A Brief Overview of the Old Testament ~

The main purpose of the Bible is to bring lost people to salvation, and it begins in the Old Testament. We need to understand each book of the Bible as best we can because we're told in II Timothy 3:16 that all scripture is given by inspiration of God, and is profitable for doctrine, reproof, and correction for instruction in righteousness. Reading the following information and looking at the Timeline will hopefully make your study of the Old Testament a little easier.

The Old Testament was derived from the original Hebrew Bible and was written about and to the Jewish nation. They were God's chosen people, as stated over and over again in the Bible. One of the earliest references to this, in Deuteronomy 7:6, says they were holy people unto the Lord thy God, and that He'd chosen them to be a special people above all people upon the face of the earth. Yes, chosen people above all others. God truly loved and favored them and wanted them to be His teachers, to preach His message and saving grace to all nations.

The Old Testament contains many references to Jesus and foretells of His earthly ministry thousands of years before His first advent. In summary, the first 5 books in the Old Testament are referred to as the Law. Joshua through Esther are the books of history. Job through the Song of Solomon are books of poetry and wisdom. Isaiah through Daniel are books from the major prophets, and Hosea through Malachi are books of minor prophets. Overall there are 39 books in the Old Testament.

To better understand the Bible, know who is speaking or being spoken to when you read each chapter and verse. Know who wrote what you're reading and to whom it was written. Most Bible books were written exclusively to the Jewish nation, while others were written to all people of the world. Knowing that alone will make the content clearer. You will probably find words and terms you're unfamiliar with. Words like Judaism, Passover, Pentecost, blasphemy, abomination, pagan, and others. You'll know them when you see them. Knowing their meaning will deepen your understanding of God's word.

In Genesis you'll read about Adam and Eve in the Garden of Eden. God told them not to eat from a particular tree. You may wonder why God created that tree and it's forbidden fruit if it was off limits to them. Well, very early on in the Bible we see that God gave humans the free will to love Him or not to love Him. The Bible tells us that God was pleased with His creation, and His creation included the tree of good and evil so God was pleased with the tree being there. He put it there for mankind to choose to believe in Him or not to believe in Him. It's the same choice we have today. He could have created us to always love Him and to always follow His laws. But if we want Him in our lives we must choose Him to be there. God knows, just as we know, that being forced to obey and love something or someone isn't love at all. If everyone had been created to love God without exception, then Satan wouldn't be among us. Satan cannot and will not ever love God. He is the enemy of the believer.

In the Old Testament you'll read about Creation, and God's covenant or promise that He made to the people of Israel. The Ten Commandments and His Laws are introduced, along with the great flood, the Judges and Kings who ruled the people, the Ark of the Covenant, and those prophets who told of the coming of Jesus Christ. Unfortunately, from the time God created earth and throughout the thousands of years that Israel struggled to become a blessed nation, the people adopted a sinful nature and disobedience toward Him. In disappointment, God would punish them as told in Ezekiel 35, but then show them His enduring love. At one point He flooded the world to rid Himself of these unrighteous people, saving only eight. Other times He sent armies from neighboring nations to conquer them.

God made a covenant and promise to His chosen people, directly to the man who God would rename Abraham. God said He would exceedingly multiply them, give them their own fertile land, and that kings would come from their midst. The highest of all these kings would be Jesus, who came approximately 2,000 years later. But the Jewish people also had to keep their part of the covenant, which was to follow all of God's Laws and commandments. All through the Old Testament there are references back to this covenant, and the failures of the Jewish nation to comply.

Through the books you'll read where God is referred to as the Father, Creator, Lord, and other Holy names. Jesus is referred to as the Messiah, Christ, Lord, I AM, the Word, Yahweh, Emmanuel, Prince of Peace, Jehovah, Redeemer, Son of Man, the Lamb, and others. The Comforter, Helper, or Spirit (when capitalized) refers to the Holy Ghost or Holy Spirit. They make up the three persons in one Godhead Trinity that Jesus speaks of in Matthew 28:19. You'll see the names of God, Jesus and the Holy Spirit used throughout the bible interchangeably. The Godhead Trinity is explained more in **Appendix F**.

The central figure throughout the Old Testament is Jesus. He may not have been called Jesus each time, but He was there. We learn from John 1:18 that no man hath seen God, so all those times when someone saw and spoke to God it was Jesus who was there, or God in the form of His Son. He is the Creator, the Alpha and Omega, the first and last. It was Jesus leading mankind from the very beginning and it's still Him leading us today. It'll always be about Jesus.

The following Timeline provides the sequences and approximate dates of the many facts and events you'll read about in the Bible, mostly in the Old Testament. There are many more, but several are shown and dated here.

Biblical Timeline with Approximate Dates

4000 BC	Adam and Eve
2320 BC	Noah's Ark and the Great Flood
2100 BC	Abraham travels as directed by God
1945 BC	God made His Covenant with Israel
1850 BC	Joseph sold into slavery
1500 BC	Moses leads exodus out of Egypt
1470 BC	Joshua leads Israelites into Canaan, the Promise Land
1050 BC	King David's rule
1020 BC	Temple built in Jerusalem under King Solomon
980 BC	Israel is divided into 2 kingdoms, Israel and Judah
720 BC	Assyrians conquer Israel and their capital city of Samaria
607 BC	Babylon conquers Jerusalem. Judeans go into exile
586 BC	Temple in Jerusalem is destroyed
540 BC	Cyrus of Persia conquers Jerusalem. The exiles return home
515 BC	Jerusalem Temple modestly rebuilt by the returning exiles
455 BC	Jerusalem walls are rebuilt
65 BC	Rome conquers Judea
20 BC	Jerusalem Temple totally renovated by Herod
1 AD	Birth of Jesus
30 AD	Jesus is baptized by John the Baptist
33 AD	Jesus' Death, Burial and Resurrection
70 AD	Romans destroy Jerusalem and the Temple
1943 AD	Over 6 million Jews murdered during World War II
1948 AD	New Jewish state of Israel is established and recognized

Genesis

The word Genesis means "origin". This book tells how God created heaven and earth. It covers the beginning of sin in the Garden of Eden, and God's punishment for Adam and Eve's disobedience. It tells about Cain and Abel, and Noah and the flood. The faithful and obedient Abraham is introduced, as well as his son Isaac and his son Jacob. Those three are patriarchs, regarded as the fathers of humanity. The twelve tribes of Israel are covered, and the life of Joseph.

- In the beginning God created heaven and earth. II Peter 3:8 and Psalms 90:4 tells us that 1,000 years to us can be like 1 day to the Lord, so some believe that creation took thousands of years instead of six days. When He'd finished His creations, He was pleased.
- Adam and Eve were created. They sin in the Garden of Eden by eating from the tree of the knowledge of good and evil, so God pronounced judgement on them.
- They had two sons, Cain and Abel. God respected Abel's offering to Him but not Cain's since it wasn't a blood offering. That angered Cain, so he killed Abel. God said Cain's life from that point forward would be that of a vagabond. In Genesis 5, neither Cain nor Abel are shown as descendants of Adam, possibly because it's only naming those in the direct lineage of the coming Messiah.
- Adam and Eve had other children; one was named Seth. Through that lineage Jared had a son named Enoch who God brought straight into heaven. His son Methuselah lived 969 years. Methuselah's son Lamech fathered Noah.
- As the population grew, God saw there were giants (Nephilim) being born. Some believe these giants were children of male fallen angels or ungodly beings. Either way, God saw they were wicked and decided to wipe them out.
- God was pleased with the purity of Noah, so He told him to build an ark and to load into it every living thing of all flesh (Genesis 6:19) plus his family. It took 120 years to build the ark, then it rained for 40 days and nights killing everything God wasn't pleased with.
- Noah had three sons, who'd be the ancestors of all people on earth. Son Ham had a son he named Canaan. Shem's son Terah was the father of Abram. From Adam and Eve to Abram (Abraham) approximately 2,000 years had passed, and another 2,000 years would pass until Jesus the Christ would be born.
- Abram wed Sarai, who was barren. Sarai assigned her Egyptian slave Hagar to have a child by Abram, who they named Ishmael. God didn't honor him as Abram's son. God changed Abram's name to Abraham and Sarai's to Sarah.
- All people at the time had only one language. In Babylonia they decided to build a tower. God was angered over their plan, so He changed their languages and scattered their people throughout the earth.
- God made a promise to Abraham, telling him to leave his home and to go where He'd send him. God promised Abraham many descendants who would become a

great nation. Abraham, Sarah, and nephew Lot entered Egypt. During a war, Lot was captured in the city of Sodom. Abraham and others rescued Lot.

- While Abraham slept, God told him his descendants would be slaves in a foreign land and be treated poorly for 400 years, but God would punish those enslaving them. In Abraham and Sarah's old age God gave them a son, named Isaac.

- Sodom and Gomorrah were two cities full of sin where God couldn't find even a handful of believers. God destroyed both cities, but angels led Lot and his family away just before it happened. They were told to run and not look back, but Lot's wife looked back and was turned into a pillar of salt.

- To test Abraham's loyalty, God asked him to burn his son Isaac as a sacrifice. Abraham was going to, but God stopped it and was therefore convinced of Abraham's loyalty. Sarah died and was buried in Canaan. Isaac married Rebecca.

- Abraham remarried and had more children before dying at age 175. Isaac and Rebecca had twin sons named Esau and Jacob. Isaac gets old and loses his sight, so he promised Esau his blessings and belongings. Jacob convinced Isaac that he was Esau and received everything. Esau vowed to kill Jacob.

- Jacob's uncle Laban had two daughters, Leah and Rachel. Jacob worked for Laban 7 years in order to marry Leah, then another 7 to marry Rachel. Rachel had a son named Joseph. Jacob was told his own name would be Israel.

- Jacob and Esau meet again, and they hug and cry. They part and go their separate ways. God spoke to Jacob and renewed the covenant He had with Abraham, telling Jacob he'd be the ancestor of kings. Jacob set up a memorial stone there, and named the place Bethel.

- Rachel died giving birth to a son named Benjamin. Jacob returned to where Abraham and Isaac had lived. Isaac died and was buried by Esau and Jacob.

- Jacob loved Joseph more than his other sons, so his brothers grew to hate him. At first, they threw Joseph into a well, but then sold him to the Ishmaelites who took him to Egypt. The brothers, all but Reuben, killed a goat and dipped Joseph's robe in the blood to convince Jacob that he'd been killed by animals.

- Joseph received blessings from God and was given authority by his Egyptian master. The master's wife accused Joseph of molestation. He went to prison.

- Joseph helped 2 prisoners then a king interpret their dreams, which came true. The king was impressed and appointed Joseph governor of Egypt. He helped the country through 7 years of plenty then 7 years of famine.

- Jacob sent Joseph's brothers to Egypt to get grain during the famine. Joseph didn't tell them who he was when he provided them their grain. Later, he tells them he's their brother, and sent for his father Jacob. They reunited in love.

- Before dying, Jacob tells his sons their future. He died and was buried in the land of Canaan and not in Egypt. Jacob had 12 sons during his lifetime, each of whom became the father of one of the 12 Tribes of Israel.

- Joseph told his brothers he'd not seek revenge on them for what they'd done to him. Before dying, he asked that his dead body be carried with them until they entered the promise land. He wanted to be buried in what would become Israel.

<u>Additional comments on the book of Genesis:</u>

In the beginning God created heaven and earth. It doesn't say when He created it. Bible scholars say Adam and Eve appeared approximately 6,000 years ago, but scientists using isotope decay and geological dating methods say that earth is billions of years old based on all the rocks, fossils and dinosaur bones discovered. Although those interpretations differ, it appears that somewhere in the past a great catastrophe occurred leaving the earth void and dark. Since Noah and the flood we have the earth we live in today, as told in II Peter 3:6-7. Much later there'll be a new heaven and earth when Jesus returns to earth to set up His Kingdom, told in II Peter 3:13 and in Revelation 21:1.

There are four major things to remember and not overlook in this chapter. First, we must remember God's important promise to Abraham, His covenant. Abraham was told he'd have many descendants, that God would make of him a great nation, and there'd be a King and redeemer to rule His people. That was God's promise to Abraham, one He'd repeat later to Abraham's son Isaac and again to Isaac's son Jacob. That covenant was not to be forgotten, and would not be fully realized until the King was born in Bethlehem about 2,000 years later.

Secondly was the tremendous faith of Abraham. God told him to leave his country and go into a strange land where he'd be blessed. Nothing was given to him at the time, so Abraham had to truly believe in those future promises. It'd take a gigantic leap of faith to leave your country and travel to strange lands at the age of 75, but he did. With his family, he had to build and dismantle his tent for decades at every stop along a journey into many countries, but Abraham soldiered right along.

The third remarkable occurrence happened in Chapter 18:1-16, when three men appeared to Abraham in flesh bodies. Abraham knew immediately that one of them was the Lord, a theophany. The other 2 were angels. Food was prepared and they all sat beneath a tree and ate. Then the Lord promised Abraham and Sarah a son, although she was 90 years old and Abraham was nearly 100. Doubtful at first, Abraham had faith so what God had promised came true in the birth of Isaac.

The fourth major event was the introduction of Melchizedek in Genesis 14:18, as the priest of the most high God. He was the King of Salem, a city later to be renamed Jerusalem. He is not mentioned again in the bible for nearly 1,000 years, in Psalms 110:4, then again 1,000 years later in Hebrews 7. Melchizedek was without father or mother, having neither the beginning of days nor the end of life, but made like unto the Son of God. Hebrews 6:20 says Jesus was made a high priest after the order of Melchizedek, so this man had to be extremely holy. Any priest to the most high God would be one who possessed ultimate knowledge who'd achieved perfect enlightenment, like Jesus.

Exodus

The word Exodus means "departure." In this book the people of Israel are freed and depart from Egypt where they'd been enslaved. It covers the incredible life of Moses, the Passover, the parting of the Red Sea, their time at Mount Sinai, and God's covenant with His people. We'll learn about The Ten Commandments, the Ark of the Covenant, and God's rules for worship.

- Over time Jacob's twelve sons died, but their descendants heavily populated the land of Egypt working mostly as slaves. The king/pharaoh felt threatened because of their numbers so he ordered all their newborn boys be thrown in the Nile River. He allowed the baby girls to live.
- From the tribe of Levi a son was born. His mother hid him for 3 months, fearing he'd be found and thrown in the river. She made a basket and placed the baby in it, then left it at the edge of the river. The king's daughter found the baby and raised him as her own, and named him Moses.
- Years later Moses married and had a child. One day an angel of God appeared as a flame in a burning bush and spoke to Moses. God told him that he'd lead His people out of Egypt and free them from slavery. They'd be led into the land of milk and honey. The king would not want to release the people, God told them, but He'd punish the king until he agreed.
- To convince the Hebrew people that Moses was their leader, God turned his shepherd's rod into a snake in front of them, then did other miracles so they'd believe him. Moses was insecure in his speaking ability, so God empowered Aaron, his older brother, to assist him.
- Moses and Aaron gathered their people. They asked the king if they could all leave Egypt for 3 days to go praise their Lord. The king asked, "who is this Jehovah?" The king said no, then increased their workloads as slaves. Later they asked him again but again he said no. God vowed to punish the Egyptians until the king released them.
- Moses told the king that God had requested, "Let My People Go." God sent disaster after disaster upon the Egyptian people, but the king still refused.
- God declared the terms for the first Lord's Passover, when He would kill the oldest sons in all of Egypt. God told the Jewish people to eat nothing containing yeast. He told them to kill a lamb and smear the lamb's blood on the doorposts of their homes. When the death angel came that night to kill, it "passed over" the homes with blood on the doorposts. Many Egyptians died that night. Scared, the king finally released the Israelites.
- 600,000 Jewish men left Egypt, plus the women, children and all their animals. As Joseph had requested when he died, they took his dead body with them. God gave them His rules for the observance of each future annual Passover.
- The king had a change of heart and wanted the Israeli slaves back in Egypt. He led his army after the Israeli people who were camping near the Red Sea. As they

approached, God told Moses to hold his rod over the sea and it would part, allowing His people to walk across on the dry sea bottom. When they reached the other shore, Moses held his rod over the sea and it closed on the Egyptians following them, drowning them all.

- As they journeyed along, the people complain to Moses and Aaron saying they had nothing to eat or drink. God heard them, and sent vast quantities of quail, water, and daily manna for the people. They put back a little manna for future generations, storing it in the Ark. On the Sabbath they rested. They ate the manna for 40 years until they arrived near the land of Canaan.

- Moses' father-in-law visited. The people continued to complain, so Moses was advised by his father-in-law to appoint judges among the Israelites to hear complaints and resolve them, to lighten the burden on him and Aaron.

- As the people moved from camp to camp, God provided pillars of clouds during the day and fire clouds at night to lead them. They arrive at the base of Mt. Sanai. God renewed the covenant with His people, and appeared to them in thunder, fire, and smoke. God gave the Ten Commandments, and many other laws His people must obey. God wrote the commandments on stone tablets.

- God instructed them to build a covenant box, a Tabernacle, tables, lampstands, and many other things. He wanted Aaron and his sons to be His priests, and to wear specific robes and turbans. On the mountaintop, before Moses left, God gave him the 2 stones containing His Ten Commandments.

- The people below became impatient since Moses had been up on the mountaintop so long. Fearing Moses had disappeared, with Aaron's blessing the people made a golden calf to worship. Angry, God wanted to destroy them all but Moses begged Him for mercy on His people. God spared them.

- With the 2 tablets, Moses descended the mountain only to hear everyone singing and dancing around the golden calf. In anger he threw the tablets, breaking them. The tribe of Levi (the one Aaron came from) sided with Moses, so they killed about 3,000 of the idol worshipers in camp. For more punishment, the Lord sent sickness upon the people there.

- The Lord had Moses prepare 2 more stones for Him to write His commandments on. Moses stayed on the mountaintop without food or drink for 40 days and 40 nights with the Lord. The Lord told him what the Israelites must do and not do when they entered Canaan, the promise land. Moses had spent so much time in the presence of God that his face glowed.

- He descended the mountain holding the tablets. The people were told what offerings to make. Using God's instructions, the people built the Covenant Box, then the Tabernacle which they adorned with many things including gold and silver. The Ten Commandment tablets were placed in the Covenant Box.

- God told them how to set up and decorate the Tabernacle. He gave them other instructions as they moved from camp to camp, following the cloud He provided, which told them when to travel and when to camp.

Additional comments on the book of Exodus:

One detail given to us in Exodus 16:4 and 16:35 can't be overlooked. As His people wandered in the wilderness for 40 years, God provided huge amounts of manna for them to eat but told them they should only gather a certain amount each day. God didn't want them to gather enough for a week or month at a time. He wanted them to rely on Him each and every day. In the Lord's Prayer we ask God to "give us day by day our daily bread". God wants us to trust and rely on his gifts and blessings day by day, not just once in a while. Pray to God daily and ask Him for everyday miracles. Thank Him each day for His blessings and grace.

The book of Exodus has two main themes. It begins with God using Moses to lead His chosen people out of bondage in Egypt, and ends with God giving them the laws and commandments they must live by. God had made a promise to Abraham that He was fulfilling. These Israelites were super special to God. He told Moses in Chapter 19:5-6 that they shall be a peculiar treasure to Him above all people, a kingdom of priests. More than anything He wanted the Israelites to love Him, and as priests to bring all others to love Him. His plan for them, as part of His covenant, was to lead them into the Promise Land where they'd become a great nation. But in return, they had to obey His laws and commandments. They struggled to keep their part of the agreement.

It's important to realize that before the Ten Commandments, the approximate 2,500 years between Adam and Moses's time, that people had no written record to guide them between right and wrong. That might be one reason why they were so disobedient and confused, not knowing the true will of God. He tried the teach them by appearing and talking to them face to face. Then at other times He spoke to His people through prophets. As we've read, even after receiving God's commandments at Mount Sanai and being told of His Laws over and over again, there were times the people were still disobedient and filled with unbelief.

When the Ten Commandments did come along they were impossible to keep. Of course they were perfect because they came from God, but man with his sinful nature was incapable of totally obeying them. Romans 3:20 and 23 tells us that all have sinned and come short of the glory of God. God loves us, so if His laws won't save us due to our sinful ways, then He'd offer us another way into heaven. But the Commandments still applied, and had to be a part of every Christian's life. The old way of trying to obey God's commandments could end in death, but a new way of belief and faith in Jesus and the cross would give us life. See **Appendix B**.

The commandments and laws were not a path that would lead a person into heaven. There may not be one instance in the Old Testament where the keeping of laws and commandments gets the credit for leading a single person to their salvation. Nearly 1,500 years later, the commandments, the slaughtering of animals for blood sacrifices, the dancing and feasts, and the Temple worships of old gave way to another road into Heaven when a descendant of King David introduced both Jew and Gentile to The Age of Grace. His name is Jesus.

Leviticus

This book opens and concludes at the same geographical location, Mount Sanai. Where Genesis was about man's creation and sinful nature, and Exodus was about freedom and God's Laws and Covenant, Leviticus is about worship and the way all people are to live to maintain their relationship with God. He states once again that He is leading them into the promise land, and that He has made a distinction between them and the people of other nations. In 19:18, this is the book that commands "Thou shalt love thy neighbor as thyself".

Here, God moves into the tabernacle and speaks from there instead of from the top of Mount Sanai. He gives them the codes of law for their well-being with Him, including moral, spiritual, physical, sacrificial, washings, observances, warnings, and more. The word atonement, or the covering or cleansing of impurities, is used over 40 times in this book and for good reason. The sacrificial blood mentioned here only covers up our sins, until the One comes who can wash them away and remove them.

- The Lord spoke to Moses from the Tabernacle, describing His regulations for many things including sacrifices, religious ceremonies, priesthoods, cleanliness, offerings, repentance of sins, animals to be used for food, atonement, the handling of sicknesses, the sale of land and homes, and others.
- The Lord proclaimed His laws of holiness and justice. He reminds us to only worship the Lord, help the poor and foreigners, and do not take advantage of others. Be honest and just in legal issues and settle grudges without taking revenge. Do not cheat anyone, and honor and respect older people.
- He tells us to be obedient. Do not curse your father or mother. Don't take advice or consult the spirits of the dead. If you're disobedient to God, you should expect punishment. Follow the Lord's commandments and celebrate your life with Him.

Additional comments on the book of Leviticus:

Maybe the most important conclusion we can draw from Leviticus is that our call as God's people is to reflect God's holiness in our lives. Being in God's presence is not just reciting Scripture verses, memorizing the Lord's Prayer, or wearing crosses. We do it by loving others and treating them right. Much of this book is teaching us how to live our lives. He wants us to be honest and not cheat people, to help the poor, and show respect to our parents and our elders. In practical terms, this means doing as much good for others through our work as we do for ourselves. Others may not initially link our kindness and care for them as a sign of our Christianity, but we want it to lead to an opportunity for us to tell them why we are how we are, impervious to trickery and deceit, and about He who gives us our strength and loving temperament.

Numbers

This book, titled as such due to the census and headcounts throughout the story, tells about the Israelites from when they left Mt. Sanai until they reach Kadesh Barnea near the Promise Land. The travel time between those two points would normally be 11 days, but due to the Jews rebellion and lack of faith, God sent them on a lengthy detour that took them the long way around. After all the miracles they'd seen God perform for well over a year since they'd left Egypt, including the parting of a vast sea, they still rejected Him and His plan to lead them into Canaan.

They didn't believe what God had repeatedly told them; that they'd win their wars in the Promise Land and become a nation, that the land there would be fertile, and they'd establish a government with a King. Instead, they wanted to appoint a person to lead them back into slavery in Egypt. Their unbelief angered God, so for punishment He made His chosen people wander in the desert for 40 years until the older generation had died. Their next generation of people were led from the desert to the land of Moab, where they would finally prepare to cross the Jordan River into Canaan. Their story is an example of what a lack of faith in God can do.

- Within the 12 tribes, a census was taken of all men 20 years old or older. Those men totaled 603,550. God told Moses and Aaron to arrange the tribes into four groups, the north, south, east and west.
- The tribe of Levites were chosen by God to be His people among the others, and each member would serve in the Tabernacle until they reached age 50. A census was taken of the Levites, and duties were set for each of their three clans.
- The Lord instructed the Jewish people on their dealings with unclean people, repayment for wrongdoings, suspicious spouses, and priestly blessings. Moses anointed the Tabernacle and the leaders brought their offerings.
- They celebrated the second Passover. They still had the fiery cloud over their worship center that lifted and moved as God directed it, to lead them from new camp to new camp during their journey. They carried the Ark with them.
- The people began complaining to Moses about lack of food. The Lord gave some of Moses' spirit to 70 others in camp so they could help him deal with the many disgruntled people there. The Lord fed them all with large quantities of quail.
- When the unbelieving people would not go freely into Canaan as the Lord had directed them, He told Moses to pick a leader from each of the 12 tribes. They would go as spies into Canaan to remove any doubts that it was as rich and fertile as He'd promised. The spies spent 40 days there before returning.
- Two spies reported the land was rich and fertile, proven by the huge grapes they'd returned with. But, the other ten lied and said it was not fertile and the cities were well fortified, and that so many warriors and giants lived there that it made them feel as small as grasshoppers. Scared from the lies, the people wanted someone to lead them back into Egypt to die. They didn't believe God.

- These people had witnessed the many miracles God had performed, including parting the Red Sea and providing them with food from Heaven and water out of rocks. So God wanted to punish the ten spies and the unbelievers, but again Moses asked God to forgive them. Caleb and Joshua, from their respective tribes, were the two who recommended the people go ahead and enter Canaan because it was everything God had said, so they were spared.
- God was angry and struck down the ten spies who had lied. The others wanted to enter Canaan but it was too late. For now, the Lord had given up on them. For punishment, He would make these unbelievers wander in the wilderness for 40 years, one year for each day they'd spend spying in Canaan.
- Korah from the Levi clan, and his followers, challenged Moses and Aaron by wanting more involvement in the priesthood leadership. They were told that their rebellion against Aaron was also a rebellion against the Lord who had chosen him and Moses. God opened the earth beneath those rebelling and they were swallowed into the ground.
- Some people continued to complain, so the Lord send a plague that killed 14,700 people. More would have died but Aaron stood between the living and the dead with a censer and incense to cleanse their impurities and unbelief.
- To prove Aaron's authority, each tribe was told to bring a rod with their leader's name on it. The one that sprouted by the following day would be from the one chosen by God. The rod with Aaron's name on it was the only one that had sprouted and produced almonds. But again, the people continued to complain.
- The Lord made it clear that Aaron and his family are the only ones who shall work in the Tabernacle, performing all sacred services. God tells him twice, "your kinsmen the Levites will be your assistants." He gave them further instructions, then also stated that the Levites would be paid with the tithes collected throughout all of Israel. They would not receive any other property or income, since He was all they'd ever need. He explained tithing in detail.
- Again, the people complain having no water. God tells Moses to speak to the rock and water will flow from it. But Moses strikes the rock with his rod. Water gushed out, but Moses didn't just speak to it as commanded. For his and Aaron's disobedience, God tells them they'll not lead these people into Canaan.
- In the land of Edom, Aaron died, and his priestly garments were given to his son Eleazar to wear. The Arad army attacked the Israelites but were defeated. Each time the Israelites asked to travel through land ruled by a king they were refused, probably because the men, women, children and livestock numbered over two million. The people still complain, so the Lord sent them poisonous snakes. The army fights and has victory over King Sihon and King Og.
- Other kings became fearful. The Moab king sent for Balaam to put a curse on the Jewish people, but God told him not to. King Balak could not get Balaam to do as he asked. Balaam would only do and say what God told him. He tells King Balak that the people of Israel will destroy their enemies and occupy their land.
- At Acacia, some younger Israelites began feasting and worshiping the idols of the Moabites. They were punished when the Lord sent a plague that killed 24,000 of

them. It only stopped when Eleazar's son killed an Israelite who'd brought a Midianite girl into camp. God said to destroy the Midianites.

- A census was taken of each tribe of men 20 years old and older. There were 601,730 counted. There were very few elderly men living since they'd died being in the desert for 40 years. God told them that their land would be divided based on each tribe's population, but the Levites would get no land to own. Joshua was named as Moses' successor. His consultant would be Eleazar the priest.

- God gave more instructions to His people, then they went to war capturing land and possessions. Balaam was killed in the battle. The tribes of Reuben and Gad asked to have the land east of Jordan instead of land in Canaan, but they would still fight in all the wars. The Lord agreed and the land was given to them and to half the tribe of Manasseh, a son of Joseph.

- The Lord told Moses to prepare to cross the Jordan into Canaan and conquer the land for Israel. He laid out the boundaries, and said the Levites would get certain cities and pasturelands. Cities of refuge would be established as places of protection for themselves, foreigners, and travelers.

- The Lord said all murderers must be executed if there were more than one witness to it. Rules, commandments, and more were given to the people of Israel while they were camped near Jericho, beside the Jordan River. They still had not crossed the Jordan River into Canaan, the Promise Land.

Additional comments on the book of Numbers:

The 12 tribes were named Asher, Dan, Ephraim, Gad, Issachar, Manasseh, Naphtali, Reuben, Simeon, Zebulun, Judah and Benjamin, all sons or grandsons of Jacob. Around 930 BC, the first 10 tribes formed the Kingdom of Israel in the north, and Judah and Benjamin set up the Kingdom of Judah in the south.

Two points of emphasis come from this book. The first one is obvious when we read the seven instances where the people grumble and complain about their hardships, food, Moses' leadership, entering Canaan, lack of water, Aaron and the Levi tribe having all the priesthood duties, and about their wellbeing. Even after they decided to appoint a leader to head them back to Egypt, which demonstrated a gross lack of faith in Him, God stayed on track although His people did not. In the end, one clear message is for us to obey God when He directs us. Forty years is a long time to travel a distance that should have taken eleven days.

The second theme of this book is how God keeps His covenant and promises to Abraham. He doesn't give up on these Israelites although He's had to punish them repeatedly to get their attention and overcome their unbelief in Him. They learn that complaining is bad, that rebellion brings judgement, and that faith brings blessings. Then there's Moses, who continually received instructions from God, communicated those instructions to the people, assembled teams, prayed for God to go easy on them, and delegated tasks. A man who God would talk to one on one and who became Israel's greatest prophet. But in the end, he was not allowed to lead the people into the promise land.

Deuteronomy

In this book, Moses addressed the Jewish people near the Jordan River where they'd stopped before entering and occupying the land of Canaan. He recalled the major events over the past 40 years, and all that God had done to get them to where they were today. He reminded them of God's Laws, His covenant, and blessings.

Moses was special, not only to the people of Israel but to God. God entrusted Moses to do His will. At God's command, he performed amazing miracles which had never been equaled. One of the greatest verses comes from Chapter 6, when Moses says, "And thou shalt love the Lord thy God with all thine heart, and with all thy soul, and with all thy might".

- Moses reminded the people detail by detail of their long 40-year journey from Egypt to where they were today. He emphasized all they'd gone through, the many blessings they'd received, and the punishments they'd endured for disobedience. He reminded them to keep the Ten Commandments.
- When they do enter the Promise Land, he told them to gather boulders from the river bottom and build a monument, coat it with lime, and record God's commandments on the stones. They are to build an alter there to the Lord, and all the people shall say, Amen. He warned them of the many things and actions that could bring a curse upon them.
- Moses specifically pointed out that they all knew God's laws and had heard them many times. In so many words, he told them that they knew their destiny if they'd just get out of God's way and let Him lead them. He told them that God's laws were not in a faraway place where they couldn't hear them, that they were not across the ocean, that they were right there in front of them. "They're close at hand, in your hearts and on your lips, so obey them!"
- Moses was old and knew he would not cross the Jordan into Canaan. Instead, Joshua would lead them there. Moses wrote a law that every seven years the Jewish nation shall all meet together and renew God's laws.
- The Lord asked Moses and Joshua to gather the people in the Tabernacle. God appeared in a pillar of a cloud and told them He already knew that in time they would break His covenant, worship other Gods, and cause many evils and troubles to befall them. When that happens, He'll hide His face & forsake them.
- God asked them to write a song, which Moses did, to witness to the future children of Israel that God had fulfilled His promises although the people broke theirs. Moses spoke the words of the song to the congregation there.
- God sent Moses into the mountains where he'd die. "You shall see the Promise Land before you," God said, "but you shall not enter the land I give to Israel."
- Moses went to the mountain of Nebo, to the top of Pisgah, and died with the Lord there with him. He was buried in a Moab Valley, but even today no one knows the exact location. He was 120 years old and still healthy when he passed. The people wept for 30 days, knowing they'd lost a great man.

Additional comments on the book of Deuteronomy:

This book was written around 1,400 BC, and completed what can be referred to as the Mosaic Law, or the Ten Commandments and other rules of religious observances given in the first 5 books of the Old Testament. Those 5 books are referred to as The Law, when God gave us His guidance and instructions. They're also called the Laws of Moses, or the Torah.

In Deuteronomy there was a transfer of authority from Moses to Joshua, a succession plan that provided the people a new leader to take them into Canaan. It also gave an order of inheritance, telling us that God's plan to bless them was a bilateral deal. First, the people had to obey his laws. Secondly, if they did He would give them a land of milk and honey. Thirdly, if they obeyed Him in the future they would have His blessings. But if they did not, He would forsake them.

God knew these people definitely needed instruction. Since the adults there were too young to remember God's original promises to them before their parents died wandering in the wilderness and desert for 40 years, time was spent recapping all that had gone on before. But even then, after repeating and reviewing the commandments and laws over and over, God already knew they would disobey Him again. We are blessed to have such a forgiving Father.

Deuteronomy is a future-oriented book, and foresees what will happen to these people as time passes. God gave Moses a song so the people would have it as a testimony when they turn against Him again, because He knows they will. In Chapter 31:16-18, God told them they'd break His covenant, and when they did He'd forsake them. And He did, when later the Israel Tribes were conquered by the Assyrians and by Babylon as written in II Kings 17:6-23 and 25:1-26.

More than a thousand years later Jesus used a parable to tell Israel's religious leaders at the time, the unbelieving Jews, the same thing. In Matthew 21:42-43, Jesus tells them they'll be forsaken when they don't follow the scriptures, and that the Kingdom of God shall be taken from them and given to another nation. They just never kept their end of the bargain so that God could bless them.

Joshua

The book of Joshua begins the 12 books of the Bible known as The History, beginning here and ending with the book of Esther. They cover the history of God's people, along with their struggles and exultations. Their history begins with the Israelites inhabiting the land of Canaan and ends with them returning from exile.

Joshua is the story of the Jewish people finally invading the land of Canaan under his leadership, the successor to Moses. They defeat armies and capture large tracts of land for their people. The fall of Jericho is included, and the division of these new territories among the 12 tribes. The Levites, the tribe of priests, are given cities to live in. Other lands are set aside as cities of refuge. Out of Chapter 24 comes the timeless phrase, "but as for me and my house, we will serve the Lord."

- They prepare to cross the Jordan Riven into Canaan land. The Lord had said that 2 tribes and part of another could occupy land east of the Jordan, so their wives, children and livestock would remain there. These were the tribes of Reuben, Gad, and east Manasseh (half of that tribe).
- Joshua sent spies into Canaan, who stayed with the lady Rahab in Jericho. The King there found out and sent men to find them. Rahab hid them, so the spies said they would spare her and her family later on when the Israelites occupied their land. The Canaanites had heard of the plight of God's chosen people, and therefore were scared of them.
- The Lord told Joshua to lead the people across the Jordan River, with the priests carrying the Ark of the Covenant box half a mile ahead of them. When those priests stuck their feet in the Jordan, it dried up to let the people cross on dry land.
- The people gathered 12 memorial stones in Cannan land, 1 for each tribe. It would remind them all the Lord their God had done.
- The miracle of the Israelites crossing the Jordan scared the neighboring kings. The "Commander of the Lord's Army" showed up and told Joshua to remove his sandals, because he was standing on Holy Ground.
- The Israelite army marched around Jericho daily for 6 days. On the seventh day, they marched around it seven times. Their army shouted, the priests blew their trumpets, and the walls of Jericho collapsed.
- The Israelites burned the city and destroyed their enemies. Joshua warned them to never rebuild it or God would curse them. Rahab and her family, who'd helped the spies earlier, were spared and saved.
- Achan, from the Judah Tribe, disobeyed God when he kept some items that he knew to burn and destroy. Joshua gathered him and his family, and the items he'd kept, and they were all stoned to death.
- Their army continued to go into battle and capture land. They captured the city of Ai, the Amorites, and much more. The Gibeonites temporarily deceive Joshua's army, but are forgiven.

- The captured lands, now a part of Israel, were divided between the Tribes and territories were assigned. Cities of refuge were established. The Levites were given their own land and towns.

- Joshua sent the two tribes and half of another, who were promised land east of the Jordan, back home to their land. They stopped and built an alter along the way on the west side of Jordan. It upset the other tribes at first, but they wanted everyone to know that although they weren't in Israel, they were still a part of the 12 Tribes and were the people of God.

- In his old age Joshua reminded the people over and over to keep the laws and not worship other Gods, or God would punish them. Other Gods could be their money, their possessions, or many things.

- Joshua and Eleazar die and are buried, Joshua on his own land and Eleazar at Gibeah. Joseph's dead body, which had been carried at his request ever since he'd died in Egypt, was buried on land owned by Jacob. As he'd wished, he was buried in God's promised land.

Additional comments on the book of Joshua:

We can envision God wiping His brow knowing this part of His covenant promise was finally over. For years and years He'd led the people of Israel over every hurdle they'd faced, including their own recurring disobedience. Finally, they'd entered into Canaan. The fulfillment of His ancient pledge to Israel's ancestors, Abraham, Isaac, and Jacob, had finally come about. The theme here may not be one of conquest by the Israelite Army, but instead a confirmation of God's Word. What He promises He delivers.

Joshua was the leader of God's Army, trained by and the successor of Moses. The name Joshua is formed from the Hebrew word for "salvation". Earlier in his life Joshua was called Hoshea, again meaning "salvation". It was Moses who changed his name to Joshua. We recall from the Book of Numbers that Joshua and Caleb were the only 2 tribe spies who told the truth out of the 12 spies who were sent into Canaan on a spying mission. Therefore, God knew Joshua could be trusted.

Some might view this book as both a win and a loss. The evil people in Canaan, according to Deuteronomy, worshiped false gods, practiced magic, and even sacrificed their own children. They lived on the land that had to be conquered in order for the people of Israel to take ownership. Adding up the numbers, more than a hundred thousand Canaanites may have died in those battles with Israel. With all the suffering and killing that occurred, this may not be one of the happier uplifting Chapters in the Bible. But it fulfilled the will of God, and the will of God could never be wrong.

Judges

This book takes us from the time the Jewish army captured Canaan until they established a monarchy form of government. Various military leaders emerged to become national heroes of the people. Samson was one of the better-known leaders.

As we've learned through the history of these people, their disobedience kept leading them away from God and His blessings. They'd sin then God would forgive them. Again they'd sin then repent, and God forgave them. A recurring pattern.

- After Joshua's death the army continued to conquer other regions within Canaan. Those from the Tribe of Judah attacked Jerusalem and burned the city, and other tribes defeated those in Bethel. Many Canaanites were not killed but were captured and forced to stay and work for the Israelites.
- An angel of the Lord told the people not to follow any customs of the people they'd captured, but the people didn't listen. After Joshua had died at the age of 110, many of the elders also died of old age. The next generation forgot the Lord and didn't realize all He'd done for them.
- When the people stopped worshipping the Lord, He let their enemies over-run them. God wanted to see if His people would follow His ways or the ways of the remaining Canaanites. The people worshipped foreign idols, so God let them be captured by the King of Mesopotamia and held captive for eight years.
- Again, after the fact, the people asked God for help so He sent Othniel as their leader or judge. He led an army that recaptured Israel, so there was peace for the next 40 years. After that, when they backslid into sin once again, they fell under the Moab King and remained there for 18 years.
- God sent Ehud to help them. He brought gifts to the Moab ruler but also a sword hidden under his clothes. He killed the king and escaped, locking the door behind him. When the servants found the king, Ehud was far away. He led the Israelite soldiers into war against Moab. After winning the battle, there was peace in the land for the next 80 years.
- After Ehud died the Israelites were ruled over and treated cruelly for the next 20 years. A prophet and judge named Deborah recruited Barak to help free the people. They both went, and with 10,000 men they defeated the enemy. Sisera, the enemy leader, escaped but while sleeping he was killed with a tent peg driven through his head. Israeli army's fought hard until they'd destroyed the Canaanite King and his army.
- Deborah and Barak sang a song of victory praising the Lord. There was peace in the land for the next 40 years.
- The Midianites overrun the Israeli people, so the Lord's angel sends Gideon to save them. He tore down the false alter which angered the townspeople.
- With only 300 men, Gideon led an army who captured and beheaded the Midianite chiefs. They win more battles under Gideon's leadership.

- The land was at peace for the next 40 years until Gideon died. He had many wives and 70 sons. A concubine bore him a child he named Abimelech. Without Gideon, the Jewish people returned to their sinful ways.
- Abimelech was made king, but he hired scoundrels and unworthy people to work for him. He killed his 69 brothers except for Jotham, the youngest. Over time the people turned against Abimelech. He died when a millstone was thrown by a woman that fractured his skull.
- Jephthah became a leader and his army defeated the Ammonites. He and others lead the people for the next 25 years until they are conquered by the Philistines, who ruled them for the next 40 years.
- The Lord's angel spoke to an Israelite woman and told her she would have a son. She was not to drink any wine or eat any forbidden fruit. She was told to never cut his hair, and that her son would defeat the Philistines. He was named Samson. He grew up strong, dedicated to God as a Nazirite.
- Samson was attracted to a Philistine girl from another clan. He wanted to marry her so he had a banquet, where he killed a lion with his bare hands. He spoke in riddles that no one understood, which angered the people there. In anger, his fiancé was given to his best man at the wedding. Samson wanted her back.
- The girls father offered Samson another of his daughters. In anger, Samson used foxes to burn the wheat fields and olive orchards belonging to the Philistines. They retaliated by killing the girl he loved then burned down her father's house. Samson then killed many of the Philistines.
- He was a hunted man, so he let some men from Judah arrest him. As the Philistines ran to harm him, he broke the ropes around him and picked up a jawbone of a donkey and killed a thousand Philistines. Samson led Israel for the next 20 years while the Philistines ruled the land there.
- Samson meets Delilah and falls in love with her. The Philistine kings told her to find out what made him so strong. He only partially tells her, so when she uses what he'd said it didn't weaken him at all. He finally tells her it's the length of his hair, which has never been cut.
- While he slept, the Philistines cut his seven locks of hair. He was captured and his eyes put out. He didn't know the Lord had left him. Slowly his hair started to grow back.
- They celebrated his capture and brought him to entertain them. Samson asked the one leading him to take him where the building columns were. He prayed for strength, then pushed the columns to collapse the building onto the kings and everyone there, including himself. He was taken and buried near his father.
- Micah stole silver from his mother and made an idol out of it. There was no king in Israel at the time, so the people did as they pleased. Micah appointed a Levite as his priest, trying to ensure God was with him.
- The Tribe of Dan was looking for land to claim and sent out 5 spies to explore the country. Their army took Micah's idol and also his priest. They conquered the city of Lavish, and rebuilt it as the city of Dan.

- A Levite and his concubine arrived in Gibeah where perverts brutally attacked them, killing her. The Levite took her body to his home and cut it into 12 pieces, one for each tribe of Israel, to show them the evilness of those who attacked her.
- The Israelites gathered 400,000-foot soldiers to attack Gibeah. After two battles against the Benjamin Tribe they were soundly defeated. God was with them for the third battle, so they defeated and nearly wiped out the entire Benjamin Tribe, all but 600 of them.
- To keep Israel from losing the tribe of Benjamin from the 12, the Israeli leaders provided a way for the remaining Benjaminite men to have a wife so they could repopulate. The Benjamin tribe was saved. There was still no king in Israel at the time, so the people did as they pleased.

Additional comments on the book of Judges:

This book takes us through the early years of the Israeli settlement in Canaan, when they had no king but only heroes of faith. Twelve regional leaders in all, selected by God, took the leadership role and led Israel through a compilation of stories and incidents. Samson, Deborah, and Gideon are the most familiar to us. Israel went from a covenant nation to one full of evil. God sent a leader (a judge) to save them from themselves, but once that leader died they committed even more sins. We've read this familiar story before. Same pattern, different time.

The period of "every man does what is right in his own eyes" had to end. Some acts of violence and blatant immorality found in this book are disturbing. The Israeli's inability to resist the sinful ways of the Canaanites eventually told them that they needed a centralized person of power going forward, someone chosen by God to show them the way.... again.

Their last great judge would be Samuel, their new king and leader, who comes on the scene later and brings them back from their disjointed occupation of the land to stabilize their need for a more permanent national leader.

Ruth

Ruth was a gentle Moabite woman married to an Israelite. She showed kindness to others, and when her husband died she continued her loyalty to his Israeli family. Later, she remarried another Israelite, and through that marriage she would become the great-grandmother to David, probably Israel's greatest king. As a foreigner who turned to Israel's God for her faith, she received the many blessings that came with her personal relationship with Him.

- Naomi and daughter-in-law Ruth were widowed living in Moab. In the midst of a famine, they heard that the Lord had blessed those in Bethlehem, in Judah, so they headed that way although Ruth's sister-in-law Orpah stayed behind. Naomi thought God had made her life bitter.
- Ruth worked in grain fields owned by Boaz. He was from Naomi's family, and had heard of Ruth's devotion and the help she'd given Naomi. He liked her and let her do work the men were doing, and helped her along.
- Naomi told Ruth that when Boaz bedded down for the night, to sleep at his feet because he was responsible for her. She did, and he and Ruth discussed the possibility of marriage, but Boaz wanted her to meet a younger man first. This younger man was asked to purchase the land Ruth's deceased husband had owned.
- Finding out that the land purchase would include Ruth in the deal, the man declined, knowing that at his death the land ownership would revert back to Ruth instead of his own children.
- Boaz married Ruth. Their child was named Obed. Later in life Obed's child Jesse would be the father of David, the future king of Israel.

Additional comments on the book of Ruth:

This book is a short and simple tale of friendship, telling us that kindness and hard work will be rewarded. Ruth, who was not Jewish, devoted her time caring for Naomi after the death of their husbands. It's one of two books of the Bible named after women, the other being Esther. It has an unhappy beginning, an uncertain middle, but a successful conclusion.

Naomi felt resentment toward God and wanted to get away and travel to a better location. Ruth clung to her, not letting Naomi leave her behind in Moab. Their relationship helped one another, as Ruth's patience and obedience brought her into the lineage of God, through David. And although Deuteronomy 23:3-6 states that no Moabite shall be admitted into the Lord's assembly, Ruth's good works brought her the Lord's blessings.

There's a message here. Like Ruth, do what you know is right and not what looks right to others. God appreciates humbleness and kindness, and the helping hands we freely offer to those in need.

I Samuel

This book moves Israel through a time without firm leadership and into a nation under the authority of a king. There were mixed feelings over this change because God was regarded as the real King of Israel. Why would they need anyone else? However, at the people's request, the Lord chose the first King of Israel.

This change revolved mainly around three men. Samuel was the last of the great judges in Israel, and Saul became the nation's first king. Then we meet David, a musician and the youngest of 7 brothers, a brave shepherd who showed signs of greatness even from an early age. He'd become Israel's second king. His reign is thought to begin around 1,000 BC and would last for 35 to 40 years.

We'll read about other characters such as Eli, and the giant Goliath. We learn of Saul's many attempts to kill David, and David's special friendship with Jonathan. Other armies press the nation to break up the new Israelite confederacy, especially the Philistines. Throughout this book God commands obedience from Israel's kings, and when they follow His orders the country prospers.

- In Shiloh, Hannah prayed for God to give her and husband Elkanah a son. The priest Eli also prayed for them. They had a son named Samuel. When he was weaned Hannah returned him to Shiloh and left him with Eli, because she felt Samuel belonged to the Lord. As young Samuel began to serve Eli in the Tabernacle of Moses, the Lord blessed Hannah with 5 more children. But Eli's sons were mean & disrespectful.
- The Lord spoke to Samuel, but he'd never been spoken to by God so he thought it was Eli speaking. This happened 3 times, until Samuel said "Speak, your servant is listening." The Lord told him what He'd told Eli, about his evil sons. The Israelites began to accept Samuel as a prophet.
- The Philistines attack Israel and kill many. The people wondered why the Lord hadn't protected them. They send for the Ark of the Covenant to protect them, and the people shouted when it arrived. But the Philistines continue to win battles over Israel, and 2 of Eli's sons are killed. The Covenant Box is captured. Hearing the shocking news, Eli dies.
- The Philistines took the Covenant Box to their temple and placed it next to their god Dagon. Twice, their god Dagon fell over, and the people there develop tumors. The kings said to take the Ark somewhere else, so it went to Gath, Goliath City, and to Ekron. Each city was punished.
- The Ark was returned to Israel along with gifts. The people there rejoiced, but when 70 people looked inside the Ark they are killed by the Lord. An older Samuel has all the false idols destroyed. When Israel was attacked again they won the battle. They recaptured their lands. There was peace.
- Samuel aged, and his sons were not worthy to become leaders. The elders wanted a king although God was their King. Samuel met Saul the Benjamite. God told

Samuel that Saul will be their ruler. Saul felt unworthy, but Samuel said he'd anoint Saul as Israel's first king.

- All the tribes gathered and Saul from the tribe of Benjamin was chosen as their king. Samuel explained the rights of a king, then everyone departed. A few didn't accept Saul and despised him.

- Jonathan, Saul's son, prepared to fight the Philistines who'd gathered a large army. The Philistines didn't allow blacksmiths in Israel who knew how to make weapons, so Saul and Jonathan were the only ones with metal swords who were armed for battle.

- Without Saul knowing, Jonathan and his servant approach the Philistine camp and kill many. The earth shook because the Lord was with them, and Israel was saved. Saul led them into more battles.

- The Amalekites who opposed Israel were to be punished and their possessions destroyed. After the battle, Saul didn't destroy all the animals or kill their king as God had directed. So Samuel captured the king and cut him up. The Lord wanted Saul replaced.

- The Lord sent Samuel to Bethlehem to a man named Jesse, to find Israel's new king among his sons. David, the youngest, was chosen by God and was anointed in the Lord's Spirit.

- Saul became tormented by an evil spirit. He was told that David played the harp, and that the harp music would drive away the spirit. Saul liked David, so David stayed on to play his harp when it was needed.

- The Israel and Philistine armies gathered on opposite hillsides to go to war. For 40 days, Goliath, who stood over 9 feet tall, challenged any Israeli to fight him. One day Jesse, David's father, sent David with some food for his brothers who were waiting on the hillside to fight.

- David saw Goliath, and was told that Saul would reward anyone who killed him. David, who'd fought wild animals and predators with a sling all his life while protecting the sheep, got Saul's blessing to fight Goliath. David dressed in armor, but it was too heavy so he removed it.

- He gathered 5 stones that would fit his sling. Goliath made fun of David's size, but God was with David. His stone hit Goliath between the eyes, killing him. With Goliath's sword he cut off Goliath's head.

- Saul's son Jonathan and David got acquainted, so Saul kept David around. Jonathan swore eternal friendship to David. The people liked David, their best fighter. As his popularity grew, Saul became jealous.

- One day while David played his harp, an evil spirit caused Saul to throw two spears at David. Saul felt the Lord preferred David so he began to fear him, although those in Israel and Judah loved him.

- If David would continue fighting the Lord's battles, Saul would offer him a daughter to wed. Saul thought eventually David would be killed in battle and he wouldn't have to do it himself. David married Saul's daughter Michal, and continued to win battles. Saul still feared him.

- Saul planned to kill David, so both Jonathan and Michal told him of Saul's plan. Saul did attack David with a spear, but he survived and was safe.
- Saul sent men several times to kill David but God's spirit only made them dance and shout when they arrived. Saul, feeling he needed to do it himself, went after David but also ended up dancing and shouting.
- Jonathan tried to find out from Saul why he was so determined to kill David, but Saul threw a spear at him. Jonathan and David swore their love for one another, and cried over the hatred that Saul had for David.
- David visited a priest in Nob who gave him Goliath's sword. David visited the King of Gath. The people there bragged of his battle victories. Afraid it would anger the king, he acted crazy so the King ignored him.
- David traveled and others joined him. Saul learned of David's visit to the king in Gath, and thinks they're planning to harm him. Saul killed those in Gath and some priests. David was told what Saul did.
- Saul tried to trap David. In a cave David had the opportunity to kill Saul but he didn't. Afterwards, they both talked and reconciled.
- Samuel died and Israel mourned. David met Abigail, whose husband insulted David. Abigail stopped David from fighting him. Saul gave Michal to another man. David married Abigail although he was already married to Michal and Ahinoam. Once again, Saul set out to kill David.
- David had another chance to kill Saul but did not. Again, Saul apologized and David accepted. They reconciled once again.
- David and his army continued to fight and win battles. The Philistines attack Israel and kill 3 of Saul's sons, including Jonathan. Fearing capture, Saul threw himself on a sword, killing himself. The Philistines brutalize his body and hang it up. His people buried him.

Additional comments on the book of I Samuel:

This book took place over a span of about 110 years. Hannah appeared first, teaching us not to ask for blessings we want for ourselves, but blessings that promote God's purposes. She had Samuel, and immediately gave him to Eli to use in the ministry. Then there was Saul, a godly man at first who got angry when David became a hero for slaying Goliath. We should all be angry over things that dishonor God, but Saul's anger was toward someone made in God's image. It wasn't aimed toward Satan.

We must all learn to wait. David waited many years to become Israel's king after God became displeased with Saul. Like David, we must wait until God uses us in His plan. Sometimes we hear God speak but don't wait for Him to finish his message, or we fail to get out of His way so He can make things happen. Acts 1:4 tells us to wait on God's promise. We know the word wait means "to expect" or to "look for", but it also means "to serve" like a waiter does in a restaurant. We can't just sit and wait for God to act in our behalf, we should be "serving" Him as we wait. Prayer: Lord, give us patience as we wait for Your will to be fulfilled in our lives.

II Samuel

The theme of this book is the reign of King David. The first half covers his triumphs and the second half covers his troubles. We see him become king over the tribe of Judah and then over all of Israel, uniting the twelve tribes into one nation and turning Jerusalem into Israel's spiritual center. He was a fierce warrior and deeply religious man.

But then, we begin to see the sinful side of David brought on by his relationship with Bathsheba. He eventually confessed his sins and was assured of God's forgiveness. He had to endure a series of deaths and tragedies to regain his focus. God never gave up on him, and even established a new covenant with David that ensured Israel would always have a land of their own. As Godly as David was at his core, he was not the best example of a person that we should follow as Christians.

- David learned that both Saul and Jonathan were dead. He grieved, and sang a lament for them and ordered the people to learn it. God directed him to go to Judah, where the people there would make him king.
- Battles broke out between Judah and Israel, and between Judah and those loyal to Saul. Abner, Saul's army commander, supported David, so David told him that he wanted his wife Michal returned to him.
- Joab, one of David's officials, killed Abner without David knowing. David mourned his death. Two of Saul's officers kill the Israeli king and bring his head to David. He had those two officers killed.
- At age 30, David became King of Israel and grew more powerful, defeating the Philistines and then capturing Jerusalem. He took more concubines and wives and fathered many more children there.
- David and soldiers go to Judah to bring home the Ark, taking it to Jerusalem. They danced in celebration, which displeased Michal. A man touched the Ark to keep it from falling and was struck down by God.
- David told Nathan that the Ark needed to be in a great building, not in a tent. David wanted to build a temple. Nathan told David that God wanted David's son to build the temple. David continued winning battles.
- David learned that a son of Jonathan was still living, but crippled. He gave the son some land, and let him eat at the king's table. War was still in the land, and David and his army continued winning their battles.
- David meets Bathsheba, wife of Uriah. They got together and she became pregnant. David tried several times to get her and Uriah together, so it would appear that Uriah was the expectant father. Unsuccessful, David had Uriah sent to the front lines where he was killed.
- God sent Nathan to speak with David, using a parable. David realized his sin and pleaded with God for forgiveness, but the newborn baby died. They had another son, Solomon, who God named Jedidiah.

- David's son Amnon forced himself on his sister Tamar. Two years later her brother Absalom had Amnon killed, then fled. David agreed to bring Absalom back, but he wasn't to see David's face for two years.
- Absalom wanted the people to proclaim him king, and some Israeli's did. David and others fled Jerusalem. The Ark of the Covenant was taken from Jerusalem but returned later.
- David was advised to cross the Jordan River to escape those pursuing him. David gathered his army to fight his son Absalom, but told them not to harm him. Absalom was killed, and David mourned his death.
- David moved back to Jerusalem. Judah and Israel argue over who they're loyal to. Sheba rebelled and Israel followed him but Judah sided with David. Joab, David's officer, found Sheba but the people of Abel didn't want a war there. They cut off Sheba's head and gave it to Joab.
- A famine came and lasted 3 years. The Lord condemned 7 of Saul's relatives for murder, and they were killed. Wars with the Philistines continued. David sang a song of victory. A count was taken of those in Israel and Judah who were available for military service. The Lord sent a plague. David built an alter to God, so the plague ended.

Additional comments on the book of II Samuel:

The story of David as much as any other shows the power of repentance. David was the murderer of Uriah, was an adulterer with Bathsheba, and still God forgave his sins because He knew David had come back to Him with a true repentant heart. The hard lesson we should all learn here is that being forgiven doesn't mean there'll be no consequences. David had truly repented, but to repent then go back into sin over and over without turning to the Lord in true humility for forgiveness will not lead you into Paradise. God knows before we repent if we really mean it.

There is probably more written in the bible about David than anyone else except Jesus. A messiah was promised through the lineage of David, through Abraham, Isaac, Jacob, Judah, and Jesse. Twenty-eight generations after David, it came to pass as we're told in the New Testament. God chose the Tribe of Levi as the priestly class, but He also chose the Tribe of Judah to be the Tribe of Kings. Saul, who never gained God's favor as a king, was not from the Tribe of Judah but from the Benjamin Tribe.

David's faith kept his descendants from being treated the way Saul's descendants were treated. Sure, his sins were punished, but his attachment to God was never renounced. God loved David, and we read about it in II Samuel 7:16 when God told him: "And thine house and thy kingdom shall be established for ever before thee; thy throne shall be established forever." This became known as the Davidic Covenant.

I Kings

This book continues the rule of Israelites by kings, advancing the story that began in the books of Samuel. It starts with Solomon and ends with Elijah. Solomon did well at first, but like his father David he had a weakness for women who led him to worship their idols. But he was instrumental in building the Temple, God's dwelling place among His people. Later though, he spent more time building his own palace.

Elijah would have the task of bringing the Israelites back to God after Solomon's death. Among the evil kings opposing him was Ahab and his wife Jezebel, who brought the sinful worship of Baal to a new level. She eventually ordered the death of Elijah but he escaped into the wilderness. He was a holy man so God saved him to use in other ways. He could be viewed as the forerunner of Christ.

Around 900 BC we learn that the people and the land split. The northern part of the country remained as Israel but the lower portion becomes Judah, each with their own king. The 12 Tribes were split among the two countries. After all it took to collectively unite God's people into one region under one king, it begins to unravel.

- David was old when behind his back, his son Adonijah claimed to be the new king. David wanted his son Solomon to be the new king. David forgave Adonijah. David told Solomon to keep God's laws as king, and also to settle a few old scores and wounds. The people recognized Solomon's wisdom.
- David died, and Adonijah married David's previous caretaker. That angered Solomon so he had his brother killed. Then Solomon had Joab killed for killing two innocent men back when David ruled.
- Solomon married the daughter of Egypt's pharaoh, and asked God for wisdom. When he wisely chose from two women who a baby's mother was, weighing their love and emotions, the people knew he was blessed by God.
- Solomon had many officials and governors, and both Israel and Judah grew in population and wealth. Others would travel to him to hear his wisdom. He composed around 3,000 proverbs and over 1,000 songs.
- With the country at peace, Solomon built a temple for the Lord. King Hiram of Tyre provided the cedars and stones. Elaborately furnished with gold, it took 7 years to build. 480 years had passed since they had exited from Egypt.
- Solomon also had palaces built for himself and his family. He had the priests bring the Ark of the Covenant to the temple, still containing the stone tablets placed there by Moses. God's presence was there. They celebrated for 7 days.
- God appeared and told Solomon He would protect the temple as long as he followed His laws. If other gods and idols were worshiped, God would abandon the temple and it would tumble into a pile of ruins.
- Solomon had the Canaanite descendants build him a fleet of ships. His wealth grew and grew. The queen of Sheba visited him to test his wisdom. She was impressed, and gave him even more gifts. He excelled over all other kings.

- Solomon loved foreign women and married 700 of them. They led him to worship their gods. That angered Jeroboam, one of Solomon's officials.
- Solomon tried to kill Jeroboam but he fled. After ruling for 40 years, Solomon died and his son Rehoboam became king. Jeroboam returned, and asked the new king to go easy on the 10 northern tribes who Solomon had always overworked, but Rehoboam refused and added to their workload.
- All of Israel made Jeroboam their king, ruling over 10 of the tribes. Before long he was worshiping other idols. Rehoboam was left with only 2 tribes in Judah.
- A prophet was sent into Bethel to denounce their false idols. While there, he disobeyed God's direction and was killed by a lion. Egypt's army attacked Judah and won, then emptied the temple of all it treasures.
- Asa, a godly man, restocked the temple. Both kings continued their sinful ways, especially Ahab and his wife Jezebel. Ahab was the most evil king.
- Elijah told Ahab there'd be no rain for several years. He visited a widow and multiplied her food. Her son died but Elijah brought him back to life.
- Elijah told Ahab to bring all their prophets of Baal and meet him on Mount Carmel. The prophets ordered Baal to send fire, but none came. Elijah asked God to send fire, and He did. Elijah killed the false prophets. The rains came.
- Jezebel wanted Elijah killed so he fled. Weakened, he wanted to die but an angel gave him food and drink. God told him that all but 7,000 in Israel would die because of their sins. Elisha met Elijah and became his helper.
- King Ahab wanted more land near his palace but the owner refused, so Jezebel had him killed. Ahab and King Jehoshaphat of Judah plan war with Syria. Disguised, King Ahab took an arrow during the battle and died.

Additional comments on the book of I Kings:

When God offered Solomon anything he wanted, he asked for wisdom. He knew he needed the wisdom to carry out what God would ask of him. Over the years, he became very wealthy and wise. His prayer in Chapter 8:22-53 was as good as it gets. But his legacy was tarnished when he married many foreign wives who worshiped Baal, the god of fertility. His wives and friends were his downfall. We learn that Christians shouldn't unduly mingle with unbelievers, and that an unbelieving family can be worse than unbelieving friends. He didn't know of the old saying, "Show me your friends and I'll show you your future."

There are other meaningful points to remember. When Elijah wished he would die, Chapter 19:4, he was touched by an angel. Often when we think we're alone... we're really not. And his victory over King Ahab and the false prophets on Mount Carmel showed that when unbelievers are moved aside, rewards will follow (the rains came). Then sadly, when Solomon died the people erupted into a civil war as foreigners chipped away at his kingdom. Israel was divided into two separate countries, erasing all that had been accomplished to get God's people all together in one land under one king. 200 years later the Assyrians would control Israel. 150 years later Judah fell to the Babylonians.

II Kings

II Kings begins where I Kings left off. We learn more about Elijah and Elisha, and the ongoing wars in the kingdoms of Israel and Judah that seemed to never end. Things changed in Israel around 722 B.C. when the Assyrian army invaded their country and their capital city of Samaria. Then in 586 B.C. King Nebuchadnezzar of Babylon and his army set out to conquer Jerusalem.

Before departing straight to heaven, Elijah handed off his prophetic role to Elisha who performed many miracles. Those miraculous events testify to God's continued support of His people, although His patience was wearing thin. Over and over He continued to deal with a number of horrible kings and leaders. At some point God may have thought about teaching them a lesson. If the people weren't going to follow His authority, then He'd let them fall under the authority of another country, and the cruelty they'd have to endure. Finally, He abandoned them due to their unbelief.

- The King of Israel was injured but asked others for healing instead of asking God. Therefore, Elijah said the king would die and he did. Twice, fifty men were sent to get Elijah, but they were consumed by fire each time.
- Elisha was a follower of Elijah. A chariot of fire appeared and Elijah was taken straight up into heaven. Elisha asked God for the powers Elijah had. After he divided the waters, men accepted Elisha as a Godly prophet.
- Israel, Judah and Edom declare war on Moab. The armies run out of water but Elisha provides it. He tells them they'll conquer Moab.
- Elisha tells a barren woman she'll have a son. The son died but Elisha brought him back to life. He cleansed food that had been poisoned.
- Naaman was a leper but the king couldn't heal him. Elisha told him to wash in the Jordan River and he was cured. An army was sent to capture Elisha but they were blinded before they could attack.
- A seven-year famine hit the land. Elisha predicted the death of the Syrian king, who was killed later by Hazael. Elisha prophesied the end of the famine. Hazael treated Israel badly.
- Jehu was anointed to become King of Israel. To settle an old score, Jehu had two other kings killed. Jezebel hears of the 2 killings and scorns Jehu, so he has her thrown down from the palace window. Already dead, Jehu runs over her with his chariot. Dogs eat her body.
- Seventy descendants of King Ahab are killed and beheaded, which fulfilled what God said would happen. All the worshipers of Baal were gathered and killed, wiping out the worship of Baal in Israel. Jehu began to sin.
- Different kings ruled Israel and Judah as war continued. King Jehoash of Israel defeated Judah's king Amaziah and restored their borders.
- The Assyrians conquer Samaria, Israel's capital. God didn't defend Israel because of their sinful ways. Assyria worshiped other gods, so God sent lions that killed many. Joash was a good ruler in Jerusalem.

- Money was collected to repair the damaged temple. Afterwards, Elisha died. For a while, Judah's kings were godly while Israel's kings were sinful. An Israeli priest taught Assyrians about God, but with little success.
- King Hezekiah of Judah destroyed all ungodly things to please the Lord. Israelites continued to sin. Assyria prepared to attack Israel but were afraid due to Hezekiah's faith in God. An angel of the Lord killed 185,000 Assyrian soldiers. Hezekiah's sons killed the Assyrian king.
- King Hezekiah became ill but was given 15 more years to live after he prayed to God. Upon his death his son Manasseh became king but sinned by rebuilding an alter to Baal. The Lord brought disaster upon Jerusalem and Judah, and abandoned them due to their sins.
- Later, King Josiah of Judah wanted to repair the Temple. The book of the Law of the Temple was read to him. He realized they weren't following the law and would be punished.
- Josiah was scared, and did away with all things related to Baal and pagan worship. He replaced the priests and killed the sinful ones. He made sure Passover was celebrated. He was later killed in battle.
- King Nebuchadnezzar and his Babylon army conquer Jerusalem and carry off the temple treasures. Sinful King Zedekiah began ruling there.
- Nebuchadnezzar built a wall around the city to starve out those inside. Then he burned the temple and palace, removing all precious metals and the items Solomon had made. Priests were taken and killed. Judah was in exile. Those remaining were in fear, so they left for Egypt.

Additional comments on the book of II Kings:

Many miracles were performed in this book. Two persons were raised from the dead (4:32-37 and 13:21) and twice the waters were parted (2:8 and 2:14). Elijah was so holy that he went to heaven without dying (2:11) just like Enoch had done in Genesis. There were also major changes within Israel and Judah about 80 years after they'd split into their two kingdoms. Not only did both kingdoms fall, but God allowed King Nebuchadnezzar to take away the temple treasures along with Jerusalem's warriors and craftsmen.

One message included Elisha's helping of a woman deeply in debt. He required the woman, in faith, to work and accomplish what she could by herself before God helped her along. In other words, the amount of faith and effort we have in our own works determines the number of blessings we receive from God. We reap what we sow. Then in chapter 11, we read about the hero Jehosheba who hid Joash for seven years to save his life and the royal line of David, from which would come the Messiah.

In chapters 18 and 19 we read about King Hezekiah who received serious threats from the King of Assyria. Instead of panicking, he prayed and God answered him. When in fear, we should go to the Lord in prayer.

I Chronicles

Chronicles retells many of the events which occurred in the books of Samuel and Kings. It was written to the Israelites who survived the Babylonian captivity and covers the history of Judah and Israel until the return of Babylonian captivity in or around 536 BC. Genealogical histories are reviewed, plus the death of Saul and the reign of King David. Many preparations are made for the rebuilding of the temple.

One important person in this book is King David. He had a lot to do with Jerusalem becoming the center for worshiping God. When the book was written, David's descendants no longer ruled as monarchs over Israel. But the writer emphasized that through David's lineage, God promised the future King and Messiah would come. The book retells stories through a priestly point of view.

- We're reminded of the lineage from Adam to Abraham, a period of approximately 2,000 years, and those in earlier Old Testament books.
- The story is retold how David became king. The names of his most famous soldiers and famous followers are given. Retracing the movement of the covenant box, and David's praise and works are highlighted.
- Nathan reveals God's message about building the temple, and that David's son Solomon would build it. David says a prayer of Thanksgiving. David's military victories are given, including killing the giants at Gath.
- David ordered a census of Israel be taken, which displeased God so He sent an epidemic on the Israeli people. David built an alter and sacrificed animals which stopped the epidemic.
- David made preparations for building the temple by having many materials gathered. He confessed to Solomon that he had caused too much bloodshed to be allowed to build it.
- David gathered the Israeli leaders and priests and Levites. They're assigned responsibilities such as temple worship and temple duties. Other groups, administrators, and advisors are named. They all praised God.

Additional comments on the book of I Chronicles:

This book primarily restates the reign and deeds of King David as described earlier in the Books of Samuel, but there's another important message to be gleaned from this story. Throughout the bible we see many "family trees" where each descendant of a prophet or important person is listed by name. That was the only way a person could prove they belonged to the family of Abraham. It also ensured that only members of the Levi Tribe were priests, and that only members from certain tribes were allowed to be kings. In our own family trees, we must remember that God knows each of us by name. He is intimately interested in each one of us, His children, because we belong to His family. He cares for us with an adopting love, and generously gives us hope and direction.

II Chronicles

II Chronicles continues the events in I Chronicles, reviewing the reign of King Solomon and construction of the temple during a time when a small group of Jews returned to Judah after the collapse of the Babylonian Empire. Tradition tells us this book was probably written by Ezra, covering the history of Judah and the nation's religious history.

Much is written about the divided monarchy of Israel after the rebellion of the northern tribes. After the death of his father Solomon, King David's grandson Rehoboam failed to win ratification from the ten northern tribes because of his arrogance toward them. So the ten tribes form the Northern Kingdom of Israel with their first king, Jeroboam, and establish Samaria as its capital city. Rehoboam retained leadership over the Kingdom of Judah, with Jerusalem its capital city.

- Solomon took control of Israel around 971 BC. He had accumulated great wealth, but prayed for more wisdom and knowledge. The temple, or portable tabernacle, was located in Gibeon at the time.
- Solomon planned a more permanent temple to be built in Jerusalem. King Hiram provided resources and materials so the building could begin.
- The covenant box was brought there. Solomon addressed the people then prayed "Solomon's Prayer". Sacrifices were offered and fire came from Heaven to burn them. Everyone celebrated the Festival of Shelters.
- After 20 years of construction the temple was completed. The Queen of Sheba visited and was impressed. Solomon ruled Israel for 40 years before passing. He was buried in David's City, and his son Rehoboam took over.
- Rehoboam increased the workload on the northern tribes so they revolted. He banned the Levites from priesthood. They turn to sin, and are invaded by Egypt who took items from the temple. Wars broke out.
- King Asa of Judah had false idols removed from the temple. There was peace for 35 years before Israel invaded Judah. Later Jehoshaphat became Judah's king, and they grew more powerful.
- Ahab, now king of Israel, was killed in a battle which the prophet Micaiah had foreseen and predicted.
- Jehoshaphat's son Jehoram became king, and Elijah told him God had condemned him for being evil. The Philistines and Arabs invade Judah and loot the palace. They took the kings wives with them.
- All of Jehoram's sons are killed except the evil Ahaziah. Later he was killed and Queen Athaliah of Judah wanted revenge. They revolted against her.
- King Joash of Judah wanted the temple repaired so the Levites collected money to do it. Meanwhile other kings came and went; some evil and some God-fearing. King Hezekiah of Judah followed God's laws and order.

- The temple was purified and rededicated, and worship started there once again. They prepared for Passover. King Hezekiah reestablished religious life in the region. Things were good and joyful.
- The Assyrians threaten Jerusalem and Hezekiah, so God shielded and rescued them. Hezekiah becomes sick, but recovers and prospers.
- When King Hezekiah died his son Manasseh took over at the age of 12. Through the years he and his descendants ruled the area.
- The book that God gave to Moses was found in the temple. It was read to the people and they were ordered to obey it. They celebrated Passover.
- Later, other kings ruled but they defiled God and the temple. The Lord sent Babylon to attack them, and the temple was burned and the people taken as slaves. The land sat desolate until God commanded Cyrus, the Emperor of Persia, to have the scattered Jews return from exile and rebuild the temple in Jerusalem.

Additional comments on the book of II Chronicles:

This period in history was a volatile time for the Jewish people. Their kings were never lukewarm in their religious beliefs. They were either invested in God's word and righteousness, or engaged in nefarious activities meant to disgrace and defile God's kingdom. We read in Chapter 36 that God will do whatever is necessary to unite and save those who've wandered off His path, even to having His holy place of worship destroyed and ravaged and the people enslaved. We see that in our lives too, when sometimes we'll lose that special person or thing we just can't do without to make us stop looking in the mirror and start looking upward.

God wants to be our heavenly Father, even if it takes a loss or a major sorrowful event for us to recognize and embrace Him. We've seen sinful people lose a precious family member then turn to God for understanding and salvation. We've seen sinful people be stricken with a serious illness before being healed, then turn to God for thanks and a rededication of their lives to Him. Things happen for a reason, even bad things. God works in many ways, and He knows that our souls are the only things in us that have real eternal value. We can lose every possession we own but still have victory in Jesus, or we can own the riches of the world but never see Paradise.

God had His temple sacrificed and destroyed, just as we must often sacrifice and give up something we really want in order to help someone, even ourselves. God surrenders and concedes many things for our benefit, and continuously tolerates our sinful nature hoping we'll repent and accept His gift of forgiveness. But His ultimate gift to us comes later, when Jesus Christ dies for us on a skull-shaped hillside in Golgotha.

Ezra

Ezra, a lineal descendant of Aaron, was regarded as the second greatest hero in the history of Israel, after Moses. After some of the exiled Jewish people led by Zerubbabel returned to Jerusalem after 70 years of Babylonian captivity, the rebuilding of Solomon's Temple began. Ezra, whose name means "help", or "helper", later assembled a second band of Israeli exiles and led them into Jerusalem. There he sparked a spiritual revival by purifying the Jewish community and restoring the temple services. All this began around 536 BC and ended around 456 BC.

- Cyrus, Emperor of Persia, commanded the Jews to return from Babylon to rebuild the temple in Jerusalem. Although reluctant, many from the tribes of Benjamin and Judah planned to return, including the priests.
- Over 42,000 people return, plus their servants, musicians and animals. The items taken from the temple by Nebuchadnezzar were also returned.
- An alter was built so sacrifices could be made. The people gave money to obtain building supplies for the temple and to pay the workers.
- When the temple foundation was completed, the exuberant Jewish people shouted and celebrated so loudly it was heard from miles away.
- Enemies of the southern tribes didn't want the temple rebuilt and tried to slow the work by frightening the workers. They also opposed the rebuilding of Jerusalem and temporarily had the work stopped.
- As Emperor Cyrus had ordered, the temple did get rebuilt and rededicated. The Levite priests set up worship services. Passover was celebrated.
- Ezra, a scholar with a thorough understanding of the Laws of Moses, gathered a second band of exiled Jewish people and left Babylon for Jerusalem. He taught them the Laws, and praised God for His blessings.
- Ezra learned that some priests and Israelites had married women from neighboring counties. He felt disgraced, and asked God to forgive them.
- The people gathered, and those with foreign wives were identified. After an investigation, the married couples were divorced and sent away.

Additional comments on the book of Ezra:

To get the exiled Jewish people back to Jerusalem God used Cyrus, a pagan non-Jewish evil king, to authorize their return. It seemed odd that someone outside the Israeli circle was chosen by God to do that, but He often uses those who are the least likely to guide us and deliver His messages. We've all heard someone speaking and felt they were talking directly to us, and have had their words move us to go somewhere or to do something we needed to do.

God uses many couriers and messengers to guide us day by day. Just like the Israelites, returning back to where we've been before can be stressful. There are unknowns, and changes have occurred. But we go where God sends us. He who forgives us and gives us grace sends His Spirit to light our paths.

Nehemiah

When Nehemiah asked his brother Hanani how things were going in Jerusalem, he was told the Jewish people who'd returned from exile were being treated poorly, and that the walls of Jerusalem laid in ruins. Nehemiah had heard that Ezra helped rebuild the temple, but felt a wall was also needed to help protect the city. Living in Susa, he was permitted to return to Jerusalem by the Persian king who'd also named him as the Governor of that region. His return was compromised when he found out the people living near Jerusalem didn't really want the city walls rebuilt.

After much prayer, Nehemiah assembled a crew and construction began on the walls in or around 445 BC. He knew the wall would protect his people from further attacks, but would also separate and distinguish the people there from those living in the surrounding areas. It would make God's special people feel special once again.

- Nehemiah, the emperor's wine steward, learned those who'd returned to Jerusalem from exile were being disrespected and that the walls and gates there laid in ruin. He prayed for guidance, and asked to go there.
- The emperor approved his trip so he went to inspect the damage. He asked the leaders to rebuild, with different groups and clans assigned to construct each section. Some there opposed the rebuilding the wall.
- Nehemiah prayed for protection. Expecting trouble, some worked while others stood by with weapons in hand. Work was guarded day and night.
- Nehemiah helped the poor and oppressed. He was unselfish and strived to do what was right, but still took care to protect himself from harm.
- The entire wall and gates were finished, so more clans of Israelites returned to Jerusalem. Duties within the walls were assigned.
- They all asked Ezra to read the law to them, to remind them. They listened and began to cry. They had a 7-day feast in celebration.
- During a Festival of Shelters, many built and lived in temporary shelters. They fasted and prayed a prayer of confession.
- Nehemiah and Zedekiah agreed to separate the people from foreigners who lived nearby. Jewish leaders and 1 out of 10 others drew lots to see who would live within the city and who would live outside the walls.
- The city wall was dedicated. Many got on top of the wall and gave thanks to God. Others set up worship in the temple. Foreigners were excluded from the community. After 12 years Nehemiah left Jerusalem for Susa.
- When he returned to Jerusalem, he saw some temple rooms were being misused and the temple had been neglected. He got upset after learning some had married foreigners, some had profaned the Sabbath, and that many had backslid. He prayed and asked for God's favor and direction.
- He reestablished his earlier reforms and made corrections. He worked hard to please God and keep things within God's laws.

Additional comments on the book of Nehemiah:

Nehemiah was a man who knew to pray often and seek God's guidance. Before he asked the Emperor to release him to travel to Jerusalem, he prayed. Before he began to oversee the wall and gate construction, he prayed. When he felt threatened, he prayed. In the past, when the Jewish people mixed with others there was trouble, so he wanted a wall to separate them so they'd remain uncontaminated from their neighbors. When he separated and protected these Israelites from others, he prayed.

In part, this book is about starting over when our lives and the things around us have been through hard times. Nehemiah wasn't a priest or preacher, but was chosen by God to help and assist others to start over after their city had been attacked and left in ruin. But he lived in Susa and Jerusalem was nearly 900 miles away. In biblical days, a journey over that distance could take weeks, but he was moved by God to head that way. His goal was not only to oversee the reconstruction there, but to renew the covenant between God and the descendants of Judah, Benjamin, and the Levites and priests living there. After the temple, the city, the walls and the gates in Jerusalem had become damaged and unserviceable, one could say that the city was starting over.

Just as in Jerusalem, how many of us need a wall around us to protect us from outside forces and temptations? When the going gets rough, we should read what God says about protection from those people or things trying to harm us. If we fear others, Luke 10:19 tells us we have authority to tread on serpents and over the power of the enemy, and nothing shall hurt us. Ephesians 6:11 tells us to put on the whole armor of God, that we may be able to stand against the schemes of the devil.

But I Corinthians 10:13 may say it best and give us our best wall of defense to escape both evil and temptation. It says that no temptation that has overtaken us is uncommon to man (in other words, you are not alone because we have all had those same temptations in life). It also says that **God is faithful, and He will not let you be tempted beyond your ability, and along with the temptation He will also provide a way for you to escape, that you may be able to endure it.** God loves us, so He always has our backs. It's comforting to know we are not alone, and that our anchor will hold during each turbulent storm of life.

Esther

Esther was a humble yet beautiful orphaned Jewish girl, raised by her cousin Mordecai in or around 480 BC, who saved a generation of people through her persuasion and bravery. She was not a strict follower of Jewish customs when she married non-Jewish King Xerxes in Susa, the capital city of Persia. Through her marriage to the king she met the king's Prime Minister Haman, who hated the Jewish people and wanted them killed. The plot thickened after the king approved the killings, not knowing his wife Esther was Jewish. The name Esther means secret, or hidden, and she certainly knew to keep the secret of her ancestry from the King.

Esther was a descendant of the Benjamin Tribe from Judah whose people had been relocated to Babylon years earlier before Babylon was conquered by Persia. She ended up being the Queen to King Xerxes only because the incumbent Queen didn't like it when the King tried to show her off to his friends, which angered and embarrassed him. He replaced her with Esther, influenced in part by her beauty. This book tells a compelling story involving trust, spiritual truths, and vengeance, with clearly defined heroes and villains.

- King Xerxes of Persia had power. He threw a big banquet for his male leaders and military which lasted a whole week. So Queen Vashti threw a banquet for the women. The King asked for the Queen to join him, to show her off, but she refused. He felt she had tarnished his authority.
- He announced that in the future all men would be masters of their houses and speak with authority. He wanted someone else as his queen.
- Women were gathered for his inspection. Mordecai had a Jewish cousin named Esther whom he had raised as his own. She came to the Kings palace, receiving beauty treatments and massages for a whole year.
- Among all the other women, the King chose her and threw a banquet not knowing she was Jewish. Two men planned to assassinate the King but Mordecai and Esther warned him, and he was saved.
- The King named Haman his Prime Minister, and everyone was to bow to him. Mordecai, being Jewish refused, so Haman wanted Mordecai and all local Jews killed. The King approved it, and gallows were built.
- Mordecai asked Esther for help. The Jewish people prayed as she went to speak to the King. She invited the King and Haman to a banquet.
- The King remembered how Mordecai had warned him about the attempt to assassinate him, so in Haman's disbelief the King put a robe on Mordecai and marched him on horseback to honor him.
- The King and Haman attended Esther's banquet, and she tells the King that Haman wanted her and all other Jews killed. That was a dangerous thing to tell the King, since it told him she was Jewish. She risked her own life by intervening, but it proved successful. In anger, the King had Haman hanged on the gallows that he'd had built to hang Mordecai.

- The King wouldn't rescind the orders he'd approved, but told Esther that the Jewish people could resist capture and put up a fight. So they felt safer.
- All Jewish people in the area received letters telling them it was okay to fight back against those wanting to harm them. The Persian people felt Mordecai had gained power, and began to fear the Jewish people.
- All ten of Haman's sons were killed by Jewish people and hung from the gallows. Others who were their enemies were also killed. Mordecai was promoted by the King to be second in command.

Additional comments on the book of Esther:

The book of Esther contains several important points, one of which is the talk of racism by Haman on the people from Israel who lived there in Susa. Mordecai wouldn't bow down to him, so Haman wanted to extinguish them all. Then without knowing how the King would take it, Esther's talk with him about Haman's plan showed her trust and faith that somehow God would make things right. The talk of racism is wrong, and the bible tells us in Romans 14:12 that we all must give an account to God for our evil thoughts and actions. Haman didn't have to wait for God's judgement; the King delt with him right away, at least in his flesh body.

Oddly, this story about Esther does not mention God even once, although His presence and involvement can be felt throughout the book. When Queen Vashti embarrassed the King, it opened the door for Esther to be selected among the many women from which the King would chose his new queen. Then she won the favor of Hegai, the one overseeing all the women there, so he gave her special treatment for a whole year and even assigned seven girls to serve her. Then wearing what Hegai had chosen for her to wear to meet the King, she was chosen as his Queen.

All those fortunate breaks, as serendipitous as they seemed as she won over each person along the way to becoming queen, put her in position to save all the Jewish people of Susa when the time came. In the end, approximately 75,000 people in the area who were against God's chosen people ended up being killed. We don't have to see God or His Holy Spirit to know when He's near, working through us or others in our behalf.

As it says in John 3:8, the wind blows and you hear it's sound, but you don't know where it comes from or where it goes. So it is with everyone born of the Spirit. We all witness good things happening to us in life but we can't always see the blessings coming or know what we've done to deserve them. The Holy Spirit is with every believer even though we can't see Him, but just like the wind we can feel His presence. We don't know when He'll intercede for us or where He'll go next, but when we need a touch from God He is there.

Job

The book of Job is about a very wealthy man who considered himself righteous because he had always avoided doing evil. He worshiped the Lord and was careful not to do anything that might insult Him. Therefore the Lord viewed Job as a true and faithful servant, and boasted of his goodness. But Satan saw it differently. He appeared before God to claim that Job was an upright person only because he had been blessed with a large family and many possessions. If he had none of those things, Satan claimed, he'd be sinful and curse the Lord to His face.

Maybe Satan had forgotten or never understood that God knows everything there is about us, because He's our Father and He made us. So to prove Job's faithfulness, God allowed Satan to torment Job but he wasn't allowed to take his life. While suffering, Job's friends visited him and offered words of encouragement and advice. The books of Job through The Song of Solomon contain spiritual guidance and advice for the Christian life, so they're known as books of Poetry and Wisdom.

- Job from the land of Uz was very wealthy; a Godly man careful to do no evil. Satan said Job would be different if he was penniless, so God gave Job's belongings to Satan who then had Job's children killed.
- Job still praised God, so Satan had sores cover Job's body to further test his faithfulness. Job still worshipped God as his friends came to visit.
- Eliphaz, Bildad, and Zophar arrived after hearing of Job's suffering. Job complained to God about having no peace or rest. Eliphaz told him to present his case to God and be rescued, then live a long life.
- Job wondered why God hadn't answered his prayers. He was miserable and wanted to die, and told his friends he was tired of living that way.
- Bildad told Job to quit complaining, that God would do what's right. He assured Job that God would never abandon the faithful.
- Job said that God hung the moon, so He was too busy and powerful for him to talk to. He felt no one spoke to God in his behalf. God knows he's sinless, so Job doesn't know what charges God has against him.
- Zophar asked God to answer Job, while admitting everyone really gets punished less than they deserve. He asked Job to reach out to God.
- Job understood what Zophar had said, but still wanted to argue his case before God knowing he'd done nothing to deserve punishment.
- Eliphaz said Job's harsh words would condemn him, so he shouldn't shake his fist at God. He said Job's bitterness would bring no harvest; he'd be like a healthy vine that loses its unripe grapes.
- Bildad told him not to be angry because it would only hurt him.
- Job was determined to keep his prayers pure. He loved the Lord just like his friends did but they weren't made to suffer, so he found that hard to understand. He was miserable, but believed God would save him.

- Zophar told Job that successful men get crushed by the weight of their misery, and that wicked men never seemed to be happy.
- Eliphaz asked if any man was useful to God. He told Job he was wicked at times, and to throw away his riches since God was his wealth.
- Job wanted his life to return to when he was known and respected, when God watched over him. Now others made fun of him, but he still wanted God to recognize his goodness.
- Job's young friend Elihu spoke up and said God was speaking but none there were listening, and none there had answered Job's concerns.
- The Lord spoke, asking why they all questioned His wisdom. "Do any of you control the seas, the animals, or new births?" He asked. "If you can do the things I do I'll praise you, but you're trying to make me unjust. Don't forget I created you, just as I did Behemoth and Leviathan."
- Job repented, and said that he knew the Lord was all powerful. He now saw the Lord in a new light.
- The Lord was angry with Job's three friends who didn't speak the truth about Him, but Job prayed for them. God restored Job and gave him twice as much of everything that he'd had before. Job feasted with his family and friends. He prospered, and lived another 140 years.

Additional comments on the book of Job:

All through this story Job felt he'd been righteous and didn't deserve to suffer. Even today, Christians can't explain the hardships and adversities they see that befall good people. We're incapable of truly understanding God's will with our narrow viewpoint, but in the end He will always reward goodness and He will always punish evil. Each time we feel punished should we automatically conclude that it was brought on by our sins? The answer is no. Everything that happens is the will of God, and man will never be knowledgeable enough to fully comprehend His reasons.

God knew that Job had built his spiritual foundation on solid ground, as we're taught in I Corinthians 3:10-13, one that would withstand the flames of the judgement fire. It tells us that every man's work shall be made manifest, put under a spotlight for the eyes of Christ to judge. We must be judicious in our works, for there are many ways to serve God and many areas of service that needs our help.

Of course the believer's foundation is God, and what we build on that foundation determines our ultimate destiny. God knew Job's life was good, and that he'd survive Satan's attacks because his base was not built of wood, hay or stubble. Just like Job, we strive to live our lives so we'll receive God's rewards. In I Corinthians 3:14 we learn that if any man's work abides (passes the scrutiny of God's judgement) he shall receive a reward, and everyone loves gifts and rewards, especially those from God.

Psalms

Psalms may be one of the most difficult books in the bible to summarize. It contains 150 poems, prayers and praises written for the people of Israel, and like all of God's word it applies to us today just like it did thousands of years ago. Principally composed by David, there were other contributors including Moses, Solomon, the Levites who served in the Temple, and others. It is regarded as one of the most widely read books in the Old Testament, expressing the innermost feelings of the Jewish people throughout their early history. These Psalms are probably at their best when read aloud, set to music, or studied in reflective solitude.

Psalms can be viewed as 5 separate books or collections which many feel are patterned after the first 5 books of the bible. They cover everything from when God is beside us, when He goes before us, and when He is around, above and among us. To truly receive the messages contained in Psalms, try to read them individually to teach, feed and guide your Christian soul.

To find a Psalm to meet a specific need, the following is a rough guide to direct you to the many subjects contained in this book.

<u>Psalms 1-10:</u> True happiness is like a tree planted by water. God is King. Morning and evening prayers always help. There are prayers for justice, protection, glory, dignity, and during times of trouble.

<u>Psalms 11-20:</u> Having confidence in the Lord. Praying for help and confidence, and what God requires. Prayers for the wickedness or innocence of men. God's creation glory, and David's Song of Victory.

<u>Psalms 21-30:</u> Cries of anguish and praise, and a victory prayer. The Lord is my Shepard and Great King. Prayers of help, praise, guidance and protection. The prayer of the good man, the Lord's voice in a storm, and in Thanksgiving.

<u>Psalms 31-40:</u> The trust and praise in God. The destiny of the wicked or good man. A prayer for help, and those of a suffering man. A song of praise.

<u>Psalms 41-50:</u> Prayers for a sick man, and a man in exile. A royal wedding song, and the Supreme Ruler who is with us. Zion the city of God, the foolishness of trusting in riches, and a prayer of true worship.

<u>Psalms 51-60:</u> A prayer of trust, and for forgiveness. God's judgement and Grace. Prayers for protection from enemies, and if you're betrayed by a friend. A prayer for safety, trust, and deliverance. God's punishment of the wicked.

<u>Psalms 61-70:</u> A longing for God. Prayers for His protection. Praise and Thanksgiving. A National song of Triumph. Prayers when you need help.

Psalms 71-80: An old man's prayer. A prayer for the King. The Justice of God. A Prayer for National Deliverance. God the Victor and Judge. God and His people. A prayer for the Nation's restoration.

Psalms 81-90: A festival song. God the Supreme Ruler, and longing for His house. A prayer to defeat Israel's enemies. Pray for the nation's welfare, and a hymn in times of trouble. God's promise to David. Praise to Jerusalem. A lament over the death of a King. Of God and man.

Psalms 91-100: God our King, Judge, and Protector. Songs of praise. God the supreme King and Ruler. A hymn of worship.

Psalms 101-110: The King's promise. Prayers for a troubled man. The love of God, and in praise of Him. God's people, and His goodness to them. A prayer for help against enemies. Complaints of men in trouble. The chosen King.

Psalms 111-120: The happiness of good people. Praising the Lord. The one true God; praising His goodness. A Passover Song. A man saved from death. The value, understanding, and all about the Lord's laws. Praying for help.

Psalms 121-130: God the Protector. In praise of Jerusalem. Prayers for mercy and deliverance. The security of God's people. Prayers for help, and God's goodness. Trust and obedience to God. Praying for Israel's enemies.

Psalms 131-140: In praise to the temple. In praise of Brotherly Love. A hymn of praise to God. Hymns and prayers of Thanksgiving. A lament to those in exile. God's complete knowledge and care. A prayer for protection.

Psalms 141-150: An evening prayer. Prayers when you need help. Thanking God for victory. Hymns of praise to God the Almighty. A call for the universe to praise God. Praise the Lord!

Additional comments on the book of Psalms:

For daily guidance and direction, the Psalms are a great source of information. They can serve as the Christian's prayer book, hymnal, and training guide.

A few of the many Psalms needed regularly:

20 – for praying for others

32 – for confession and forgiveness

41 – for sicknesses and illness

54 – for when you're in trouble

61, 91 – for need of security and confidence

23, 27, 103, 138, and 146 – for private devotion and praise

Proverbs

We learned in I Kings that when God offered Solomon anything he wanted, Solomon asked for wisdom. We read of that wisdom in many of these Proverbs since Solomon was the principal writer. This book often distinguishes between what a wise man might do in a certain situation compared to what a foolish man might do. The emphasis is placed on having the wisdom and good judgement to make correct decisions, and understanding that a successful Christian must be able to ascertain that good moral behavior and righteous conduct is what pleases God.

It has been said that B-I-B-L-E could be giving us **Basic Instructions Before Leaving Earth**, and Proverbs certainly provides all the instructions needed for us to live an effective life of discernment and enlightenment. Some of these Proverbs apply to younger people while others apply to everyone. Like Psalms, these Proverbs should be read individually to fully comprehend the knowledge they contain. They're full of life principles and great advice. The following is a condensed outline of this book, by chapter (C), capturing only a small part of the invaluable wisdom within.

C 1-2: Young people should learn from their fathers and mothers. Don't be tempted by sinners, and be knowledgeable instead of being foolish. Don't reject wisdom but seek it. Resist immoral men and women. Be righteous.

C 3-4: Be loyal and faithful. Trust in the Lord to give you plenty. He corrects young men and women. Do good to those who need it. The Lord dislikes conceit and wickedness. Strive for knowledge and education. Walk the straight path.

C 5-6: Be faithful to your spouse; avoid adultery. Don't involve yourself in the debts of others. The Lord hates lying tongues and killing hands, evil thinkers and doers, false witnesses and troublemakers. Good sons avoid bad women.

C 7-8: Don't give in to an immoral woman, the ruin of many men. Don't go where sin awaits you. Learn to be mature without foolishness. Wisdom is better than gold and jewels. Young men who find wisdom find life.

C 9-10: Correct a wise man and he'll respect you. Reverence for the Lord brings wisdom and years to your life. Don't let stupidity call out to you. Wise children make parents proud. Good people are remembered. Hate stirs up trouble. Too much talk breeds sin; the wise keep quiet. Righteous people will survive.

C 11-12: Be modest. Riches won't save you from death. Don't scorn others; keep quiet. Hard work brings prosperity. Pretty women without judgement is like a gold ring in a pig's snout. Help others, and you'll be helped. Accept being corrected. Wisdom is praised. Your rewards will equal your actions. Worry can rob your happiness. Care for your animals. Useless projects waste your time.

C 13-14: Wise sons listen to fathers. Don't act rich if you're not. Ask for advice when needed. Stay hopeful. Punish your children if you love them. Wise people are calm people. Helping the poor brings happiness. Hot tempers show ignorance. If you mistreat the poor you are mistreating God.

C 15-16: Accept honest correction. God loves it when good men pray. Happy people smile. Patience brings peace. Love your mother. Good people think then speak. God has final approval, ask for his blessings. Grey hair is a crown.

C 17-18: Forgive people when they wrong you. End arguments quickly. Avoid the debts of others. Cheerfulness means happiness. A fool tries to show his intelligence. Be humble, speak carefully and kindly, and bring gifts to others.

C 19-20: Don't blame God for your stupid actions. Sensible people control their tempers. A nagging wife is like a dripping faucet. It's disgraceful to be greedy. Avoid arguments. Be fair in dealings. Don't battle without a plan. Don't brag.

C 21-22: God judges our motives. Dishonest riches disappear. Listen to cries of the poor. Be kind and honest. Be careful what you say. Victories come from God. God made the rich and poor. Correct your children. Honor property lines.

C 23-24: Discipline children. Wise children make proud parents. Live wisely and seriously. Don't envy evil people. Being wise is better then being strong. Show strength in a crisis. Worship the Lord. Don't mislead anyone.

C 25-26: Don't pretend to be important. Don't promise what you can't deliver. It's okay to help an enemy. Don't try to win praise. Control your anger. Don't praise foolishness. Don't argue. You can get caught in traps set for others.

C 27-28: Anger is destructive but jealousy is worse. Don't forget your friends. Sensible people see trouble coming before it arrives. Learn from one another. Obeying the Lord brings happiness. Give to the poor and you'll be blessed.

C 29-30: Anger doesn't have to be openly expressed. Humble people are respected. Trusting in God brings safety. God protects, and keeps promises. It's good to be truthful, and to be neither rich nor poor. Give, don't always receive. Be able to move in formation even when no one leads you.

C 31: Alcohol is for the miserable. Speak for those who can't speak for themselves. A capable wife knows the value of things, and the value she adds. Speak with gentle wisdom. Give others due credit. Beauty and charm can disappear, but anyone honoring the Lord will continue to receive complements.

Additional comments on the book of Proverbs:

If you read only a few books from the Bible, you should include Proverbs. It covers many topics, many dealing with self-control, patience, controlling anger, humility, and respect for the poor. Where unwise people have no respect for learning or improvement, wise people know that to have knowledge you must first have reverence for the Lord. These Proverbs can make anyone, regardless of their age, more inspired and ingenious.

Ecclesiastes

What is life? Can we comprehend its fullness as complex and convoluted as it is? The writer of Ecclesiastes asks those questions, then concludes that life is useless because the righteous and faithful don't always come out on top like we feel they should. Righteous people may often end up with the same fate as the unholy. It's true that we don't always understand why things happen to us or around us, but our instincts are to move forward even without all the answers. If we knew why we didn't get that job we were qualified to have, or why we weren't blessed with children, then life wouldn't be so frustrating. But on the other hand, if life were easy we'd be less likely to pray and ask God for His guidance. Ecclesiastes helps us realize that everything happening to us is all part of God's plan.

In a way we all experience the same issues in life. We have no guarantees that we will prosper, or that everything will happen just as we've planned. We work hard then struggle to see what we have to show for it. As the years click by we gain experience in many areas of life, but still have questions about our future. That's where God enters the picture, our one constant who knows what lies ahead for each of us if we'll keep the faith. Ecclesiastes examines many of the frustrations and doubts we're confronted with, and provides a biblical perspective to accept them on the basis that our time here on earth is only temporary. Only God can show us how to understand and appreciate our lives in full distinction and glory.

- Our eyes never see enough; our ears never hear enough. Everything in life repeats itself over and over. There's nothing new, so life can seem useless.
- We accomplish great things but feel they're of no use, it's like chasing the wind. What happens to us also happens to fools. At death, all we've gained we must leave for others. We can only eat, drink and enjoy.
- God sets our birth and death. In between there's time for sorrow and joy, for loving and dancing, for finding and loosing, for war and peace. In the end we all go back to dust, and hope our spirit goes upward.
- The disadvantaged aren't always helped. Neighbors envy other neighbors. Be pleased with the blessings we receive. Having a partner is better than being alone. Stay wise as you age. People may forget your contributions.
- Don't make rash promises to God. The more you talk the more chance you'll speak foolishly. We're often denied justice and our rights. All wishes don't come true. At death we lose everything, so enjoy life now.
- We aren't allowed to enjoy what we have, so life is useless. We never have enough. Is a wise man better off than a fool? Be pleased with what you have. Every person has a higher authority. What happens at death?
- The day we die can be better than the day we were born. Don't think that things were better in the past. God sends both happiness and trouble. We were made simple but then we complicate ourselves.

- Only a wise man knows what things really mean. We cannot cheat death. Don't praise the wicked. We can't understand all that God is.
- A man's loves and passions die when he dies. The brave don't win every battle. Poor men aren't listened to although many are wise. Listen more to a man whispering the truth than an unwise man shouting.
- A fool lets others know he's foolish by his actions. It's not uncommon for an unwise sinner to ride the horse while the man with wisdom walks behind. Plan ahead, a dull axe means harder work. Don't charm a snake after it's bit you. Your criticism often comes back and hurts someone.
- Spread your investments over many areas to decrease your risk. If you wait until conditions are perfect you'll never start anything. We will all be dead for more years that when we were alive.
- Young people should enjoy their youth and follow their heart's desire. When you're young don't let anything worry you or cause you pain. You won't be young very long.
- A time will come when you may say you don't enjoy life. Your arms will tremble, and your eyesight will fade. You will lose your desires, and age will rob you of any pleasures. When the silver chain and golden lamp snaps and falls one last time, we will die. Our bodies will return to dust, but our breath of life will go back to the Father who gave it to us.
- Life may appear useless but our reverence for God is why we were first created; it wasn't to be rich and famous. He'll judge us all for our works, whether good or bad, even things we thought were done secretly.

Additional comments on the book of Ecclesiastes:

Most of us worry about our future, our homes, our possessions, but the writer of Ecclesiastes (assumed to be Solomon) tells us those things are useless since they all obliterate over time. People come and go in life, and old things are removed to make way for newer and improved versions. The human condition is simply a recurring pattern. At death all we own goes to those who inherit it, so the cycle continues.

Although things do happen to us to darken our outlook on life, it doesn't mean life is useless as the writer implies. This book describes a man who experienced those truths, but in the end developed a wiser and more positive perspective to combat the injustices he'd encountered. It tells us that life doesn't always deal us the rewards we'd hope for, but we need to still enjoy life knowing God gives us all a lasting purpose. Eat, drink and enjoy, because God has a plan for this unfair but wonderful world, and we want to be there with Him to rejoice in it.

Along with the books of Psalms, Proverbs and Job, Ecclesiastes has been called a book of wisdom. One piece of that wisdom found in Ecclesiastes 12:7 breeds a lot of discussion. It reads that when we die "Then shall the dust (our bodies) return to the earth as it was: and the spirit shall return unto God who gave it." Most of us can agree that we have a spirit, and of course it came from God. In Luke 23:46, Jesus says "Father, unto Your hands I commit My Spirit." In Acts 7:59, Stephen says "Lord Jesus, receive my spirit." The word spirit is written and used many times throughout the bible.

Based on the wording in 12:7, Christians have different interpretations of what it means. Some think that our spirit returns to God immediately when we die, but others think our spirit doesn't meet up with Jesus until the saved are caught up in the air with Him, referred to as the Rapture. It's really not important here if we agree or disagree when our spirits meet up with the Lord. The only thing that really matters in all this is that through faith you believe in Jesus Christ, which means your spirit will be with Him in Paradise.

Only God knows when our death or the Rapture will come. The good news for believers is knowing that we'll end up with the Lord regardless of when those events occur. It's more rewarding to hope that our spirit goes to the Lord immediately at our death since it's more probable that our death will precede the Rapture. We can all agree that the sooner our spirits go to be with the Lord, the better. Meanwhile, we eat, drink and enjoy. A good simple rule in life is that before we die we should live, and before we pray we should believe.

Yes, it's a hardscrabble life at times, and we wonder why better things aren't happening to God's children. But as we're advised to do in Ecclesiastes, look for the good in life and enjoy it; make it useful and rememberable. Pray and talk directly to God each morning for daily guidance, then read your Bible so God can talk to you too. There'll always be disappointments in life, but there's a place that's free of hardships, afflictions and sorrows. The divine and precious words found in Revelation 7:17 may describe it best: "For the Lamb who is in the midst of the throne shall feed them, and shall lead them unto living fountains of waters: and God shall wipe away all tears from their eyes."

And all the people shall say, Amen.

The Song of Solomon

This book, also called The Song of Songs, was probably composed around 950 BC and is a passionate exchange between a man and woman both full of heated emotions. Their words paint a deep yearning and desire to be together in a commitment of everlasting love. Although this book and the book of Esther are the only two books in the Bible that don't mention God at all, it does symbolize the endearment and tenderness of God toward His Church and signifies the deep and fervent love He feels for each of His children.

- <u>The First Song:</u> No woman could keep from loving you; it's your kisses and fragrance. Don't look down on me because I'm dark but beautiful. I must work, so I can't spoil or care for myself. Where do I look for you?
- But you my love, your beauty excites all men. You're like a lily among thorns. I want my left hand under your head as I caress you.
- <u>The Second Song:</u> My man is mine and I am his. I dream of you nightly. I search for you but can't find you. Nothing should interrupt our love.
- Then come to me my darling. It's a time for singing. The figs are ripening and vines are blossoming. I want to see your lovely face.
- <u>The Third Song:</u> Women of Zion, come see King Solomon on this day of joy. He comes through the desert with bodyguards, wearing the crown placed on him on his wedding day. My fragrance will fill the air.
- Come with me my bride from the Lebanon Mountains. Your face glows behind your veil. The look in your eyes, my bride, has stolen my heart.
- <u>The Fourth Song:</u> I opened the door for him but he had left. I called for him without an answer. Women of Jerusalem he is strong and majestic, and enchanting and sweet to kiss. If you see him tell him I need him.
- Here I am, so come to me my darling. My head is wet with dew and my hair is damp from the mist. This woman is like my garden.
- <u>The Fifth Song:</u> I will dance and he and the others will watch me. I belong to him, and I know he desires me. Women of Jerusalem, you will not interrupt my love for him.
- My love, you are breathtaking and you hold me captive. The king has many loves, but I love only her. I am trembling and eager in love. Your beauty is great; what a magnificent girl you are.
- <u>The Sixth Song:</u> We are now arm in arm with one another. Our passion is as strong as death itself. Farmers have vineyards, but we have our own!

Additional comments on the book of The Song of Solomon:

This dialogue between a man and woman demonstrates what a loving dedicated relationship between a husband and wife should sound like. It is intense, full of respect, and with a commitment that God would anoint. It's full of faith, hope and love, but the greatest of these is always love.

Isaiah

This book contains messages revealed to the prophet Isaiah about the cities of Jerusalem and Judah during the reign of Hezekiah and other Judean rulers. It's the first of several books from the Major Prophets, and a man like Isaiah who God prophesied through was certainly an important figure during a key period in the history of the southern kingdom. The prophecies given in this book and in several of the following books are repeated because some prophets lived during or around the same time, each receiving messages from God of the pending destruction of Jerusalem and punishment of the Jewish people. An important feature in the book of Isaiah covers the second coming of Jesus and the setting up of His kingdom, and the vision of a new heaven and earth.

Isaiah's prophesies began around 740 BC and lasted for about 60 years. He tried to get the people of Judah, who had turned away from God in the worst of ways, back on track by telling them the Messiah was coming. Many scholars have stated the book covers three distinctive periods. Chapters 1-39 explains the numerous sins of the people. Chapters 40-55 covers the period when many in exile returned to their homeland. In Chapters 56-66 His people are back in Jerusalem seeking reassurance with God, and from the coming Messiah.

- God reprimanded His people who'd rejected Him. Jerusalem would come under siege, with foreigners taking over their land. God couldn't stand their corruption, and would not listen to their prayers any longer.
- Jerusalem had lost it's righteous men, so God would take revenge on the sinners. Any who repented would be spared, but all human arrogance would be destroyed. People will try to escape His power and glory.
- The Lord will destroy everything His people depended on. They'd have no leader. The righteous will be happy, but sinners will be doomed. The people should prepare for their coming judgement.
- The day will be coming when the women will be punished, and be dressed in rags. Strong men will be killed in war. Afterwards Jerusalem will be restored, and all who are left will be holy. The evil will be doomed.
- The Lord will send a distant nation to take over Israel. Isaiah saw the Lord sitting on His throne, asking who His messenger will be. Isaiah answered "Here I am! I will go; send me." God sent a message by Isaiah saying the lands would become wastelands, full of tree stumps.
- The armies of Syria and Israel unsuccessfully attacked Jerusalem. Isaiah told King Ahaz of Judah that a son would be born there and named Immanuel, and by the time he's grown Judah would be prospering.
- The Lord will bring the Assyrian army upon Judah, and the land will be full of briars and thorns. The few survivors will have milk and honey.
- God told Isaiah not to follow or fear anyone but Him. The people are not to seek fortunetellers, mediums, or spirits of the dead.

- A child will be born to them. He will be called Counselor, Father, the Prince of Peace. He'll be King David's successor, and rule forever.
- The Lord will punish Israel. They hadn't repented although they'd been punished. The poor had been given no rights. The country is doomed.
- The Lord used Assyria to punish Jerusalem, but afterwards punished their emperor for his boastfulness. A few in Israel would come back to God.
- Later a new King will rise among the Israelites. Wolves and sheep will live together in peace. Many in exile will return. Judah and Israel will no longer fight one another. They'll sing a hymn of Thanksgiving.
- Isaiah prophesied that God would punish Babylon, and every star would stop shining. The Lord will overthrow Babylon like He did Sodom and Gomorrah. The people of Israel will once again rule over their enemies.
- Then God will destroy the Assyrians, Philistines, and Moab. He'll establish Zion for the people's safety. Moab's situation will be hopeless.
- Then He'll punish Syria and Israel. Damascus will be in ruins, and Israel's wealth will turn into poverty. There'll be incurable pain.
- All enemy nations will be defeated, including Sudan and Egypt. The Egyptians will fall under a tyrant king. The Nile waters will run low. Egypt will fear Judah, and the Lord's presence will be felt there.
- Eventually Israel, Egypt and Assyria will worship together and be a blessing to the world. They will turn to God and He'll heal them.
- The Lord told Isaiah to remove his clothes as a sign of what will happen to sinful countries. They have a vision of the fall of Babylon.
- Jerusalem's sins were so deep they may never be forgiven. The Lord will send Eliakim to have authority under the king, but for a short while.
- The Lord will devastate earth and leave it desolate. The earth and sky will decay. Happiness will be gone, but those who survive will sing for joy.
- The Lord will prepare a great banquet on Mt. Zion. Death will be destroyed forever. Everyone will know God and that He saved them. His people will have victory. The dead will rise; bodies coming back to life.
- Leviathan, symbolizing Israel's enemies, will be punished. Then a trumpet will sound to bring back all Israelites in exile. The northern kingdom must lose their pride or be doomed. Zion will be the foundation.
- Prophetic visions will be hid from God's people, but there's hope for their future when the deaf will hear and the blind will see. They'll be disgraced no more. Isaiah recorded the disobedience of God's people as a record.
- God will bless and protect His people, and join the fight against their enemies. A King is coming who'll bring His glory and integrity.
- There'll be a restoration, full of peace and security. His people's greatest treasure is their reverence for the Lord. There'll be a glorious future for Zion, where they'll have festivals. Everyone in Jerusalem will feel safe.
- Anyone or any country who didn't follow God's road to Holiness will be punished. Those who did will see the Lord's splendor.

- The Assyrians threaten Jerusalem. Their king asked "are they still relying on the Lord their God? No other Gods have saved those we've attacked."
- King Hezekiah asked for Isaiah's advice, and prayed for the Lord to rescue Jerusalem. Isaiah told him the Lord will have the Assyrians return to their own country where they'd be killed.
- Isaiah told Hezekiah their crops would be scarce for two years, but the following year they'd have good crops. King Hezekiah became sick and was preparing to die. The Lord promised him fifteen more years.
- Babylonian messengers visited Hezekiah. Isaiah told Hezekiah that the Babylonians would soon carry off all his treasures. God gives assurance to Israel and tells them He is coming soon! They offer a song of praise.
- The Lord assures Israel of His love. He asked why some worshiped false gods who'd bow to a carved wooden idol. The Lord has Cyrus to fulfill God's purpose to rebuild Jerusalem after Babylon had ravaged it.
- God promised an end to Jerusalem's suffering and disgrace, and would take the beatings, punishment and death for all who really deserve it. If they honor Him, their names would never be forgotten. If they seek other gods, they'll find out that those gods can't save them.
- Jerusalem's future will shine like the sun. "You'll be called the city of the Lord, and I'll be your eternal light." They say, "Lord, part the skies and come to us now!" The Lord said, "I will come to claim My people."
- The Lord says, "I'm making a new earth and heaven. All the past will be forgotten. Heaven is My throne and earth is My footstool. I will come with fire, and many will go to other nations to proclaim My greatness."

Additional comments on the book of Isaiah:

An important feature in the book of Isaiah is the foretelling of the birth, Good News, death and return of Jesus. In 65:17 the creation of the new heavens and earth is divulged, with the new Jerusalem on Mount Zion. In Chapter 53 we read the tearful and emotional words "He is brought as a Lamb to the slaughter, ... so He openeth not His mouth."

When Isaiah volunteered in Chapter 6 to be God's messenger to the people of Israel and Judah, he may not have realized he'd be bringing them news of their doom and destruction for all their years of disobedience. His affection and fondness for his people made his prophecies difficult to proclaim, but he loyally obeyed God's will. Amid the destruction of God's people, enough of them would be spared to continue the holy covenant God had made with their ancestors.

It seems obvious after reading the books of Isaiah and the following book of Jeremiah that God's precious and chosen people had broken His heart. Their unbelief and gross defiance in Him was described over and over again, along with the punishment they'd receive for it. It's hard to imagine the pain He felt bringing destruction to His people.

Jeremiah

Jeremiah, the son of a Levi priest, began to prophesy when he was nearly twenty years old in or around the year 625 BC and continued for another forty years into the period when Jerusalem fell to the Babylonians. A courageous man who fearlessly delivered messages from God, he spoke bluntly to the Judaeans who at times were so unappreciative that his friends needed to protect him from bodily harm. His scope of prophecies covered the futures of Judah, Jerusalem and even foreign nations and their dealings with the Israeli people. Unfortunately, most of his emotional counseling was ignored.

His own views and those he prophesied are disclosed in the prayers given throughout this book, many of which highlight the everlasting patience and endless love God has for the Jewish people. The capture and destruction of Jerusalem in 586 BC came over 800 years after God had made His promise and covenant with Abraham, more than enough time for the people to grasp onto and apply His laws. But the continued unbelief of many brought on God's wrath and judgement, a theme which dominates a large portion of this book. The realization that their salvation was ultimately going to require a more personal relationship between God and His people through the person of His Son was becoming more and more evident.

- The Lord told Jeremiah He'd chosen him as a prophet before he was born. He was still young, but said he'd go wherever God sent him. Many would be against him, but God would give him strength.
- The Lord said to proclaim this message to Jerusalem, that He'd led them through a desert because they were His. Now they've exchanged Him for useless idols. When in trouble, God knows those idols won't save them.
- An unfaithful Israel must repent. If they do I will take two from each clan to Mount Zion. Their time is short; a scorching wind is blowing in from the north that will pronounce God's judgement on them.
- Jerusalem will be doomed, gasping for air. They haven't listened to My prophets. Many will die but not all. The people of Benjamin should run for safety. Jeremiah, tell them I'll no longer accept their offerings.
- Jerusalem will be invaded. They will not be safe even in the Lord's Temple. "Jeremiah, tell them to change their ways now, and do not pray in their behalf. Tell them I know that even their priests are evil."
- Even animals know when to migrate, to turn and go back, but not these people. You have sorrow for them, but all other gods they have must be destroyed. They'll be under siege, and some will go into exile.
- Tell them I've cursed all who don't honor My covenant. Announce if they seek Me that I'm not listening. Don't plead for Me to spare them, because many are wanting to harm you for proclaiming My messages.
- With sorrow, the Lord abandoned Israel. "They turned against Me, and now because of My anger their homes are a wasteland. But in time Israel's neighbors

will each occupy their own lands, and if they'll accept the religion of My people they'll become Mine and will prosper."

- The Lord brought a drought upon the land and people, and told Jeremiah not to plead in their behalf because other prophets were telling lies. The people confess their sins, but God showed no mercy.

- "God, everyone curses me although I've pleaded with them in Your behalf. Let me have revenge on those persecuting me. Haven't I served You well?" The Lord said, "return to Me and I'll protect you."

- Jeremiah was told not to marry and have children in Judah, because they'd die there. "They should know why they receive no mercy. Soon I'll be known as the God who scattered His people and took their treasures." "Spare me Lord," Jeremiah said. "Don't terrify me."

- The Lord said, "They must observe the Sabbath. I can mold them like a potter molds clay. Jeremiah, they'll plot and set a trap for you. Break a clay jar. Like them, they'll see it can't be made whole again."

- The priest Pashhur had Jeremiah beaten, so he was told he'd die in Babylon. Jeremiah asked why people ridiculed and scorned him.

- Jeremiah prophesied about the sad fate of Jerusalem, but that later God would gather the survivors back home. He'd choose them a new King, a descendant of David, who'd be their Lord of Salvation.

- The prophets were saying things God hadn't said. God said, "Tell them they're the Lords burden, and use those words."

- The Lord had 2 baskets of figs. "My people who were captured and taken to Babylon are good figs; I'll watch over them. Those who stayed behind, King Zedekiah and others, will be treated worse than bad figs."

- "I tell you what your God says," said Jeremiah, "You have made Him angry so He'll send King Nebuchadnezzar to destroy you and your lands. You'll all drink from His cup of anger, for seventy long years."

- He told these things to the Jewish people, and that God would destroy their temple. The priests and prophets wanted to kill Jeremiah.

- God told Jeremiah to wear an ox yoke, symbolizing how the Jews and all surrounding nations would feel under Babylonian rule. God would allow this, and also for all temple treasures to be taken to Babylon.

- Hananiah spoke to Jeremiah in the temple. He removed his ox yoke, broke it, and said that's how God would free all people under Babylonian rule. Jeremiah knew God didn't send that message to Hananiah, so he told him God would have him die within the year, and he did.

- Jeremiah wrote to the prisoned Jews taken into Babylon. He told them God wanted them to settle down and prosper, and not to be deceived by the false prophets there. In 70 years, He'd come for them.

- Lies about God and Jeremiah continued. God told Jeremiah to record in a book all He'd told him. He again said the Jews would suffer for all their sins, but later He'd restore Jerusalem and the temple. Jews would return home from everywhere, because God is Father to Israel.

- God promised a new covenant with Israel, replacing the older one. "Everyone will know Me. I'll forgive sins, and not remember them."
- The Lord told Jeremiah to buy land and put the deeds away. "Later, houses, fields and vineyards will once again dot the land," He said.
- The Lord gave Jeremiah a promise of hope. "Jerusalem and the temple will be restored. There'll always be a descendant of David."
- Zedekiah was told he'd not be killed in battle. He freed the Hebrew slaves but then forced them back into labor, displeasing God.
- Jeremiah was told to write on a scroll all the Lord had told him about Israel and Judah. Baruch did it for Jeremiah. It was read aloud for all to hear. The king burned it, so Baruch & Jeremiah went into hiding.
- Jeremiah was arrested, then lowered into a well. He was moved to the courtyard when Jerusalem fell. Zedekiah was captured and his eyes put out, and his sons were killed per Nebuchadnezzar's orders.
- Jeremiah was placed under the care of Gedaliah, the governor. Ishmael, a chief officer, killed Gedaliah and many more.
- Jeremiah prayed for the safety of the leaders there. The Lord said He'd protect them only if they stayed in Judah. They'd die if they left for Egypt. They didn't believe it so they left for Egypt and took Baruch and Jeremiah with them. God sent Nebuchadnezzar to defeat Egypt.
- The Lord humbled and destroyed Moab, and their god Chemosh. He knew of their arrogance, and they were made fun of.
- The Lord passed judgement on Ammon, Edom, Damascus, Hazor, Elam, and the Tribe of Kedar. Later, He would rise some of those back up to prosper again.
- After Babylon had followed God's demands to destroy cities and enslave many unbelievers among the Jewish people, He would now send nations and armies from the north to capture Babylon.
- The people of Babylon would be punished and disgraced just as the Assyrians were. Just like Sodom and Gomorrah, Babylon will be so devastated that no one will ever live there agin. They are doomed.
- Jeremiah had written down all the destruction coming to Babylon and sent it there to be read by Seraiah. Afterwards, he was to throw it in the Euphrates River to symbolize it would sink and never rise again.
- King Zedekiah had become King of Judah and had ruled for eleven years. After being blinded, he stayed in a Babylon prison until death.
- When Nebuchadnezzar entered Jerusalem and burned down the temple, palaces and homes of important people, he'd stripped the temple of its belongings. They broke into pieces the tall bronze columns, bronze tanks and carts, then the ash containers and shovels used to clean the alter. They took the tools used for the lamps, the bowls used to catch blood from animals being sacrificed, and bowls used to burn incense. Everything made of silver or gold was taken, plus bowls used for wine offerings and everything King Solomon had made for use in the temple including the twelve bronze bulls used for support.

- In total, Nebuchadnezzar took 4,600 Jewish prisoners during his attacks on Judah, and those who survived remained in exile until they were called back to their homeland to join those who'd stayed.

Additional comments on the book of Jeremiah:

Although the theme of this book may be the many warnings God sent to His people through Jeremiah, and the detailed gloom and doom many suffered from not following those warnings, we can't overlook Jeremiah and how important he was during a time in history that was before, during, and after the fall of Jerusalem to the Babylonians. Compassionately conveying unpopular messages to the Jewish people got him beaten and imprisoned, but he maintained his courage and hope. His sincerity and communications with God were bold, and it seemed to bring them closer. His concerns for his own safety and those of his people often drove him to tears.

Just as we did in the book of Isaiah, we get a glimpse here of God's "New Covenant" that He'd make when Jesus walks the earth. It would tell us that through faith and belief we can all be saved through grace without continuously struggling and failing to keep His Ten Commandments. The Holy Spirit within believers will tell them what's right and what's wrong, so they'll not need a teacher or the Commandments to remind them. As stated in 31:33, "I will put my law in their inward parts, and write it in their hearts." God's Spirit in the hearts of believers would never tell anyone to sin, never.

God tells us that we really won't become one of His children until we discard our sinful nature and embrace a new nature. We must recognize that we need a new heart before we'll receive one. We need to take the first step, one which no longer requires going to a temple to worship, sacrificing animals, or only eating Kosher foods. To know God personally we need to believe in Jesus, because if we know Jesus personally then we know God.

For more about God's New Covenant and the Gospel of the Age of Grace, which is the gospel given to Paul by Jesus to be taught first to the Gentiles and then to the entire world, see **Appendices B, C and I.**

Lamentations

After reading through this book of poetic laments by an unnamed author, several indicators point to Jeremiah as the writer since he was in Jerusalem during its destruction and possessed a way of describing and expressing events with raw unfeigned emotion. Since we know the Babylonians attacked and destroyed Jerusalem and Solomon's Temple in 586 BC, we can date this book around then. The temple had stood for approximately 400 years before being plundered of its treasures and burnt to the ground.

- Jerusalem was once full of people, but had fallen into slavery. Now no one worshiped at the temple where Gentiles weren't allowed, and it's treasures have been taken away. God took note of our sins because we disobeyed Him. We ask God to make our enemies suffer too, just as we have.
- Without mercy, the Lord destroyed every village in Judah. Old men sat in silence, and my eyes are worn from weeping. The Lord had done what He said He'd do to the old and young alike. He put an end to our holy days and Sabbath. O Jerusalem, how can I comfort you?
- I cry for help but God no longer listens. We've forgotten what peace and happiness were. Our homelessness is a bitter thought. Hope returns when we remember the Lord's unfailing love. Though beaten, we accept it. He'll not reject us forever. Reexamine our ways and return to the Lord.
- Jerusalem has fallen. Children are begging for food. The Lord turned loose His fury because the prophets sinned and her priests were guilty. Zion has paid for her sin. The Lord won't keep us in exile much longer. Our enemies laugh now, but soon He'll expose their guilt as well.
- Lord look at us, and all our disgrace. Foreigners are living in our homes. No one sits at the city gate, and no one makes music. We must pay for a drink of water. We're always hungry. But You, oh Lord, are our ruler. Bring us back to You Lord, bring us back. Restore all our ancient glory.

Additional comments on the book of Lamentations:

These laments are words of punishment and defeat, and we feel like Jeremiah is telling us what he sees as he walks through the empty mangled streets of Jerusalem. We can feel the enormity of the destruction God has inflicted on His people, just as He had warned them about over and over again through His prophets and messengers.

The persistent sins of the Jewish people eventually caused God to stop listening to their pleas for mercy. God is overflowing with love and compassion, but we cannot continue to sin and worship our money and belongings as they did in Jerusalem and expect God to remain on hold until we get back to Him later. Jeremiah was called the weeping prophet because he cried for his people. We pray to God that someone will cry for us.

Ezekiel

Ezekiel was around 30 years old when the invading Babylonians captured and destroyed most of Jerusalem, and was one of the many thousands of prisoners taken back to Babylon. After being there several years, he began serving as the leader and counselor to those in his colony in their camp by the river. This was around 595 BC. He would advise his fellow Jewish captives and give them prophetic messages for the next twenty years. Since the people there were being punished for their rebellion against God, Ezekiel knew how they'd suffer for their sins, described here and earlier in the books of Isaiah and Jeremiah. His visions and influences brought about their Judaism beliefs, centered around a singular transcendent God, and their faithfulness to Jewish rites, ceremonies, practices, and the laws of the Torah.

The Book of Ezekiel contains three sections, each with a different subject and focus. Chapters 1 through 24 covers the capture and fall of Jerusalem. Chapters 25 through 39 contain a series of visions and predictions about Israel's neighboring nations, and Chapters 40 through 48 cover the reestablishment of Jerusalem and it's temple. Ezekiel's visions covered the future of Israel, and the need for each of its people to confess and take ownership of their own sins. He was a man of deep faith and holiness.

- During his captivity, the priest Ezekiel saw the skies open up and heard the voice of God. A windstorm blew in from the north, and in the center were four creatures in human form. Each had 4 wings and hands, with 4 different faces pointing in different directions, with 1 wheel per creature.
- This vision made Ezekiel fall to the ground, but God stood him back up. God told him He was sending him to Israel to tell them His warnings. "They'll defile you but give them my messages. Eat this scroll I give you and speak what it says to those in exile. It's full of grief and wails."
- "You'll be a watchman for the nation of Israel, and you alone are responsible to give them My warnings. Your own life will depend on it. Go home, where I'll paralyze your tongue so you can't tell them My plan."
- God gave Ezekiel a representation of how the Israelites must eat once they're scattered, until some run out of food. God told him, "Shave your beard, cut your hair, then burn it. It'll show them that I'm their enemy."
- "A third of My people will die from sickness and hunger, another third from swords, and a third will be scattered. I despise their false idols. Their land is doomed, disaster is coming, these are not empty threats."
- Ezekiel had a second vision of God, which took him to the Jerusalem Temple. It was defiled and defaced, and women wept over their idol Tammuz. God sent a man dressed in linen to mark the foreheads of those against what the sinners there had done. All the others were killed.
- God promised those being exiled that they'd get their land back one day. "They'll be My people, keep My Laws, and I will be their God," He said.

- Then in Ezekiel's vision the 4 creatures flew off with their wheels. The vision faded and Ezekiel was brought back into Babylonian exile. He told all those in exile what God had shown him in the vision.

- Ezekiel was told by God to pack up and leave, making sure the others see him depart. "Go when it's dark, with your eyes covered. Later, tell them it was God's warning, that they don't see the harm awaiting them."

- "Those in exile should be trembling," God said. "They have a proverb that predictions never happen, but tell them that all they've heard is coming true. Their prophets told them all was well. Their false men and women prophets are doomed. Plus they must leave their disgusting idols."

- All sinners will have their food supply destroyed. Or wild animals may be sent upon them, or an epidemic. They sacrificed their own children to idols. They are much worse than Samaria and Sodom ever were.

- For now all will be treated as they deserve, but later My covenant will again be with you. I'll forgive your sins, but you'll never forget them.

- God gave them a promise of hope. Know that the exact person who sins is the exact person who will die. There'll be individual accountability. Good sons will not suffer from their father's sins, but be rewarded.

- Ezekiel sang a song of sorrow given to him by the Lord. Then leaders came to consult Ezekiel, but the Lord would not answer any more questions. "You'll end up worshiping Me from a mountain in Israel."

- The Lord gave Ezekiel another riddle but he complained, saying the people were tired of riddles. Ezekiel was told to groan in sorrow, telling others it's because of the terrible things about to happen to them. Someone is coming to destroy Jerusalem. Tell them of their crimes.

- The Lord gave Ezekiel a riddle about 2 sisters, one representing Samaria and the other one Jerusalem, and the punishment headed their way due to immorality and false idols. "The cities of murderers are doomed."

- The Lord told Ezekiel He would take away his wife, and she died. He said not to mourn her. The Lord will also take all that these sinners love. The Lord gave him prophecies over many nations and their punishments.

- God appointed Ezekiel as the watchman over Israel. "I don't enjoy seeing sinners die," said the Lord. "They will be held accountable only for their deeds. If they repent I will surely forgive them."

- The Lord said He'd look for those who are lost, as a shepherd watches over his sheep, to bandage those who are hurt and heal those who are sick. God punishes Edom. He blessed Israel, not for their sake but for the sake of His holy name. "They may again ask for My help", He said.

- The Lord led Ezekiel into a valley with many dry bones and told him to prophecy to them. As he did they joined together and the wind breathed life into them. "I will also put life back into My people," the Lord said.

- The Lord said He'd join Judah and Israel into one nation. "They'll be one nation under one King," he said, "like King David was, with a temple."

- The Lord denounced Gog, who was an enemy. "When Gog invades Israel I'll be furious," He said. "Their bodies will be food for the animals."
- After 25 years in exile, Ezekiel saw in a vision a divine man standing at the gateway holding a tape. He told me to tell the Israeli people all I will see. He described the temple to him, how it would look, all the dimensions, the alter, the doors, and all about it. He was also given the rules to enter the temple.
- Only certain Priests and certain ones from the Levi Tribe may serve there. They'll wear linen turbans and trousers with no belt. They must not shave their heads or have long hair. They must only eat what they are told, and they cannot touch a corpse.
- The land there will be divided among the tribes, and the Lord shall have a plot there for the temple. The ruling Prince will have land there. You must sacrifice animals and bring offerings so your sins will be forgiven.
- "You will have festivals there," the Lord said. "The priests will put blood on the temple doorposts, and there'll be Passover festivals and a Festival of Shelters. Some gates only open for New Moon Festivals and sabbaths."
- There'll be 12 entrances into Jerusalem, three in each of the four walls and each one named for a tribe. The city will be called, The Lord Is Here.

Additional comments on the book of Ezekiel:

God, with His eternal powers and encompassing oversight of life, permits many things to happen to us in His world. He can cause things to happen, He can prevent things from happening, and He can allow things to happen. So after centuries of prophecies, counseling and reprimands that unsuccessfully persuaded His people to reform, God allowed Jerusalem to be overrun and decimated by a foreign nation. Since God's Temple was located there, some probably felt that Jerusalem would always be protected from foreigners. But God is willing to take whatever actions are necessary to save the Jewish people, and each of us today, to the point of sending Jesus to die for our sins.

It was insightful to read about the new temple, with its precise and specific details and dimensions, and the lands around it that God would dedicate to the people, the Prince, and others. The people had constructed and used temporary tents and sanctuaries for centuries in many locations. Their new temple would be built away from the center of Jerusalem, and tighter controls would be enforced to keep it Holy since God would return there. Around 515 BC, this new and second temple was constructed.

We read in Ezekiel that the neighboring nations around Judah were also subject to God's laws, whether they knew it before then or not. He holds all of us accountable for our individual actions. He doesn't punish us for our disobedience just because He wants to, He does it to make us wake up and repent of our sins. God will do whatever is necessary to save us from ourselves.

Daniel

Daniel, while still a teenager, was one of the many Jewish people exiled to Babylon from Jerusalem when they were first attacked in or around 605 BC. There, he would be renamed Belteshazzar by the Babylonian leadership and live through the seventy years of Jewish captivity. He was the last of the major prophets, after Isaiah, Jeremiah and Ezekiel, who wrote about the fall of their homeland and what God did to punish His people and then restore them back into Israel. In chapters 1-6 we read about Daniel and others and their triumphs over their enemies. Chapters 7-12 are prophetic with Daniel's visions of empires rising and falling and his summarization of the kingdom of God, and God's eventual plan for the whole world.

Along with Daniel in exile were three of his friends, Shadrach, Meshach, and Abednego, who were given those names by the Babylonians. We learn the story of them being thrown into a furnace as punishment for not worshiping a false image, but surviving unharmed due to God's saving hands. We read about Daniel surviving a night in the lion's den, and also of Daniel's explanation of the "writing on the wall." Many of those characters and their stories, along with God's intervention, we learned as children. Daniel's interpretations of signs, dreams and images won him favor with the king and made him an important person with entitlement within the Babylonian society.

- After Nebuchadnezzar's army attacked Jerusalem and it's temple, he took prisoners back with him to Babylon. He wanted some to learn to read and write and to serve in his royal court. They trained for three years.
- Daniel, along with Shadrach, Meshach, and Abednego (their new names) were chosen, all from the tribe of Judah. Ashpenaz, a chief official, was sympathetic to Daniel and gave the four healthy foods to eat.
- God gave the four a knowledge of literature and philosophy, plus to Daniel He gave the skill to interpret dreams and visions. They served in the king's court for years, until Cyrus conquered Babylonia.
- Nebuchadnezzar had a dream and wanted it interpreted. His advisors told him no one could interpret such a dream, which angered him. He ordered them all to be killed, including Daniel and his three friends.
- God had the dream revealed to Daniel in a vision, so he explained it to the king. He said there would be four empires, but one would crush the others. At that time, God would establish a kingdom that never ends.
- The king was impressed, and awarded Daniel with a high position within Babylon. At Daniel's request, his three friends were also promoted.
- Nebuchadnezzar had a gold statue made, and everyone had to worship it. Shadrach, Meshach, and Abednego told the king they wouldn't worship his gold statue. He had the three tied and thrown into a blazing furnace.

- The king was amazed to see four men walking around unharmed in the fire, the three men and a holy person. He called their names and they came out, with no burns. He praised their God, and promoted them.
- Daniel interpreted another dream. He said the king was a great tree, but an angel said to cut it down. That's what would happen to the king unless he recognized God as ruler. He refused, so he was punished.
- After suffering for seven years, the king gave glory to God. His royal powers returned even greater than before. He praised and honored God.
- The king's son Belshazzar held a big banquet, during which a human hand appeared and began writing on the palace wall. His advisors couldn't read the message. They sent for Daniel to read it.
- Daniel told Belshazzar what had happened to his father Nebuchadnezzar, and now since he had not humbled himself before God just like his father, he would die and the kingdom would be given to Darius the Mede.
- Darius chose Daniel and others to look after the king's interests. The others in power convinced the king that all requests for anything must be asked of him first. But Daniel only asked God, so he was thrown into the lion's den. The king was glad when God saved Daniel from the lions.
- Daniel had a vision of four beasts rising from the sea; the four empires that would rise to power, but only God's empire would survive. Later Daniel had a vision of a ram and goat, which the angel Gabriel explained.
- Gabriel further explained that God would restore Jerusalem and the people there in seven times seventy years. But later God's chosen leader would be killed and the new ruler would be there for seven years.
- Daniel received another vision. An angel and Michael told of kingdoms in Egypt and Syria and their eventual war against each other. He said "times will be bad, but those names written in God's book will be saved. Those who've died will either live again or suffer eternally. Seal that book until the end of the world. All those events will end in three and one-half years, but keep all this secret."

Additional comments on the book of Daniel:

If we try to fully understand the book of Revelation, the book of Daniel would be a great place to start. It provides the most detailed prophecy of future events found in the Old Testament, and a timeline when Jesus will come again to set up His kingdom. Daniel's vision of the four empires or beasts, who most think were Babylon, Persia, Greece and Rome, tells of one who will dominate and from which the 'little horn" or antichrist would appear. His vision of the ram and goat was insightful, with the defiant goat taking over and forbidding holy worship and sacrifices. The Tribulation, with its disasters and suffering, is foretold and will proceed the judgement of sinners and test our faith before Jesus' Second Coming. The Seventy Weeks are mentioned, the time allowed to end unlawful acts or duties, to end sin, atone for our wickedness, to become righteous, to seal prophecies, and to anoint the Holy One.

Hosea

Hosea was active as a prophet in or around 750 to 710 BC, so he lived among other prophets like Isaiah and Micah before the fall of Samaria in 721 BC in Israel. But his story was quite different than theirs, at least in the beginning, when God told him to marry a woman who'd be unfaithful to him. So he did, and his adulterous wife named Gomer had three children by other men that God said weren't his people. But throughout his bitter relationship with her, Hosea still cared for her and wanted her to be faithful.

Gomer's unfaithfulness to Hosea parallels and mirrors our relationship with God, since we're often unfaithful to Him and fall short of His expectations. God uses that comparison in this book, and we can see how an unfaithful relationship between a husband and wife could be compared to Israel's unfaithfulness to God. But He'll always love us no matter how sinful we are, and is willing to take us back if we'll only repent and change our ways. That's what God told Hosea, so he paid money and barley to get Gomer back and away from her sinful life. We need to understand that God paid much more than that for us.

- The Lord told Hosea to get married, although his wife would be unfaithful just like the Jewish people had been to Him. His wife Gomer has 3 children. God would be faithful to Judah but not to Israel.
- God compared an unfaithful Gomer to an unfaithful Israel. He said He'd end their festivities and punish them. Gomer continued to sin.
- God told Hosea to get Gomer back, and love her just as He loved Israel. Hosea bought Gomer back from the others, then told her to wait for him just like Israel would need to faithfully wait for God to return.
- God accused the Priests of rejecting His teachings, so He'd turn their honor into disgrace. God condemned their pagan worship and false idols.
- The Jewish people insincerely repented, and although God could take them back He would always remember their evil ways. He had brought them there and made them strong, but they still plotted against Him.
- The Lord said, "The more alters the people of Israel build, the more places they have to sin. They have forgotten their Maker."
- God had sent Hosea to announce punishment for Israel. There are consequences for sin. Israel's greatness will fly away like a bird. God loves His rebellious people, but in sorrow passes judgement on them. "How can I give up on you Israel, and how can I abandon you?"
- "I will make you live in tents again, as you did in the desert. I have given you kings, and in My fury I have taken them away."
- Hosea pleaded for Israel to return to the Lord, because they had stumbled and fallen.
- "I will love them again. Like an evergreen tree I will shelter them. They'll be as famous as the wine in Lebanon."

Additional comments on the book of Hosea:

Before the earthly ministry of Jesus, only the Jews were considered to be God's people. He had spoken directly to them for thousands of years, and sent them messages through the holiest of men and prophets. He had led them, performed miracles for them, disciplined them, and given all of His attention to them. Anyone outside of Israel was not thought of as a child of God. But in the book of Hosea we read that Gentiles would also be a part of God's plan, although it would come some 700 years later.

In Hosea 2:23, God says, "And I will sew her unto Me in the earth; and I will have mercy upon her that had not obtained mercy; and I will say to them which were not my people (non-Jewish Gentiles), Thou art My people; and they shall say, Thou art my God." The apostle Paul repeats that message in Romans 9:26, when he writes: "And it shall come to pass, that in the place where it was said unto them, Ye are not My people; there shall they be called the children of the living God."

Through God's mercy and grace, He gave Jesus to the world so that whoever believeth in Him shall not perish but have everlasting life. That means anybody, and everybody. The gift of Jesus to the world was a secret or mystery that God had kept us from knowing ever since Adam and Eve were in the Garden of Eden. He had withheld it from the knowledge of men until He'd determined it was time to reveal it, mostly to Paul, who would share it to us along with other "mysteries" through his letters. In Romans 11:25, Paul writes (paraphrasing): "blindness in part has happened to Israel, until the fullness of the Gentiles come in." For more on all the powerful and remarkable mysteries that God initially withheld from mankind, **see Appendix C**.

As we can see from the above notes, there is much to learn from reading the book of Hosea, and in the following books that come from those referred to as "minor prophets." They're only called minor because their books are so much shorter in length than those from the other prophets. In II Timothy 3:16, it reads: "All scripture is given by inspiration from God, and is profitable for doctrine, for reproof, for correction, for instruction in righteousness." So although the 12 books at the end of the Old Testament are brief, Hosea through Malachi, they contain nuggets of important information to deepen the faith of every believer.

Joel

Joel was a prophet who lived in or near Jerusalem around 840 to 830 BC, prior to the fall of the Northern and Southern Kingdoms. His writings show a familiarity with the temple and the worship rituals and duties of the priests, so he was near the center of activities within the city. He gives us his prophetic insight on the coming judgement of Judah, and what is referred to as "The Day of The Lord", when God's almighty wrath is swiftly cast upon the wicked and the evil in all nations.

His story begins with swarm after swarm of locusts invading Judah, attacking the land and destroying the crops. The event is viewed symbolically as a call of repentance, describing the enemies of Judah and how they will overrun the land if the people there don't change their ways. But God could show mercy on His people, uplifting them to a level never to be despised again. God will avenge those who died when foreign armies scattered the Jews throughout other countries and divided the land of Israel.

- The Lord gave a message to Joel, a son of Pethuel. Locusts would attack Judah and their crops. There'd be no grapes for wine; no figs on their trees. People will put on sackcloth, and weep and mourn in their temple.
- The locusts are a warning that the Day of The Lord is coming. What once looked like the Garden of Eden would become a barren desert. But even in the late hour, the Lord wanted them to repent and return to Him.
- In the end, God will punish any enemy of the Jewish nation. He'll bring His people back from the lands they were sold into. There'll come a time when God will punish sinners for their inattention to His word. He'll restore the land and bring many blessings to His people.

Additional comments on the book of Joel:

A big part of this book is about judgement, and when we think of judgement we think of The Day of the Lord, the day of Jesus' Second Coming. He'll warn us of His arrival, when the sun shall be turned into darkness, and the moon into blood. Joel 2:28 states "And it shall come to pass afterward, that I will pour out My spirit on all flesh; and your sons and daughters shall prophesy, your old men shall dream dreams, your young men shall see visions". On the other hand, those who are His enemies will be terrified and will hide from God's wrath.

If through faith we believe in Jesus, in His death, burial and resurrection, then we'll have nothing to fear during those apocalyptic times. But we must be ready. I Thessalonians 5:6 tells us, "Let us watch and be sober," and in 5:2 we are told "for yourselves know perfectly that the Day of The Lord so cometh as a thief in the night." Each day that passes brings us one day closer to that truth.

Amos

Amos was a herdsman and fruit grower from a small town about ten miles south of Jerusalem, and was one of the first prophets to have a bible book named after him. He wrote his story around 750 BC, a few years before a devastating earthquake hit the region. Although being from Judah, God sent him north to Bethel in Israel to deliver His message of judgement. At the time, the northern region was basking in unprecedented success after conquering several nations, but was drifting further and further from the ways of the Lord.

How something looks on the outside doesn't always tell the whole story. Celebrating the Sabbath and following God's laws the best they could didn't make them holy. Since they knew their history, they felt they could do anything they wanted and God would forgive them and look the other way. So God sent Amos to tell them they'd be held accountable for taking advantage of the poor and treating others with disrespect and contempt. Little did the Israelites know at the time that the Assyrians would be sent to invade their country and overrun them about thirty years later.

- God revealed to Amos that judgement would come to many of Israel's neighbors. He would burn cities, remove inhabitants, and run the rulers of Syria, Philistia, Tyre, Edom, Ammon and Moab into exile.
- The people of Judah and Israel would also suffer because they had false gods, they took from the poor, and disrespected others. Their sins felt worse because God truly cared for and loved these people.
- Samaria would be doomed for mistreating the weak and oppressing the poor. Bethel alters would fall. Every house would be destroyed.
- The Lord said Israel had learned nothing from the past. He had destroyed cities, scorched crops and brought famine, but they would not come back to Him. If they did what was right they would live.
- God hated the pride of those in Israel. Amos saw a vision of locusts and fire, and a plumb line that showed the people were out of line.
- The priest Amaziah told King Jeroboam that Amos' speeches would destroy Israel. For that, some in Amaziah's family would be killed.
- Amos understood what the Lord would command. The people would be put to death. Then later, the Lord would bring them back and replant them there.

Additional comments on the book of Amos:

Throughout all of Scripture, Amos reminds us more than in the other books that we're expected to treat others with respect and fairness. For a Christian, worshiping God and serving others are both equal in His eyes. Carrying a Bible and wearing a cross doesn't fulfill God's expectations of us. We must remember on judgement day that true Christians have already been forgiven for repented sins. It's our good works to God's glory that'll bring us our rewards in heaven.

Obadiah

Obadiah, a name meaning "worshiper of Yahweh", has the shortest book in the Old Testament. He provides very little for us to date his writings, but the best guess places it in or around 840 BC. His reference to Jerusalem makes us feel he lived there or somewhere in southern Judah. His name also appears elsewhere in the bible, either referring to him or another man with that name.

Most of this book chronicles the prophetic vision and judgement on the nation of Edom, land bordering ancient Israel but presently in southwest Jordan. Edom was founded by Esau, the brother of Jacob. Obadiah tells of Edom's narcissism and vanity, traits unimportant to God that usually bring disappointment to a nation.

- Obadiah prophesied after hearing from the Lord that pride had deceived Edom. They would lose their wisdom, and their fighting men.
- They had killed descendants of Jacob, and gloated over the misfortunes in Judah. They would be punished and made weak.
- Edom thought it couldn't fail but the Lord would pull them down. They laughed at the distress of others. They'd get back what they'd given. The Lord would punish them and all the nations.
- The people of Judah would occupy Edom and rule over it. The Lord Himself will be King.

Additional comments on the book of Obadiah:

There is no place among us for boastful self-pride, but those in Edom didn't feel that way. They took advantage of opportunities to build themselves up at the expense of others. Social standing in God's eyes means absolutely nothing. James 4:6 teaches that God resisteth the proud, but gives grace to the humble.

The pride we feel for a job well done is good. But the pride we get from discrediting others for a weakness they might have, or what we have that they don't have, is sinful. We're telling ourselves that we're better than them since we don't have their weakness. Prideful people have a feeling of superiority.

Why do people make fun of another person's torn coat, or laugh when a person trips and falls into a creek? If their coat isn't torn they feel wealthier than others, and if they didn't fall in the creek they think they're more aware of their surroundings and not as clumsy as others. Egotistical people can't build up their own pride and feed their arrogance just by themselves, so they look for any flaw in others to comparatively judge themselves against to refuel their own prideful nature. Sadly, the majority of lost people are that way. We see that in people every day and everywhere. The fact is, what we say and think about ourselves means absolutely nothing to God. It's what God thinks about us that really matters, and He knows everything we think and do.

Jonah

The prophet Jonah lived during or just before Assyria attacked and conquered Israel, so we can date this book in or around 770 BC. God told Jonah to go to Nineveh, a sinful Assyrian city and enemy of Israel, to tell them of their pending destruction. But Jonah was reluctant to go there with God's message because he knew God was so loving that He might forgive them and not destroy them. So he defied God's command and headed off in the opposite direction toward Tarshish trying to escape his assignment.

God knows everything we do, so Jonah had no chance to avoid his mission. Luckily, God is slow to anger so He let Jonah board a ship to begin his journey toward Tarshish before sending a strong storm that placed the ship in danger. Jonah was blamed for putting the ship in harm's way so he was thrown overboard, and we all know the story of Jonah being swallowed by a whale.

- The Lord spoke to Jonah and told him to travel to Nineveh to speak out against their wicked people, but Jonah headed in an opposite direction.
- In Joppa, he boarded a ship headed toward Tarshish. At sea, the Lord sent a strong storm that terrified the sailors so they threw their cargo overboard, The captain woke Jonah from his sleep and told him to pray.
- They drew lots, and Jonah's name was drawn and therefore blamed for the reason they were about to sink. He told them he was running from God so he knew he was at fault. He asked to be thrown overboard.
- Sailors couldn't get the ship safely to shore, so Jonah was thrown overboard. The storm immediately ended, and the sailors worshiped God. A large fish swallowed Jonah and he was inside the fish 3 days and 3 nights. He prayed to God for help, so the fish spit him out onto the shore.
- Jonah was again told to go to Nineveh. He went and warned them of their pending destruction. They believed him, so the king ordered the people to stop sinning and pray. God heard them, so He didn't destroy them.
- Jonah was angry that God had forgiven them just as he'd predicted, after all he'd been put through to warn them. He asked the Lord to let him die.
- The Lord told Jonah why He'd spared Nineveh, where 120,000 innocent people didn't know the difference between their right and left hands.

Additional comments on the book of Jonah:

There are two main themes in this book. We are to follow God's plans without question, and God forgives repentant sinners. It took time and punishment, but Jonah eventually aligned his plans to God's plans for him. But we shouldn't be faithful just to be obedient; we must know God's way is right. Jonah's 3 days and nights in the fish's belly are referenced in Matthew 12:40, where Jesus says: "For as Jonas was 3 days and 3 nights in the whale's belly; so shall the Son of Man be 3 days and 3 nights in the heart of the earth."

Micah

Micah was born around 740 BC in a small town just south of Jerusalem, where he lived in and among the poor and disadvantaged. He sympathized with them for the way they were treated, so he wrote against the powerful kings and leaders of larger cities like Jerusalem and Samaria who lived in luxury and reaped the rewards of the pauper's labor. Like some others who lived in Judah and Israel during this time, the leaders knew of their history and God's protection of them so they felt they could do as they pleased without penalty. Micah was not the first to criticize the rich and their treatment of the afflicted, and he wouldn't be the last. His prophecies to them ranged from gloom and despair to hope and peace. They'd feel God's wrath, then they'd feel His love.

- The Lord gave a message to Micah about the sin and rebellion going on in Jerusalem and Samaria. He'd punish them and smash their idols.
- The rich there took what they wanted, so no man's family or property was safe. After God punished them, they'd not walk as proudly anymore.
- Those left after God's punishment would be gathered like sheep, and they'd be free from exile. God Himself would lead them to safety.
- Micah denounced Israel's leaders, and told the false prophets they'd no longer have visions. They can't build God's city on a sinful foundation.
- In coming days, the Lord will reign in peace. He'd settle disputes among nations. There'd be no more wars, and He'd rule over mankind forever from Mount Zion. Jerusalem would again be the capital of the Kingdom.
- From the small town of Bethlehem a Ruler will come. He will love and protect His people with the majesty of God Himself. They'd be required to do what is just and live in humbleness with God.
- God warned sinners through watchmen and prophets but they didn't listen. But they'll rise again from the light of the Lord. He'll love the descendants of Abraham and Jacob once again with compassion.

Additional comments on the book of Micah:

This book is one of many in the bible describing the judgement coming to all who are disobedient to the Lord, not because He detests us but because He loves us. Prophecies about the birth of Jesus are given, which don't come for another seven hundred years, plus His judgement on the heathen and His promises of world peace. Bethlehem is specifically mentioned in Micah 5:2.

The future kingdom of Jesus, during His millennial reign, will bring an earth where many nations will live harmoniously in peace. Both heaven and earth will be transformed because the Lord will pardon our iniquities so we can delight in His mercy. If you've ever seriously asked yourself what the Lord requires of you, Micah 6:8 will tell you. The Lord requires us to do justly, to love mercy, and to walk humbly with thy God.

Nahum

Nahum was the second prophet directed by God to warn the sin-filled city of Nineveh, located in the Assyrian empire. He had Jonah warn them first, hoping they'd repent and change their ways, then God had Nahum warn them again some 140 years later in or around 650 BC. Assyria was a long-standing enemy of both Israel and Judah, and after Jonah's initial warning they worked to refine themselves. But a generation or two later they were back to their evil schemes and were plotting against the Lord.

Nahum's focus was to make sure the people in Nineveh knew of their pending fate and destruction. God had seen enough of their plundering and reprehensible behavior. Later in the same century, Nineveh would be overrun and besieged by the Medes and Babylonian armies.

- The Lord doesn't easily become angry, but Nahum saw in a vision that He was ready to punish Nineveh for their oppression and tyranny. The Lord told Israel that He'd end Assyria's power over them.
- The Lord was their enemy. He'd fill their palaces with terror, and take away everything they'd pillaged and stolen. They'd all be wiped out.
- The people of Assyria will be scattered with no one to bring them back home. All those hearing of your destruction will celebrate and be joyful.

<u>Additional comments on the book of Nahum:</u>

Just as God waited to see if Nineveh would heed His warnings and repent of their sinful ways, He'll wait for us too. He wants all sinners to end their disobedience and with a truthful heart ask for His forgiveness. We all intuitively know when we do something wrong or sinful that we'll be punished for it; we learned that as children when we were scolded or went without TV for a week.

God gave us a free will to make choices, just as Adam and Eve had choices. He doesn't make us follow Him. He wants us to love Him because we choose to and not because we're made to. We know that either during our lifetimes or at our deaths there'll be a day of judgement and reckoning. It cannot be avoided. It will happen.

He also wants His followers to promote Him. Our works, which are those things we do to tell and show others of His love through faith and belief, will determine our heavenly rewards. Titus 2:10 tells us "adorn the doctrine of God in all things." And in I Peter 3:15, we're directed to "sanctify the Lord God in our hearts: and be ready always to give an answer to every man that asks you the reason for the hope that is in you with meekness and fear."

Habakkuk

The prophet Habakkuk probably wrote this book between 610 to 590 BC, just before Judah in the southern kingdom was invaded by Babylon the second time. The northern kingdom of Israel had fallen around 722 BC, but many of God's people who lived in Judah had stayed put although they were concerned about the other nations around them growing in power.

Habakkuk feared the Babylonians might invade Judah and wondered what God was doing to protect His people. God had delivered this land to their ancestors long go, but now it appeared it'd be taken from them. He didn't understand why God hadn't intervened, especially since the Babylon nation was more corrupt and immoral than the Judeans ever were. He felt forsaken.

- Habakkuk complained to the Lord that he felt evil was taking over the righteous. God, how can you look at violence and not do something?
- The Lord replied that He'd bring a neighboring nation to power, and they'd conquer other lands. They'll come, but then they'll be gone.
- Habakkuk complained again. You are my God, he said, but why did you choose the Babylonians? They are wicked. They destroy the righteous.
- The Lord told him to write this down: The evil will not survive, but those who are strong and faithful to their Lord will survive.
- The Lord told him that wealth is deceitful and greedy men are never satisfied. The unrighteous bring shame on their families. They build cities based on crimes and murders. Their false idols have no life.
- Habakkuk prayed, acknowledging all that God had done for His people. He'd wait for God to punish the wicked. He'd stay joyful to his Savior.

Additional comments on the book of Habakkuk:

Habakkuk was a prophet who brazenly questioned God's plan. Just as Jonah did, he didn't understand God's wisdom. He was troubled when he didn't see anything being done to curb the violence being perpetuated all around him. Although perplexed at first, he later began to understand God's decisions and conceded in prayer that he had absolute trust in the Father.

Just as Habakkuk struggled to understand, how do we feel when God's plan doesn't make sense to us? Where does your belief go when your prayers go silently unanswered, and you feel God doesn't hear a word you say? Is God a part of your everyday life, or do you only pray to Him when you're troubled and don't know what to do? God's timetable to act in our lives is not our timetable. We must be patient, knowing that He'll never forsake a believer. Even when things look bleak we must remember what Paul writes in I Corinthians 10:13, that God is faithful and He won't make us suffer more than we can bear. He'll always give us a way to escape our temptations and our troubles.

Zephaniah

The prophet Zephaniah wrote this book in or around 635 BC. Being a descendant of Hezekiah, a believer and early king in Judah, he prophesied to the people of Jerusalem from 640 to 610 BC. His writings and insights tell us he was familiar with the religious services there, which he expanded by proclaiming to the people the visions and messages he'd received from God.

He continued the warnings other prophets had given Judah many times before, that the Day of the Lord was approaching so they needed to repent. The Lord was disappointed and angry with the false idols they worshiped, the irresponsible priests there, and the way the inhabitants twisted His Laws to their advantage. God promised their survival, but first there'd be punishment.

- The Lord gave messages to Zephaniah, telling him that He'd destroy the wicked. Those in Judah would pay for their sins. The day was getting closer when He would sit in judgement, and tears would be shed.
- The Lord had passed sentence on those nations around Israel, because they had insulted and taunted His people. The Lord would terrify them.
- Jerusalem was accused of oppressing its own people. The unrighteous there kept doing wrong without feeling ashamed, but they'd be punished. He would change them, making them humble and needing His help. They'd prosper and be secure, afraid of no one.
- Sing and shout a song of joy, those in Israel. You have no reason to be fearful any longer. I'll bring the exiled back home. You'll all be famous throughout the world. You'll have new life, and the love of the Lord.

Additional comments on the book of Zephaniah:

As told throughout the Bible, our Savior has a master plan of action for us that culminates in The Day of the Lord, mentioned several times throughout this book. Before then there's the familiar pattern beginning with His warning for us to repent, then His destruction and punishment of those who have disobeyed Him, and His promise of restoration and rebuilding. The day will come when He gives His final judgement and sets up a new heaven and earth. What a glorious day that will be for all of humanity, for those who believe in Jesus Christ through faith.

God's people often take a lot of scoffing and ridicule, but the day will come when we'll be envied. We'll no longer feel different from those around us, because after judgement we'll only be among other believers. Can we even imagine being in spiritual bodies in a place where there's no more pain, no sadness, no shame, and no sin? There'll be love all around us, and peace. In Ecclesiastes12:7 it tells us when we die "then shall the dust return to the earth as it was (reference Genesis 2:7), and the spirit shall return unto God who gave it." Quoting the words from Philip Doddridge (1702-1751), "O Happy Day."

Haggai

Approximately eighteen years after the Jewish people began returning to Judah from Babylonian in 520 BC, the prophet Haggai wrote this book. Earlier, God had directed King Cyrus of Persia to allow the exiled Jews in captivity to return to their homeland. With many of them back, Haggai challenged them to rebuild the Temple in Jerusalem, knowing there'd be opposition from the locals and the Persians.

He hoped the Jewish people would become more spiritual just by helping in God's work. God would use Zerubbabel, the governor of Judah, to support His temple plans. Haggai wanted the Jews to reclaim the birthrights given them along with a renewed faith for their future, strengthened by their God and encouraged by His rebuilt temple standing there before them in full view.

- God spoke through Haggai and told Zerubbabel, the governor of Judah, to rebuild the Temple. God didn't like the people there living in fine homes while His temple still laid in ruins. If they did the work, He promised the drought they were experiencing would end.
- They obeyed the message Haggai had given so the work began, and the Lord blessed them with prosperity. Haggai prophesied that the new temple would be more splendid than the one before, filled with wealth.
- The Lord said He disapproved what the locals brought to His alter, items defiled due to their sinful lifestyles. But He promised them blessings since the temple foundation had been finished.
- The Lord made a promise to Zerubbabel through Haggai. He would overthrow nations and end their power, then He'd name Zerubbabel to rule over them in His name. For their obedience, He would give them blessings.

Additional comments on the book of Haggai:

There must be a large storage facility somewhere in our universe where blessings have accumulated since the beginning of time, blessings that God had in store for us but we never earned due to our unbelief and sinful nature. They have a shelf life with no expiration date, so we have until the day we die to be worthy enough to receive them. Sadly, some will be there forever.

The astonishing event in this book was when God told Haggai to direct the people in Jerusalem to rebuild the temple, and they actually listened and obeyed. Throughout the Old testament we'd read dozens and dozens of instances when the Jewish people did the exact opposite of what God wanted. But this time, after they'd been captured and exiled, they finally surrendered.

If we could all live a devotional life as best we could, and allow God to bestow and enact the plan He has for each of us, there'd be less of God's blessings "returned to sender". First we must have faith, then we must obey.

Zechariah

Zechariah's visions and prophecies took place around the same time that Haggai was encouraging the Jewish people returning from exile to rebuild the temple, in 520 BC. He was both a priest and prophet who received as many as twelve visions over a two-year span, some which covered the future and restoration of Jerusalem and others which foretold the first and second comings of the Messiah. The visions he saw and spoke of emulated those addressed by the prophet Isaiah approximately 200 years earlier.

Zechariah's visions included four horsemen who inspected earth to confirm how helpless the world seemed to be. Another one told of those nations that had worsened Israel's existence and the four hammers that would seek revenge on them. He saw how the Jewish nation had been scattered from their homeland, and how the Lord would pass judgement on their wicked enemies.

- The Lord expressed His anger with Zechariah's ancestors. They wouldn't listen to Him or His prophets, but they eventually repented.
- Zechariah had a vision of four horsemen who traveled the earth and found it to be helpless. Some nations had preyed on Jerusalem, but the Lord would gather the Israelites back home and show mercy on them.
- There was a vision of four ox horns representing the nations who'd scattered God's people. Four men with hammers would punish them.
- In a vision it was said that Jerusalem would grow in people and livestock. Sing with joy, because the Lord is coming to live among them.
- Another vision saw the prophets Joshua and Satan standing together. An angel told Satan that he'd be condemned, and Joshua was told that if he obeyed the Lord then he'd be put in charge of God's temple.
- In a vision Zechariah saw a gold lampstand with 7 lamps with 7 wicks, and an olive tree and two gold pipes. The lamps allowed the Lord to see all the earth, and the tree branches were the 2 men who'd serve God.
- Zerubbabel was told he'd rebuild the temple. The vision of a scroll told of the punishment coming to liars and thieves. A lead basket held a woman representing world sin, carried to Babylon by two women to build a temple.
- Four chariots came from behind two bronze mountains, sent to inspect the earth. The one that went to Babylon softened the Lord's anger.
- The Lord told Zechariah to make a crown for Joshua to wear. He condemned those who had been artificially fasting.
- The Jewish nation had disobediently oppressed the poor and needy, so the Lord hadn't listened to their prayers. But now, He promised to restore the survivors so that others would know that God was with them.
- Neighboring nations would be punished for hoarding their wealth. The Philistines would be humbled. The Israelites had suffered enough.

~ A Brief Overview of the New Testament ~

In the Old Testament we read about the history of the Jewish people, their prophets, the Commandments they were given to live by, and the struggles they had following God's direction. In the New Testament, the main focus is on the life and death of Jesus Christ, the Messiah and Savior who God had promised to the Jewish nation. He came to teach the Kingdom of God, and how we must live to become one of His children. It begins with the four gospels, Matthew through John, followed by the acts of His disciples and the growth and challenges of the early Christian churches. Then we'll read the letters written by the apostle Paul, first to the believers throughout Asia Minor and then to others. After a few short books written by other apostles, the book of Revelation gives us the future of the Christian church and the creation of a new heaven and earth where believers will spend eternity with their Lord and Savior. In all, there are 27 books in the New Testament.

The books of the Bible, from Genesis up into Acts chapter 11, deals with Israel. But the New Testament deals with the Christian movement during and after Jesus' walk on earth, and the fulfilment of older prophecies. The period of time between the Old and New Testaments when there was no recorded history, an estimated span of around 400 years, is referred to as the Intertestamental Period. Also, where most of the bible addresses the Jewish nation, the New Testament books Romans through Philemon were written to the Gentiles or non-Jewish people, often referred to as the uncircumcised. As it clearly states in Ephesians 2:12, until Jesus arrived the Gentiles had no hope of salvation and were without God.

The term "Gospel of Law" could apply to the period that was covered in the Old Testament, since the people during that time were under God's Laws and Commandments. But when Jesus came to show us that the path to heaven was not through the Commandments but through faith and the belief in His death, burial and resurrection, mankind entered the "Gospel of Grace" or "Age of Grace". It's called that since it'd be by His grace that we'd be saved and not by anything we'd done to earn it. The huge differences between the two gospels, and their abilities to save us, is explained in more detail in **Appendix B**.

After Jesus' earthly ministry and after God revealed His mysteries and secrets to mankind, explained in **Appendix C**, the principal teacher of the gospel after the crucifixion of Jesus was Paul. He played a major role in God's plan of salvation in his letters to the new Christian churches and their believers. Paul teaches us that the "Good News" about Jesus wasn't that He died, because that alone wasn't good news. Instead, we learn that He died for us but then rose from His death to live, and that if we believe in Him we could be with Him through eternity. Now that's what we can really call "Good News".

Matthew

The gospel of Matthew begins the New Testament and tells us more about Jesus and His ministry to the Jewish people of Israel. His arrival fulfilled the covenant promise God had made to His chosen people approximately 2,000 years earlier, a promise that expanded through the death and blood of Jesus to the entire world. After many centuries of anticipation their King had arrived, living among them and offering them the Kingdom of God. Sadly, many never fully accepted Him as their Savior even after He'd died for their sins.

The teachings of Jesus and the healings He performed throughout this book are endless. We'll read about His Sermon on the Mount, and about the twelve disciples who followed Him and witnessed His miraculous life. His baptism and His teaching of the Law are told, and how they drew criticism and hatred from the Gentile nations around Him and even from some of His own people. In the end, He was punished because of the things He taught and foretold, a death He knew awaited Him.

From the cross, He continued to speak of His love for mankind when He asked God to forgive those who were putting Him to death. **As heartbreaking and tragic as it is to read about His crucifixion in the bible, an equally tormenting thought is the ignorance and unconscious unawareness of the Roman soldiers who had no idea that the wood and nails they used to nail Him to the cross were created by the One they were crucifying.**

- The ancestors of Jesus are shown. There were fourteen generations from Abraham to David, and another twenty eight from David to Jesus' birth.
- Mary, who was engaged to Joseph, was told by an angel that she'd have a child by the Holy Spirit. So Joseph married Mary to prevent her from being publicly disgraced. Jesus was born in Bethlehem, a town in Judah.
- King Herod was upset, so he found out where the child had been born and sent others to find Him. Visitors from the east followed a star to where the child was, and worshiped Him and gave Him gifts.
- An angel told Joseph that Herod wanted the baby killed, so they took Him into Egypt and stayed there until Herod had died years later.
- An order went out to kill all boys in Bethlehem, two years old or younger. Afterwards, an angel told Joseph to take his family back into Israel. But still afraid, they went to Galilee and settled in the town of Nazareth.
- John the Baptist began preaching. People came to confess their sins and be baptized by him. He told them a much greater man was coming.
- Around age 30, Jesus came to John at the River Jordan. Jesus was baptized then the heavens opened up and He saw the Spirit of God. A voice from heaven said, "This is My Son, with whom I am pleased."
- Jesus spent forty days and nights in the desert. The devil tempted Him there, then at the temple, then on a mountain. Jesus remained faithful.

- Jesus heard that John the Baptist had been put in prison. He called four fishermen to follow Him. He began teaching in synagogues and healing.
- From Jesus' Sermon on the Mount, He taught of true happiness. He told His followers of the persecutions they'd receive, but they'd be rewarded.
- He had not come to do away with God's laws but to endorse them. He told them to love their brothers, and not to covet what others may have.
- Jesus taught of vows and divorce. He taught to not take revenge, but to love and pray for our enemies. Try to be perfect, as God is.
- Don't be boastful when being charitable. Do it privately and you'll be rewarded. Pray without always being seen. God knows all our needs. Use the Lord's Prayer as an example. To be forgiven, forgive others. Don't be a slave to two masters, you can't serve both God and money.
- Do not judge others. Do not worry about tomorrow. The log in our eye is larger than the speck in your brother's eye. Ask to receive; seek to find.
- The gate to hell is large and wide open. The gate to life is narrow and hard to find. Recognize false prophets by their actions and what they do. Do what God wants of us, or He may say He never knew us.
- Jesus healed a man then told him not to tell anyone. Jesus healed a Roman officer's servant and many others. He calmed a storm, because even the winds and waves obey Him. He asked Matthew to follow Him.
- After more healings, Jesus gave His disciples their mission. He told them to preach to the lost in Israel and declare Him publicly for God to see.
- Jesus did not come to bring peace, He brought a sword. We must love Him more than our own family and support those who follow Him.
- Jesus said come to Him those who are tired, and He'd give them rest. But some wanted to harm Him. The Pharisees made plans to kill Him, and Jesus heard of it. He said anyone speaking against God's Spirit would never be forgiven. Everyone would be judged, either innocent or guilty.
- They asked Jesus to perform miracles, but He told them of Jonah. Jesus' mother and family arrived. He said those who follow God are His family.
- Jesus gave and explained many parables, and the people were amazed. But they still rejected Him. King Herod had John the Baptist beheaded.
- With five loaves and two fish, Jesus fed five thousand. Jesus walked on water, and Peter tried to but lost his faith. Jesus helped him to the boat.
- Jesus continued to heal. With seven loaves and a few fish, Jesus fed 4,000 men who'd been following Him, not counting women and children.
- Jesus asked if the Jewish people realized who He is. He told the disciples not to tell others that He was the Messiah. Jesus told of His punishment and death. Jesus went atop a mountain. His face shined as He spoke with Moses and Elijah. God spoke, saying He was pleased with His Son.
- Jesus said John the Baptist was Elijah, who came before Him. He said when two or more agree on earth, their wish will be granted from heaven.

- Jesus spoke of divorce, and that the Commandments must be followed. He spoke again of His death, and that He had come to serve people and give His life. He went to Jerusalem and entered the town riding a donkey.
- Jesus spoke in the temple, and threw out those buying and selling there. The priests and elders questioned His authority. He speaks in many parables. They asked Him which commandments were the greatest of all.
- Jesus scorns all not following His Laws, and predicts their punishment. He warns of a false messiah. He tells of the temple's destruction. He tells them the Son of Man will return one day, but no one will know when.
- Jesus tells of a final judgement, the "sheep and the goats". They'll be separated, and will receive punishment or rewards based on their faith in God and whether they helped the homeless, the hungry, and the sick.
- The chief priests and elders plot against Jesus. They offer Judas silver coins to betray Him. Jesus had a Passover meal with His disciples, saying one there would betray Him. They ate bread which stood for His body and drank wine, which sealed God's covenant. They sung a hymn.
- Jesus predicted Peter's denial, then He goes to Gethsemane where He prays to God three times. A crowd came with swords and clubs, then Jesus was betrayed by Judas and arrested. One who followed Him took his sword and cut off the ear of a priest's slave. The disciples ran away.
- Jesus was taken before the council. No evidence was presented that would put Him to death. Jesus spoke of His death, and afterwards being at the right hand of God. They beat and slapped Him for what He'd said. Peter was identified as His follower, but he said he didn't know Jesus.
- Judas repented, and returned the thirty silver coins. He then went and hung himself. Jesus was taken to Pilate, the Roman governor, who asked if He was the king of the Jews. Jesus wouldn't defend Himself.
- It was the Passover Festival, so the tradition was for the governor to pick one person to pardon. He felt Jesus was innocent, but the crowd demanded His death. So Pilate pardoned Barabbas and not Jesus.
- The soldiers made fun of Jesus then took Him to Golgotha where He was crucified. There was an earthquake, and many believers were raised from their graves. The temple was damaged. Mary Magdalene and others watched from a distance. Jesus was buried. Extra guards were assigned.
- On Sunday morning, Mary Magdalene and Mary went to the tomb. An angel rolled away the stone covering the tomb. The women saw Jesus wasn't there, and ran to tell His disciples. The guards were paid to lie about Jesus' body, saying the disciples took it away during the night.
- Jesus appeared to His disciples on a hill and told them to go preach His gospel and baptize others in the name of God, the Son, and Holy Spirit.

Additional comments on the book of Matthew:

This is the first book in the Bible that provides all the details surrounding the birth and death of Jesus. Once we get past the pain of reading about His death, the news going forward is all good. The Old Testament prophets said He was coming and He came. They spoke of His deeds and He did them. He was born as the Savior/Son of God and He is.

As foretold in the Old Testament, Jesus initially came to earth in order to fulfill the promises that God gave to Abraham in His first covenant with Israel. He came to save those who were lost, as He said Himself in Matthew 10:5-7. Jesus told His disciples, "Go not into the way of the Gentiles (the non-Jewish people), but go rather to the lost sheep of the house of Israel." But after Israel rejected Him, He bore the sins of all mankind when He died on the cross so that both Jew and Gentile who believed in His name could be saved. This is explained in more detail in **Appendix A.**

In Chapter 16, Jesus asked His disciples a monumental question. He asked, "Who do men say that I the Son of Man am?" Keep in mind this was after Jesus had performed miraculous healings in their presence, calmed ferocious storms, brought the dead back to life, fed thousands with very little food, and even walked across a lake without sinking. They answered by saying the Jews believed He was John the Baptist, or maybe a prophet, or maybe Elijah. We wonder why the Jewish Nation couldn't recognize their Savior when He stood right there in front of them. If that happened today, I hope we'd know it was Jesus. They knew from earlier prophets that He was coming, but their unbelief rejected who He was and all He offered.

We should keep in mind when we read the book of Matthew and the following three books that Jesus was still preaching God's Laws and the Ten Commandments. He was there to reach the lost souls in Israel and tell them about God's Kingdom. Although we associate His earthly ministry with His death on the cross, none of that had happened yet when He told His disciples what would become of Him. They were shocked hearing Him tell about His death, first in Matthew 16:21-22 then in Luke 18:31-34. Quoting Luke 18:34, "And they understood none of these things." Jesus knew that all the efforts to save souls through the Laws and Commandments would fail due to man's sinful nature. He knew He'd have to die for us in order to save us from ourselves. When He did, it wasn't only for the Jews but for whosoever believed in Him, as John 3:16 tells us.

In Matthew 24:32, Jesus tells us to learn the parable of the fig tree. He wants us pay attention and learn it's lessons. When new leaves appear on a tree, we should know that summer is near. Likewise, when things begin happening that He describes beginning in Matthew 24:4, we should know His return is near. He doesn't want us to be blindsided. He asked that we learn and remember that. He will come and save all who believe.

Mark

Mark's gospel, like the next two books in the Bible, repeats many of the same events given to us in Matthew since those four knew of the miraculous feats and examples of service given to us by Jesus. John Mark, as he was also known, was a follower of Jesus but not one of the twelve. He refers to Jesus' ministry as Good News, and certainly it is. His gospel tells more of what Jesus did and taught than some of the others.

- John the Baptist preached and many went to hear him. Jesus traveled from Nazareth and was baptized by John. A voice from heaven confirmed who Jesus was. A Spirit took Him into the desert where Satan tempted Him for 40 days and 40 nights. Angels came and helped Him.
- John was imprisoned. Jesus went to Galilee preaching the Kingdom of God. He met Simon, Andrew, James and John, and they followed Him.
- He began healing people, and ordering evil spirits out of the bodies of the sick. His powers and miracles spread quickly as people spoke of Him.
- Jewish teachers accused Him of blasphemy, but He continued teaching about fasting and honoring the Sabbath. Levi, a tax collector, joined Him.
- He chose His apostles, and from a boat healed many in the crowd who was following Him. The Jewish elders said he had the demon Beelzebul in Him, giving Him His powers. They planned to kill Jesus.
- Jesus' mother and brothers arrived. He said those who did what pleases the Father are His family. He gives and explains several parables.
- Jesus was asleep in a boat when the waves grew larger, threatening to sink it. He commanded the waves to be still and they calmed down. Jesus transferred evil spirits out of a man and into some pigs.
- King Herod, who'd married his brother's wife, was told it wasn't right by John the Baptist. She had him beheaded, and the disciples buried him.
- Jesus and the twelve were in a boat when a large crowd assembled to see Him. With five loaves and two fish He fed all five thousand of them. Later He spoke of a woman's faith, and of all the things that makes us unclean.
- He healed a deaf-mute, then another crowd gathered to see Him. He took seven loaves of bread, gave thanks to God, and fed the 4,000 there.
- Jesus asked the disciples who the Jewish people thought He was. None thought of Him as their Messiah, but Peter knew of His deity.
- Jesus and a few disciples went upon a mountain where He transfigured Himself and became shining white. He spoke with Moses and Elijah.
- Jesus spoke of His death and resurrection but none of the disciples understood Him. They were afraid to ask Him exactly what He'd said.
- Jesus warns about the temptations of sin, and about marriage, divorce and money. He tells a rich man to sell his riches so he can feed the poor.
- Jesus said He was going to Jerusalem, where He'll be killed. He sent for a colt to ride on, and they all went there. At the temple, Jesus drove away those who used

the space for trading, reminding them that it's a place for prayer. The elders challenged His authority. They wanted Him killed.

- Jesus said the most important commandment is to love God with all your heart. The second one is to love your neighbor as you love yourself.
- Jesus warns of false teachers, and tells of the temple's destruction. He tells His followers they'll be beaten and hated, then taken to court.
- He foretells of the coming of Man, but no one will know the hour or day. The priests plot against Jesus, and Judas plans to betray Him. They have the Lord's supper. Jesus speaks how the bread and wine is His body and blood. They sang a hymn then left for the Mount of Olives.
- Jesus told Peter he'd deny Him three times. Jesus was arrested and the disciples ran away. He was asked if He was the Messiah, and He said yes. They sentenced Him to death. Pilate could have pardoned Jesus, but the crowd said no. They wanted Him killed. He was taken to the cross.
- He was killed along with two bandits. When He died the temple curtain tore in half, symbolizing that there'd be no separation anymore between God and man. The old covenant would be replaced with a new one.
- Joseph of Arimathea asked Pilate for Jesus' body. He wrapped the body in a linen sheet and placed it in a tomb dug from solid rock. Jesus' mother and Mary Magdalene saw that a stone covered the entrance.
- Early Sunday morning, Mary Magdalene and two others saw that the stone had been rolled away. A man inside the tomb told them Jesus had been raised. He briefly appeared to Mary Magdalene and two followers.
- He met with the eleven apostles and told them to preach the gospel to all mankind. Then He was taken into heaven to sit at the right hand of God.

Additional comments on the book of Mark:

The gospel of Mark is considered to be the first book to be written about Jesus' earthly ministry, probably recorded in or around 58 AD before any of the others. It's unique in that it begins with Jesus' baptism, with no mention of His birth or His earlier years. Bible scholars feel that most of what Mark knew of Jesus' ministry was obtained from his friend, the apostle Peter. He's not considered to be an eye witness to Jesus' teachings.

He was a companion to Peter, Paul and Barnabas, and traveled with them on occasion. He's mentioned several times in the book of Acts. His death around 68 AD in Alexandria didn't end well. The pagans there didn't like his untraditional teachings and the way he tried to move them away from their earlier beliefs. He was roped around his neck and dragged through their city until dead. He tried hard to be a good servant to those he met, just like Jesus did. At their deaths, neither of them were respected.

Luke

Luke was a physician by trade who probably wrote this book in or around 62 AD. Scholars consider his writings to be intelligently detailed both here and in the book of Acts, two good examples of his compositional style. He was not one of the original twelve apostles selected by Jesus, and it's believed that he never actually met Jesus since he was thought to be non-Jewish. Both of his writings were addressed to Theophilus, not someone known in the immediate circle of Jesus' followers.

Luke was a friend of Saul, who was later named Paul, and Paul references Luke in Chapter 4 of Colossians. It's thought that Luke accompanied Paul on some of his visits to Gentile churches, where they tried to convert the people there away from their pagan beliefs. He was a religious man who strived to include the impoverished and displaced in the teachings of Jesus by spreading the word of God's kingdom and new covenant. He died around the age of 84.

- Luke wrote to Theophilus with an account of what had taken place. He told of the angel Gabriel who appeared to Zechariah telling him that he and his wife Elizabeth would have a son, who they would name John.
- Zechariah didn't believe it would happen, so Gabriel made him unable to speak. Six months into her pregnancy, God sent Gabriel to Nazareth to tell Mary that she'd have a Son, that they would name Jesus.
- Mary visited Elizabeth, and gave a song of praise for the blessed child she carried. They stayed together for three months. John was born, then Zechariah was able to speak again and was filled with the Holy Spirit.
- The Emperor ordered a census so everyone had to return to their hometown. Joseph traveled from Nazareth to Bethlehem. There, Mary had the baby Jesus and laid Him in a manger.
- Some shepherds left for Bethlehem, sent there by the Lord. First-born males had to be dedicated to the Lord, so Jesus was presented in the temple. A holy man named Simeon told of the baby's powerful eminence.
- When Jesus was twelve they went to Jerusalem for Passover. Afterwards they left for home but Jesus stayed behind. They returned for Him, and found Him in the temple listening and asking questions to the teachers.
- When John the Baptist was around twenty years old, he began preaching near the River Jordan. Jesus came and was baptized. A voice came from heaven confirming Jesus was the Son of God, and God was very pleased.
- Jesus was led into the desert where the devil unsuccessfully tempted Him for forty days. Later as He taught in synagogues, the news of Him spread. Some were angered by His teachings and wanted to harm Him.
- Jesus began to heal people and cast out evil spirits. He began choosing His twelve disciples. He taught them to love their enemies, and to be merciful to others. He told them not to judge, because the speck in the eyes of others was nothing compared to the log in their eyes.

- Jesus healed a Roman officer's servant. Then, He went into a home to eat and a sinful woman showed up. She wept, and washed His feet. He forgave her sins. They asked, who is this Man who forgives sins? He traveled with the twelve, with Mary Magdalene and others accompanying them. He spoke in parables, and healed those with demons.
- An ill woman approached Jesus and touched His cloak, then fell at His feet. He told her that her faith had made her well. Then He heard that a daughter had died. He brought her back to life.
- Jesus sent out the twelve to preach the Good News. They returned, and a large crowd followed them all. With 5 loaves and 2 fish, 5,000 were fed.
- Jesus asked if the crowds knew who He was. Peter knew He was the Messiah. Jesus spoke of His suffering and death. He transfigured, and on a hill He spoke to Moses and Elijah. God said, "this is My Son".
- A Samarian village refused to receive Jesus, so He rebuked them. He sent out 72 followers to go ahead of Him into towns. When they returned, they said that demons had obeyed them when they spoke in His name.
- Some claimed that Beelzebul gave Jesus His powers. Jesus insulted those who complained to Him when they tried to catch Him saying something wrong. He told them to trust in God, and to fear God.
- The story of the rich man and Lazarus was told, and how the rich man in Hades was being punished. He wanted water, but there was a pit or gulf between him and the water that couldn't be crossed.
- Jesus explained the power of faith. He told a rich man to sell his things and give to the poor. He spoke of His death again, and again the twelve didn't understand what He was talking about.
- Zacchaeus climbed a tree to see Jesus. He confessed his sins but said he'd repent, so Jesus forgave him. Jesus asked for a colt that'd never been ridden. He rode it into Jerusalem, and drove merchants out of the temple. They questioned His authority. He told and warned of false teachers.
- Judas agreed to betray Jesus. The Passover meal was planned, and Jesus and the twelve had the Lord's Supper. Afterwards, Jesus told of Peter's denial of Him. Jesus went to the Mount of Olives to pray.
- Jesus was arrested. Peter denied knowing Him. Jesus was taken before the council, then before Pilate and Herod, and was sentenced to death. He was crucified. Above him on the cross were the words, "This is the King of the Jews."
- Two others were being crucified. One humbly asked Jesus to remember him, and Jesus assured him that he'd be with Him in paradise.
- Jesus cried out for His Father, then died. On Friday, Joseph from Judah asked for His body. He wrapped it and placed it in a tomb.
- On Sunday, women went there with their prepared spices, but the stone that covered the tomb had been rolled away. Two men in shining clothing told them He had been raised. They told the apostles what'd happened.

- In Emmaus, two followers discussed Jesus's death. Jesus drew near and walked along side. They didn't know who He was, and they told Him of the death and resurrection. It was near dark, so Jesus stayed with them.
- They sat to eat and Jesus said a prayer. Then they knew who He was, but He disappeared from their sight. They told this to the remaining eleven disciples. They reported that the Lord had definitely risen.
- Jesus appeared to them, and showed them the scars on His hands and feet. They gave Him some fish to eat, and He ate in their presence. He opened their minds to understand the scriptures. He led them to Bethany. He blessed them, raised His hands, and was taken into heaven.

Additional comments on the book of Luke:

Luke's gospel is the longest book in the New Testament with over 1,100 versus. That's enough content to tell us about the unpardonable sin, the gulf between the holy and the unrighteous, and even more about Jesus. The unpardonable sin is what every believer must know, because we all pray for our sins to be pardoned. In Luke 12:10, Jesus says, "whoever shall speak a word against the Son of Man, it shall be forgiven him: but unto him that blasphemeth against the Holy Ghost it shall not be forgiven."

The story of Lazarus and the division between good and evil begins in Luke 16:19. Jesus tells of a rich man who died and was being tormented with flames, while the poor man Lazarus was being comforted in death. In verse 26, Jesus said "between us and you (between those in comfort and those in flames) there is a great gulf fixed: so that they which would pass from hence to you cannot; neither can they pass to us, that would come from thence." So at death our souls will either be in flame (Hades) or in the comforting place (Paradise), and there's no passing from one side to the other. In this narrative, Jesus illustrates a rich man as a sinner and a poor man as a believer, although money doesn't determine our salvation. So the time is coming when sinners will exhaust their opportunity to "switch to the other side" and be saved. Once they're in the flames, they'll remain there.

Since Luke was the only author in the New Testament who was non-Jewish (a Gentile), he didn't quote or repeat many of the Jewish writings from the Old Testament. He does tell us that Jesus on earth was humanistic in that He ate, wept, slept and walked beside others. After resurrection, Jesus showed them His hands and feet. Then they knew He'd died for them.

John

John was a leader in the early Christian church in the latter part of the first century. This gospel was probably written around 90 AD, much later than the first three gospels in the New testament. It was during a time when Christians were being persecuted by the Romans and non-Christian Jews. He particularly wanted everyone to know that Jesus was the true Son of God, the Christ, and that through Him one could have eternal life. In the first half of this book John tells of Jesus' miracles and ministry, then we read about the instructions he gave to his disciples so they could continue His work.

Through John we learn of Jesus' earthly mission along with the seven miracles He performed. He explains them not as historical events, but as proof and evidence that Jesus is who He says He is, the Son of the living God and our Savior. John is credited with writing this book, plus his three epistles and the book of Revelation contained toward the end of the New Testament. Many bible scholars, when asked where a new reader should begin studying the bible, will recommend beginning with this book. It gives the reader a solid overview of Jesus' ministry, death and resurrection. After that, the books of Genesis, Acts, Psalms, and Ephesians provide details about God's creations, the actions of the early Christians, the guidance needed to navigate through life in faith, and reminders to believers of how God's grace will show them the way.

- Before creation, the Word already existed and He was the same as God. Through Him, God made all things. He is the source of life. He's the Light.
- God sent John the Baptist to tell about the Light that was to come. John told of His greatness, so the Jewish elders challenged him. He told them the Messiah was coming. One greater than life, and One who can give life.
- John told them that God gave us the Law through Moses, but grace and truth comes through Jesus. No one had seen God, but His beloved Son was in the bosom of the Father, and He was bringing His fulness.
- The next day Jesus came, and John called Him the Lamb of God. He was baptized, then the Holy Spirit came down from heaven to be with Him.
- Jesus selected some disciples to follow Him. Later at a wedding, His mother told Him they needed more wine. Jesus told her that His time hadn't come, but He turned the water into wine and revealed His Glory.
- Jesus told Nicodemus, a Pharisee, that people had to be born again of water and Spirit to enter heaven. There was darkness, but He had light.
- John the Baptist confirmed that he must become less important while Jesus becomes the most important. The one from heaven is above all.
- Jesus passed through Samaria and stopped at Jacob's well for water. He asked a woman there for a drink, but she said Jews couldn't drink from water cups used

by Gentiles. Jesus said their water would leave them thirsty, but water from Him was everlasting. She understood His words.

- Jesus told her the Holy Spirit would make her people worship God. She knew the Messiah would come someday, and Jesus said, "I am He." She left and told her people about this Man. He stayed there 2 more days.

- Jesus went to Galilee where the people welcomed Him. A government official asked Jesus to heal his son who was dying. Due to the man's faith in Him, Jesus told him to go home because his son would live.

- In Jerusalem many had been sick, one man for 38 years. He told Jesus that he wanted to be healed, so he was. The man picked up his mat and walked away. The Jewish authorities used that to persecute Jesus.

- Large numbers of followers stayed with Jesus. With no food there, He used 5 loaves of bread and 2 fish to feed 5,000 with 12 baskets of food left over. They called Him their Prophet. He went alone into the hills.

- The disciples rowed their boat out onto the lake when they saw Jesus walking on top of the water toward them. They were amazed.

- Jesus spoke on the shore, telling those there that He is the bread of life, and those who ate that bread had eternal life. The people were confused, because they knew His earthly father and mother, and they were normal everyday people.

- Jesus saw the people grumbling, knowing they didn't believe. Some left, so Jesus asked if His disciples also wanted to leave. Peter said they knew He'd come from God, but Jesus knew one would betray Him later on.

- The Pharisees brought a woman to Jesus who had been caught in adultery. He said, those of you who have never committed a sin can throw the first stone at her. They all left. Jesus told her to sin no more.

- Jewish authorities asked who He was. Jesus said, "I Am Who I Am." He told them that they came from this world, but He was not of this world.

- They continued to reject Jesus and accused him of blasphemy. Jesus told them that the Father was in Him, and He was in the Father.

- Lazarus became sick, but Jesus told the people he would live. Jesus stayed where He was for 2 more days, during which time Lazarus died.

- After Lazarus had been buried 4 days, Jesus arrived and told them he would rise to life. His sister Mary greeted Him, and said if He'd been there her brother Lazarus wouldn't have died. Seeing their sorrow, Jesus wept. He said, "Lazarus come out." Lazarus did, and walked away.

- The Pharisees plotted against Jesus again. At the home of Lazarus, Mary washed Jesus' feet with expensive perfume, drying them with her hair.

- The people learned that Jesus would be entering Jerusalem on a donkey, so they laid palm branches along His path. The elders grew angrier.
- Jesus spoke of His death, and that He hadn't come to judge the world but to save it. At supper with the disciples, Jesus washed their feet as an example of how they should serve and love one another. Jesus handed Judas some bread, pointing him out as the one who'd betray Him. He told Peter that he'd deny Him when He was being led to His death.
- He told the disciples that the Holy Spirit would come, to show and remind them all He'd said because the world would make them suffer.
- Jesus was arrested, and in anger Peter cut a soldier's ear. Peter denied knowing Jesus. Pilate found no reason to punish Jesus and could have pardoned Him, but the crowd shouted to crucify Him. They made a crown of thorny branches for His head, and took Him to Golgotha.
- They hung a sign above Him on the cross that read "King of the Jews." Soldiers threw dice to see who got His clothes. Jesus asked and received a drink, then died. They stuck Him with a spear to make sure. His mother, Mary Magdalene, and Mary the sister of Lazarus were all there.
- Joseph from Arimathea took His body, wrapped Him in linen and placed Him in a tomb. On Sunday, Mary Magdalene saw the tomb's entrance was opened so she ran to tell Peter and another follower (probably John).
- They saw Jesus' body was gone. Two angels inside the tomb told Mary Magdalene He'd been taken away. She turned and Jesus was there, but she didn't recognize Him. He spoke her name and she knew who He was.
- Later that evening Jesus appeared where the disciples had gathered. He showed them His nail-scared hands and feet, and they received the Holy Spirit. Thomas doubted Him at first, then realized it was really Him.
- Jesus appeared a third time to seven of His disciples. Peter went fishing, and the disciple who Jesus loved (John) recognized Him on the shore. Jesus made their fishing nets bring in many fish, and they sat and ate. Jesus told them to take care of His sheep. He told Peter to follow Him.

Additional comments on the book of John:

John's gospel gives us a lot of details surrounding Jesus' earthly ministry, including His death, burial and resurrection. We read in John 3:16 the magnitude of God's love for us, a verse that's probably the best known in all the bible. In John 11:33-35 we read about Lazarus, and how Jesus after seeing those around him grieving over his death, groaned in the spirit and wept. In Chapter 5:28-29, Jesus briefly talks about life after death, and how His judgement on the believers will be so much different than His judgement on those who were evil. Then in Chapters 18 through 21, we learn the details of His arrest, sentencing and crucifixion. It provides a heartbreaking depiction of the suffering He endured for each of us.

Much earlier in the Old Testament, Jesus was speaking to Moses when Moses said that His followers would want to know His name. Jesus replied, in Exodus 3:14, "I AM THAT I AM", and "I AM hath sent Me unto you." Jesus repeated that in John 8:58 when He spoke of Abraham and said, "Before Abraham was, I AM." That was a point Jesus made over and over again in John's gospel, telling us that God sent Him and that He and God were one in the same. He tells us "I and the Father are one", and "you Father are in Me and I in You", and in John 14:9 He tells us "he that hath seen Me hath seen the Father." They are the same, for God, Jesus and the Holy Spirit are the Godhead. **Appendix F** explains the Godhead trinity.

In this gospel, Jesus made it clear to us who He is. He stated:

I AM the bread of life

I AM the light of the world

I AM the door

I AM the resurrection and the life

I AM the Son of God

I AM the door of the sheep

I AM the gate

I AM the good shepherd

I AM the way, the truth, and the life

John wanted to ensure we knew who Jesus was and all He offered mankind. His miracles were great, and they showed us how His supreme and unlimited power could even bring the dead back to life. But His I AM statements tells us who He is and what He offers us now, today, not just in the past. We only need to accept Him and believe in Him through faith.

Acts

The book of Acts chronicles the work of those who first began to spread the Christian faith outside the borders of Israel and into every nation in the world. After the death and resurrection of Jesus, those who followed and witnessed His ministry began to spread the Good News with the divine guidance of the Holy Spirit. Their efforts grew across each neighboring country and played a huge part in the growth of the early Church. There were many key players, but the tireless work of Paul and Peter were most instrumental.

Paul's story is remarkable. His frenzied pre-Christian persecution of Jesus' followers took a sudden turn after the Lord got a hold of him. To get his attention, Jesus took his sight away on the road to Damascus, then three days later Jesus had Ananias lay hands on him as He converted him into the servant He wanted. His transition to become the "preacher to the Gentiles" was a miraculous journey, one which every Christian should know. He's one of the most important biblical figures outside of the Godhead, on a level with Moses, David, Joseph, Noah, Abraham, Elijah, Mary, Adam, and others. Paul's journey and God's use of him is explained in great detail in **Appendix C and Appendix I.**

Luke is credited as the writer of Acts, probably in or around 60 AD. In the first half of Acts he tells all that Peter and others did to advance the Christian movement, then he switches to what Paul did to convert Gentiles throughout Greece and the Roman Empire. It is a key book of the bible, one which explains how the teachings of Jesus moved from an exclusive Jewish audience into the church doctrine and principles that many of us believe today.

- Writing to Theophilus, Luke tells of a forty day span before Jesus ascended into heaven when He told His apostles to stay in Jerusalem and wait for the Holy Spirit to empower them to become His witnesses.
- Jesus was taken into heaven, then two angels appeared saying He would return the same way that He left. Later, Peter tells of Judas' betrayal, and how when he fell to his death all his insides had spilled out.
- The apostles discussed the need to select a replacement for Judas. Matthias and Joseph were proposed, and Matthias was chosen. Then they all received the Holy Spirit, and spoke in different languages.
- Peter spoke to the crowd, telling how a descendant of King David became their Messiah. They had witnessed Jesus' life and knew He was the One. Three thousand people believed him, and were baptized.
- Peter healed a lame man, making sure the crowd knew his power came from Jesus, the one they'd killed. The priests heard this and arrested Peter and John, but the believers there grew to five thousand.
- Peter and John were warned not to speak of Jesus any longer, then were set free. The number of believers grew, and they began selling their possessions and sharing everything with one another within the group.

- People came from all around to witness the healing work of the apostles. The apostles were arrested but an angel opened their cell. They were caught and whipped, and warned again not to speak of Jesus.
- Stephen, a man blessed by God, performed miracles. Some men were bribed to speak evil of him. The Council had him arrested, then saw his face light up like an angel. He spoke of Moses, David, and others throughout their early Jewish history. He told of God's covenant with His people.
- The Council was furious, but Stephen just stared toward heaven. They had him stoned to death, and Saul of Tarsus approved of his murder.
- Philip began preaching and performing miracles. Even Simon, who claimed to have powers, was astonished. He wanted the Holy Spirit that was within Philip, so he offered money for it. Peter and John scolded him.
- Saul of Tarsus continued his threats of murder toward Christian believers. As he neared Damascus, a light and voice from heaven asked why he was persecuting Jesus. He was blinded, and was led away.
- Jesus told Ananias, a believer, to find Saul. He asked why, since Saul hated believers. He found Saul, who was suddenly filled with the Holy Spirit and was able to see again. He began preaching the word of God.
- The Jews gathered to try and kill Saul, but his new followers sneaked him away. He tried to minister to any who'd listen, but they feared him knowing of his past. He told of his conversion and many accepted him. He was now called Paul.
- Peter was shown it was okay to preach to Gentiles, realizing God treated everyone the same. He spoke of Jesus, and the Holy Spirit came upon both the Jews and Gentiles. Word spread that Gentiles were being saved.
- Many Jews and Gentiles came to believe in the Lord. King Herod began to persecute them. He had James, John's brother, put to death and had Peter chained and put in prison. Angels appeared and released Peter. The prison guards were put to death, and the Lord struck Herod down.
- The Lord sent Barnabas and Paul out to preach the gospel together, and John Mark went with them for a while. In Antioch, Paul spoke at length about the life of Jesus and the Christian movement throughout Israel.
- Paul told them that their belief would set them free, something the Law of Moses could not do. Unbelieving Jews ran Paul and Barnabas off. The same happened in other towns. Paul was stoned but not killed.
- In Jerusalem, Paul and Barnabas spoke to those still preaching the Law of Moses for salvation. Peter told how God's message was for everyone, then Paul and Barnabas told of all the converted Gentile believers. They all agreed to include Gentiles in their messages about Jesus. They also agreed that Peter would preach mainly to Jews, and Paul to the Gentiles.
- Paul and Barnabas split up, with Timothy and Silas joining Paul. In Philippi, Paul and Silas were whipped and chained for doing God's work but an earthquake caused the chains to fall off. They left and went to other locations but the non-believing Jews kept punishing them.

- In Ephesus, Paul wanted a merchant to stop making models of a goddess, which caused a riot. Paul said farewell to believers before returning to Jerusalem. He visited James, then later was arrested for bringing Gentiles into the temple. Again he was put in chains.
- Paul spoke at length to defend himself, telling of his conversion and his call to preach to Gentiles. The Lord told him not to worry, but some Jews still wanted to kill him. After 2 years, Paul appealed to the Emperor. They could find no reason to keep him imprisoned, so he sailed to Rome.
- Their ship fought strong waves and storms before it was finally broken into pieces, but everyone made it to shore. Finally in Rome, Paul preached the Kingdom of God for several years to all who came to him.

Additional comments on the book of Acts:

One of the main points to take away from Acts is the realization that after thousands of years of witnessing miracles, followed by multiple warnings and punishment for their disobedience, the majority of Jews still didn't believe in God's word or that Jesus was sent to them as their promised Messiah to fulfill God's covenant to Abraham. So, Jesus converted Saul of Tarsus (later called Paul) from being the worse persecutor of Christians anywhere into His chosen disciple who'd bring His name and divine grace to the Gentiles. Still, God never gave up on the Jewish people and He never will, but after approximately 4,000 years He had to move on with His message without the unbelieving Jews so that anyone anywhere who believed in Him through faith could receive His gift of eternal life.

All through the Old Testament and up until this book of the Bible we have read about the blood sacrificing of animals, temple worship, circumcisions, and other actions regularly observed within the Jewish nation as methods of worship and holiness ordained by God. Proper worshiping of our heavenly Father as He's directed us to do could never be wrong. But after Jesus' death on the cross, a new and easier way into heaven became available to any and all who accept Him and believe. Jesus chose Paul to share that message with all mankind.

In the Gentile nations throughout the world, many people follow certain practices and perform certain deeds in order to earn favor with God and earn their way into heaven. Anyone seeking God must understand that going to church, singing in the choir, talking to coworkers about Jesus, and helping the poor and underprivileged doesn't give them salvation. Leading a self-righteous life of kindness and goodness with no cursing or unlawful acts doesn't give a person salvation. Refraining from stealing, not coveting what belongs to others, and honoring your father and mother doesn't give anyone salvation. Nothing is more heartbreaking than when a saved believer asks someone they love if they will be going to heaven, and they respond by saying "Gosh, I sure hope so." We should be sure of it. It's not something we should ever be uncertain about.

None of the actions listed above will bring salvation. They're the results of salvation. A true Christian will always help the needy, keep the Commandments, be honest in business dealings, and treat others with kindness because the Holy Spirit within him or her won't allow it to be any other way. Getting saved requires belief and faith, but afterwards God certainly instructs us to do good deeds and works. And when we do help others we're not to boast of it but show humility, so that the glory of our deeds will go to the Father. Jesus told us in Luke 12:48 that to whom much has been given, much will be required. Although Ephesians 2:8-9 clearly states that we're saved by God's grace through faith and not a result of works, Romans 2:6 tells us "(God) will render to every man according to his deeds." Revelation 2:23 says "I will give unto every one of you according to your works." Christians should share their faith, and work in Jesus' name.

Being saved requires us to repent of our sins and invite God into our lives in the belief that Jesus died for us, rose again, and was resurrected. Through faith in the cross and the resurrection we are saved as stated in Romans 10:9, and by believing in Jesus as we're told in John 3:16. Jesus doesn't tell us in John 3:16 that whosoever believeth in Him and does good deeds and works would have everlasting life, He just says to believe in Him. That's a huge part of what Paul shared to the world. If you only act like a Christian without ever accepting Jesus as your savior, then Jesus might be speaking to you on judgement day when He says, "I never knew you."

A believer's good deeds and works are seen by God, but in a way apart from awarding us our salvation. On judgement day, none of us will be judged by Jesus to determine if we're saved because we already are if we've repented and accepted Jesus as our Savior and continued to confess it and live as a true Christian until death. The Bible tells us that. The believer's judgement in heaven will be based on our works and deeds as Christians, which will determine the rewards we'll receive. In Revelation 22:12, Jesus tells us "And behold, I come quickly, and my reward is with Me, to give every man according as his work shall be."

One belief that some have about salvation and how Jesus will judge them is expressed in the phrase "once saved, always saved." Viewpoints differ on whether that phrase is true. It's really not about whether we believe that to be true, it's about what the Bible says about it. To read what the Bible says, see **Appendix D.**

Romans

The apostle Paul wrote this letter to the Gentile believers in Rome in 57 AD, before he had traveled there himself. After telling them he was called to preach the Good News, he immediately explained the power of the gospel and every man's need for salvation. He gave them many reasons they should continue to believe, and how their beliefs should be seen in their actions. It's an essential book in the bible, telling everyone who reads it about the gospel of Jesus, how we can become a member in the body of Christ, and how being born again changes every aspect of who we are.

He reminded them early on in 3:23 that "all have sinned and come short of the glory of God", a critical reminder to all of us. Compared to the holiness and omnipotence of God, there's no way we measure up in His eyes without the finished work of the cross to sanctify us. Paul's letter to the Romans is strong yet personal and instructive. In 1:16 when he writes "For I am not ashamed of the gospel of Christ," he's telling the believing Roman Gentiles that the pride he has for his Christianity they could also have. As it's written in 1:17, "the just (righteous) shall live by faith", and Paul was certainly full of faith.

- Paul was anxious to preach the Good News to those in Rome. He wanted to first reach the Jews, but also the Gentiles. He said God is ashamed of mankind's sinful ways, and that men have no conscience.
- He said don't judge others, because God is our judge, and He'll reward us for what we've done. God judges all by the same standard although the Gentiles don't have His Laws. Even our secret thoughts will be judged.
- No one is righteous whether Jew or Gentile. His Laws lets people know when they've sinned. The free gift of God's grace means all can be saved through Jesus Christ. A believer's faith forgives their sins.
- Even though we can be saved through faith, we must still uphold God's Laws. Abraham was made righteous by God because of his faith, and became the spiritual father of us all. Believers become a friend of God.
- God's Law allowed man to keep account of his sins. Adam's one sin condemned all mankind, just as one righteous act can give us life. The work of the cross released us from sin, if through faith we believe.
- Human nature is weak, so we must be controlled by the Holy Spirit which pleads to God in our behalf. Nothing can take us from God's love. He has mercy on anyone He wishes, and makes stubborn anyone He wishes. Jesus ended the Law, so believers are right with God. Don't ask who is going to heaven and who is not. Confess your sins; be saved.
- God hasn't given up on Israel, those He'd chosen from the beginning. He has kept for Himself a remnant of 7,000 men who have not worshiped false gods, chosen by His grace and not from their actions. Most Jews stumbled, so salvation was given to Gentiles to make the Jews jealous.

- The stubbornness of Israel's people isn't permanent. Once the complete number of Gentiles come to God, Israel will be saved. God doesn't change His mind on whom He has blessed. He can transform us inwardly to completely change our thoughts. Be a modest believer.
- One body has many parts, each with a different function. All believers are joined into one body in union with Jesus. We're to use the gifts God gave us in accordance with His grace. Do what He has called us to do.
- Love one another, show respect, and work hard. Serve the Lord with devotion. Ask God to bless those who persecute you. Live in peace without taking revenge. Do not judge. Please others, not yourself.
- Christ's life of service was on behalf of the Jews. Now the Gentiles can also receive Him. Paul asked that they greet his friend Phoebe who was delivering his letter. Tertius identified himself as Paul's scribe for this letter. Paul stated that he taught about Jesus according to the secret mysteries revealed to him after they'd been hidden from men for ages.

Additional comments on the book of Romans:

Many of the great themes and messages in the Bible come from Paul in his letter to the Romans, so it's a book that can help anyone understand the scriptures a little better. After his letter to them, Paul made it to Rome but was confined most of the time and under guard. Among his many messages to the Romans he reminded them that being a believer doesn't free them from their sin nature, but it does free them from their sins through repentance. Sadly, approximately 10 years after Paul's letter to these Romans, it's believed that the emperor Nero had him beheaded.

After Paul's conversion from the person who punished Christians to the person chosen by God to preach the gospel to the Gentiles, it was revealed to him the "revelation of the mysteries." These mysteries or secrets were withheld from mankind by God until He'd decided the time was right to share them, mainly through the apostle Paul. Many of them are the main components of the Grace of God, explained in detail in **Appendix C.**

God's use of Paul can't be overstated when it comes to spreading the gospel outside the borders of Israel. He was so immersed in his love and understanding of God's message that he tried to share it with all the non-Jewish nations around him. In 11:13 he clearly stated that "I am the apostle of the Gentiles." Then in 2:16 Paul said, "... God shall judge the secrets of men by Jesus Christ according to my gospel." He knew his calling and he took ownership of it, claiming it as his own. He was truly a principle apostle of God, explaining to all the practical implications of Christian faith.

I Corinthians

Paul wrote three letters to believers in the Greek city of Corinth. The first one mentioned in 5:9 must've been lost or irrecoverable, then this one dated around 55 AD, then his third letter is the next book in the bible. He had spent more than a year in Corinth preaching and working as a tent maker, so he knew those in the church there that he'd established. He'd learned there'd been quarreling and division among the people since he'd left, centering around immorality and the age-old problem of worshiping false idols, among others. This letter told them that God's word could be used to address those issues, even if it took chastising and forcing out those who were bad influences on the others. Paul could tell their faith had withered, so his letter covered a wide scope of subjects including marriage, lawsuits against other believers, maintaining order in the church, and the many parts of the body of Christ.

- Paul asked them to keep the quarrels among believers out of the church. Some said they followed Peter's teachings, and some followed Apollos. He reminded them that it was Christ who died on the cross, not Peter or the others. Christ is the power and wisdom of God, so follow only Him.
- If you must boast, then boast of what God has done through you. He is the one with the power. Paul's wisdom comes from God's secret wisdom, in place before the world was made and given to Paul through His Spirit.
- To a sinner Jesus's death on the cross means nothing, but to those being saved it's God's power. There's no difference between the man who plants and the man who waters. God will reward both according to his works.
- Paul writes that those in Corinth are like children in their Christian faith, so he must feed them milk since they're not ready for solid food.
- God placed Jesus as our building foundation, and on the Day of Christ what we've built on that foundation must withstand fire. If it does we'll receive a reward. We belong to Christ and Christ belongs to God. We're God's Temple and God's Spirit lives within us.
- Paul is sending Timothy to remind them of Christian principles. They'll all celebrate Passover since Jesus their Lamb had been sacrificed. Don't sit and eat with an immoral person, and don't associate with them.
- Our bodies are a part of the body of Christ, so only use the body to serve the Lord. Do nothing immoral, and don't initiate lawsuits against other Christians because you'd be judged in court by unbelievers.
- Join yourself to the Lord and become spiritually one with Him. Marriage of a believer to a nonbeliever shouldn't end in divorce if one agrees to stay with the other. If a person is unmarried it's okay, or if he/she is married it's okay. The unmarried avoid the troubles of married couples.
- A married person must work to please the spouse, but a single person can work to please the Lord. Avoid idols since they stand for something that doesn't really exist. Jesus Christ is the only Lord, so don't test Him.

- We'll all be tested in life, but God will not allow us to be tested beyond our power to remain firm. He'll provide us our strength, and He'll give us a way out if it becomes unbearable. Christians all eat from one loaf of bread, and since we're all one body in Christ we share the same loaf.

- God is supreme over Christ, and Christ is supreme over man. On the night Jesus was betrayed, He said that the bread they broke was His body and the drink was His blood. So take it in His memory. If man doesn't recognize the meaning of that, he brings judgement upon himself.

- Although there are different spiritual gifts the same Spirit gives them all. Christ is one body with many parts. Believers have been baptized into His body. The strong parts of Christ's body must support the weak parts, since they have a concern for one another. Use your gift for God.

- Faith without love is nothing. Love has patience, kindness, is unselfish, and is never happy with evil. So have faith, hope and love, and the greatest of these is love. Give people encouragement and comfort.

- Speaking in a strange tongue only helps yourself, but speaking to proclaim God's message helps everyone. Speaking 5 words that are understood is better than 1,000 words not understood. Speaking in strange tongues is proof for unbelievers, not for believers.

- If someone speaks aloud in strange tongues, then someone must explain what was said or it was of no use. If no one is there to interpret, then speak in strange tongues to yourself only.

- Never forget that Christ died for our sins, was buried then raised to life 3 days later, then He spoke and appeared to as many as 500 at one time. All will die because of their union with Adam, but you can live forever.

- There are both heavenly and earthly bodies. A planted seed doesn't sprout unless it dies. We are buried as mortal, but raised as immortal. We might be buried ugly and weak, but raised beautiful and strong.

- When the last trumpet sounds, we'll all be changed as quickly as the blinking of an eye. We must die to change into what can't die. The scripture tells us "Death is destroyed; victory is complete."

Additional comments on the book of I Corinthians:

Corinth was in south-central Greece and was a major city during those times, a place of retreat with lots of visitors passing through which brought wealth and prosperity. The church there was moving away from God, so Paul reminded them that they were a part of Christ's body and they needed to keep the faith and rid themselves of pagan beliefs and worships.

Paul used many wise truths to awaken those in the Corinth Church before it was too late, and these truths still apply to us today to strengthen and guide us through times of allurement and uncertainty: He wrote:

I Corinthians 1:25 – For the foolishness of God is wiser than man's wisdom, and the weakness of God is stronger than man's strength.

I Corinthians 8:2 – Those who think they know something do not yet know as they ought to know.

I Corinthians 7:9 – It is better to marry than to burn.

I Corinthians 6:19 – Your body is the temple of the Holy Ghost.

I Corinthians 13:11 – When I was a child I spoke as a child, I understood as a child, I thought as a child; but when I became a man I put away childish things.

I Corinthians 14:8 – If the trumpet give an uncertain sound, who shall prepare himself to the battle?

I Corinthians 12:4 – Now there are diversities of gifts. But the same Spirit.

I Corinthians 15:51-53 – Behold, I shew you a mystery; We shall not all sleep but we shall all be changed. In a moment, in the twinkling of an eye, at the last trump; for the trumpet shall sound and the dead shall be raised incorruptible, and we shall be changed.

I Corinthians 13:13 – And now these three remain: faith, hope and love. But the greatest of these is love.

I Corinthians 2:5 – Your faith should not stand in the wisdom of men, but in the power of God.

I Corinthians 4:20 – For the Kingdom of God is not in word, but in power.

I Corinthians 15:22 – For as in Adam all die, even so in Christ shall all be made alive.

I Corinthians 5:13 – But them that are without God judgeth. Therefore, put away from among yourselves that wicked person.

I Corinthians 10:21 – You cannot drink the cup of the Lord and the cup of the devils: you cannot be partakers of the Lord's table and of the table of devils.

I Corinthians 12:12 – For as the body is one and has many members, and all the members of that one body, being many, are one body. So also is Christ.

II Corinthians

The church in Corinth that Paul had established was struggling, but when Titus told him they were repentant and unified, Paul wrote this letter to them around 56 AD. He applauded and encouraged them to keep the straight and narrow way, assuring them that he cared deeply for each member and their renewed faith in the Lord. He also encouraged them to continue collecting for the impoverished believers in Jerusalem.

- Paul had made plans to visit them, to remind them that God had placed His mark of ownership on them, but decided to write this letter instead.
- He told them that if some in the church make you sad, tell them you still love them. Have forgiveness for the offender, and keep Satan from getting any advantage.
- There is victory through Christ. We are led by Him. For those of us who are saved, there's a fragrance that brings life. We're God's servants.
- God has placed His Spirit in our hearts, not written it with ink and not written on stone tablets. The capacity we have for good works and our faith comes from God. Written law brings death; the Spirit gives life.
- Paul tells them the Law brought death when it was in force, but the death and resurrection of Jesus brings eternal life to those who believe in Him through faith. The Lord's Spirit brings freedom wherever it is.
- We should know that the God who raised up Jesus to life will also raise us up and into His presence. We must live by faith. What we can see only lasts a short time, but what we can't see through faith will last forever.
- When the tent we live in on earth (our body) is torn down, God will have a house for us in heaven which will last forever. First, all of us must appear before Christ to be judged whether good or bad. The truly saved are good. Turn to God now.
- Don't judge others by human standards, but by the new standards received when we joined with Christ. Don't let the grace God gave us be wasted. God's servants show kindness and patience, and true love. Do not try to work together as equals with unbelievers, it cannot be done.
- Titus told Paul that those in Corinth wanted to see him. His last letter to them made them sad, but that sadness made them change their ways. Paul asked them to finish the work in Corinth that he'd started.
- We thank God for the willingness of Titus to help us. He is Paul's partner. Show your love to him, since he and the others represent the churches and bring glory to Christ.
- Give to help your fellow Christians. He who planted many seeds will have a large crop. God loves those who gladly give. God will give us more than we need, so we'll have enough to support every worthy cause. God will make us rich enough to be generous. Boast for what the Lord has done.
- Avoid all false prophets. Satan can disguise himself like an angel of light. Paul is not ashamed of the gospel, and will defend his ministry to all.

- Paul asked them not to think of him as a fool. He had been in prison many times, been whipped, and been near death. He had worked hard, but had been stoned for his faith. He was shipwrecked and once spent 24 hours in the water. He had gone hungry, and been in danger from Jews and Gentiles.
- Paul is content with his weaknesses, because the Lord told him that His grace was all he needed. So when Paul is the weakest, he is the strongest.
- Paul planned to visit them a third time. They'll see that Christ speaks through him. Christ was weak when He was put to death on the cross, but by God's power Jesus lives. The church there should live in peace and harmony. All of God's people send their love and greetings.

Additional comments on the book of II Corinthians:

There is so much important and pertinent information given in this book that it's difficult to summarize. One theme is God telling us, through Paul, how He wants His followers to live and that their journey with Him will not be easy. Christians can be ridiculed and rejected for their beliefs since so many others in mainstream America follow those who look up to idolatrous leaders, or look up to anything representing what they perceive to be pleasurable. Sinners accept their misguided affections and presume them to be true.

Paul mentions and compares the Mosaic Law, given to Moses on Mount Sanai and named after him, to the Gospel of Jesus and the age of grace. He tells the Corinthians that the Law will lead them to death but the ministry of Jesus' Holy Spirit within believers leads to eternal life. We must understand that Jesus and His death on the cross is the fulfillment of the Law within us. For a thorough discussion on that topic, see **Appendix B**.

Other directives we glean from this book includes our desire to be a comfort to others, just as God is a comfort to us. This is stated very early on in Chapter 1:3-4, an indication to us of its importance. We're told in Chapter 9 that God loves a cheerful giver, reminding us that he who sews his seeds bountifully will reap bountifully. We aren't to give reluctantly or feel pressure to give, but to do so with a cheerful heart. In 5:10, we're reminded that we'll all appear before the judgement seat of Christ to receive what is due for what we've done, whether good or evil.

Jesus is the light at the end of our tunnel, and the things we do today may be the things we'll need to explain to Him later when we look Him in the eye. We should look forward to judgement day. Imagine if you will a blind Christian who lived his life glorifying God. When dying, he's smiling and full of joy when he says, "Wow, the first thing I'll see in my whole life will be the face of Jesus!" <u>Does anything else really matter?</u> What a glorious day it shall be!

Galatians

Paul had earlier taken a missionary journey to Asia Minor which resulted in a few churches being established in the southern part of Galatia. Later, around 49 AD, after he'd learned the Gentile Christians there were being pressured to be circumcised and to follow the commandments and Mosaic Law given to Moses, he wrote them this letter. It is thought to be the fourth letter that Paul wrote to these churches that he'd started throughout the region.

Paul knew from his own history and experiences that man could not be saved just by following a checklist of laws. He wanted to remind the Galatians that there were false teachers everywhere who'd love nothing more than to make them doubt their beliefs. Using Abraham as an example, he pointed out that Abraham was righteous in the eyes of God not because he followed the Commandments (which didn't even exist until Moses came along) but because he had faith in God. Only faith and belief are needed.

He wanted them to understand that the Mosaic Law was meant to be a guide for mankind to use until their Savior arrived. The early Laws would point out what sins a man had committed, but the Law did nothing to remove those sins or forgive man for committing them. Paul explained in detail how a person could be saved. He compared what faith in God could do versus what following the Law could do. His bottom line was this: **If the Laws and Commandments could save a person, then that meant Jesus suffered and died on the cross for no reason.**

- Paul greeted them in the name of Jesus and God the Father. He expressed his concern that they were accepting "another gospel".
- He told them that if they were trying to agree and be popular with others then they couldn't be a servant to Christ. He reminded them that his message was not of human origin, but that it came straight from Jesus. He was called to preach to the Gentiles.
- By God's power, Peter was called as an apostle to the Jews just as Paul was to be an apostle to Gentiles. They met and agreed on it. The difference in Jewish and Gentile beliefs and their saving powers are made clearer in **Appendix B.**
- Now both Jews and Gentiles can be saved by faith, not by following the Law. Paul confessed that he no longer lived, but that Christ lived in him. All who believe in faith are blessed, just as Abraham was.
- The Law has nothing to do with faith. Christ redeemed us from the curse brought on by the Law. The blessings given to Abraham can be given to all. God made a covenant, and He promised to keep it.
- The Law shows us what wrongdoing is, but it is not against God's covenant promises. The Law was in charge until Christ came.
- There is no difference between Jews and Gentiles, men and women, or slaves and masters because we're all in one union with Jesus Christ.

- Paul introduced God to the Gentiles so they knew Him, but had the Gentiles accepted Him? He worried whether they'd prayed and asked God to forgive them. They'd need to keep away from all false teachers.
- Christ has set us free. When we're in union with Christ it doesn't matter if we're circumcised or not, what matters is our faith and belief. The Commandments tell us to love our neighbors as ourselves.
- Let God's Spirit guide us. Human nature opposes His Spirit. The two are enemies. Human nature makes us be jealous, immoral, and want to argue and fight, but the Spirit produces love, joy and patience.
- When you see others doing wrong, correct them in a gentle way. Carry the burdens of others. Judge your own conduct, not the conduct of others. Help others, especially those belonging to the family of God.
- Paul asked them to end any troubles within their church. His own scars showed there would be division, but we need to work through them with love.

Additional comments on the book of Galatians:

Paul told those in Galatia that when one is filled with the Spirit of God he is drastically different from those bowing and submitting to the ways of the flesh. When one walks in God's grace it is evident because they're obeying what the Holy Spirit within them would have them do. We should try our best to live a holy life, and ask God for forgiveness if we fail. If we produce good fruit, others will notice and want what we have. All Christians should be setting good examples for others to follow. Paul was insistent that Christians keep their faith.

We live in an expansive society and among those with different personalities and varying lifestyles, amid people who had an inexhaustible number of both good and bad role models growing up. Some were raised in peaceful surroundings while others grew up in an atmosphere of varied resentment toward their fellow man. The underprivileged and poor may resent those who are wealthy, seeing them waste their money and not giving to those needing a helping hand. The wealthy may put themselves in a class above others, feeling privileged without thanking God for the blessings they have. In a random group of diversified individuals, some of us will fall into one of those categories. But through the grace of God, none of those attitudes or conditions matters in the least when determining who among us is worthy of being a child of God. God loves all people. Yes, He loves you.

It may be difficult to influence someone who understands nothing of God's love, but we're asked to be a beacon of light to others. Just as Paul emphasized, to be a child of God doesn't require money, a flawless past, or a silver spoon. If you have true faith God will know you, and the Holy Spirit will require you to obey His Laws.

Ephesians

Paul took several missionary journeys during his lifetime, either by walking or riding animals throughout the region. Between his second and third missionary trips, he preached at a church in Ephesus. Many there were converted by his preaching but others were opposed to his message. Feeling threatened, he left the city only to end up being imprisoned in Rome. It was from his prison cell that he wrote this letter to the Ephesians, sometime around 60 AD. It was one of four letters he'd write to churches from behind bars, now commonly referred to as Paul's four Prison Epistles.

Paul instructed them to keep the body of Christ pure and holy. He wanted them to be true children of God, and to live out God's will in their lives. He emphasized God's power within them, telling them they held a place in God's ultimate plan through oneness with Jesus. Their church would be a body with Christ as the head. This letter addressed many moral behaviors that Christians needed to embrace to please God the Father.

- Greetings from Paul, an apostle of Jesus. Give thanks to the Father, who had chosen us even before the world was created through our union with Christ.
- Praise God for the gift He gave us in His Son. Open your minds to know the hope to which He has called you. In time, God will bring all of heaven and earth together, with Jesus as the head.
- Christ rules above all authorities, powers, and lords. He is above all things. The church is Christ's body. God's grace has saved you.
- We have been saved through faith and His grace, not of our own doing. We have been created for a life of good deeds.
- In the past, Gentiles were foreigners and did not belong to God's chosen people. They were not a part of God's covenants to His people. They lived in a world without any hope, and without God.
- But now, in union with Christ, He has made Jews and Gentiles one people. God abolished the Jewish Law with its commandments and rules. Gentiles are not foreigners or strangers any longer.
- Gentiles are now built on the same foundation laid by the apostles and prophets, with the cornerstone being Christ Jesus Himself.
- Jesus gave Paul, for the sake of the Gentiles, the work to do for their good. God revealed to Paul His secret, that by means of the gospel the Gentiles along with the Jews have a part in God's blessings. God achieved His eternal purpose through Jesus Christ our Lord.
- Be always humble, gentile and patient. Show your love by being tolerant with one another. Keep the unity which the Spirit gives.
- The One who came down then went back up filled the universe with His presence. We are the body, and under Christ's control all the various parts of the body fit together to grow through love.

- Be kind. Earn an honest living and help the poor. Do nothing to make God's Holy Spirit sad. Get rid of bitterness and anger. No more shouting and insults, and no hateful feelings. Forgive others as God has forgiven you. Be tender-hearted, and try to be like Him.

- Don't let others deceive you, and stay away from those who do. Try to learn what pleases the Lord, and what He wants you to do. Always give thanks for every blessing and everything in life to God the Father.

- The scripture says that a man and woman should bond and live as one. Children should obey their parents. Parents are to raise their children without anger, but in Christian discipline and instruction.

- Remember the Lord will reward everyone for the good deeds they do. Carry your faith as a shield. Use the word of God that the Spirit gives. May the Lord give you peace and love with your faith.

Additional comments on the book of Ephesians:

Paul used this letter to remind the Ephesians what good things God has done for them, and how their lives could bring blessings if they'd follow His light. He gives them many reasons they should stand unified in their faith and work through any struggles they'd encounter. Paul understood it was difficult to maintain one's faith day after day through trial after trial, when the mind and body wants to live an easier life in a routine that is not as challenging. Being a Christian isn't easy.

Another point Paul revealed to them is what could be referred to as the "secrets or mysteries of the church", making sure they understood that God had given both Jews and Gentiles an equal part of His blessings. Anyone and everyone who believes through faith in the cross and the life and death of Jesus can have eternal life without strict adherence to Jewish laws and it's commandments. These secrets were known by God since the beginning of time, but had been withheld from the knowledge of man until God determined it was time to reveal them to the world. When the Jewish nation didn't acknowledge Jesus as the One sent by God to fulfill the promise He'd made to Abraham, the secrets of the gospel were disclosed to Gentiles and the grace of God was offered to everyone. God used Paul as a key player in making these secrets known to all mankind. These secrets or mysteries are mentioned in the Bible several times, especially how all Christians, Jews and Gentiles alike would make up the church with Jesus as the head. Read more about God's secrets in **Appendix C.**

Philippians

This was another of the letters Paul wrote while in custody, a prisoner in Rome under the Emperor Nero. It was written to the church in Philippi, considered to be the first Christian church founded in all of Europe. He had continued to receive backing from that church, and he wanted to write and let them know how much he appreciated their support. He was relieved not to be writing them due to a setback in their faith, which had become the theme and basis for many of his letters. He wrote this in or around the year 62 AD.

Paul had first visited Philippi during one of his missionary journeys, and was arrested when the leaders there claimed his preaching caused a public nuisance. They still believed salvation came according to the requirements and provisions of the old covenant and Laws, something Paul didn't preach. Paul's letter was delivered to the Philippians by Epaphroditus, who had visited Paul and brought him finances from the Philippi church. This letter was full of Paul's joy and humility, but he also reminded the church to stay clear of anyone trying to impose Jewish observances and rites on them. Paul's preaching didn't base salvation on whether a person followed the old Commandments, but on accepting Christ and His death on the cross.

- From Paul and Timothy to God's people in Phillipi. May our Father give you grace and peace.
- You have helped me in the work of the gospel and have shared in this privilege that God has given me. I am writing to you from prison.
- I pray your lives be filled with all the qualities only Jesus can give. The guards here know God has given me the job of defending the gospel.
- I know I'll be set free, and that my whole being will bring honor to Christ whether I live or die. I want to live for Christ, but also die to be with Him.
- Don't be afraid of your enemies. Be courageous, because God will give you victory. You are strong because you have fellowship in the Spirit.
- Always be humble to one another. Consider others better than yourself. Jesus took the nature of a servant, and walked the path of obedience all the way to His death. Have an attitude like the one Jesus had.
- Keep working in your church, We're God's perfect children who live in a world full of corrupt and sinful people. Stay innocent and pure.
- I hope to send Timothy to you soon. He cares deeply about you. Watch out for those doing evil things. We put no trust in external ceremonies. Worship God by means of His Spirit. Be in union with Christ.
- I am an Israelite by birth from the tribe of Benjamin, a pure-blooded Hebrew. For the sake of Jesus, I have thrown everything away. I no longer have a righteousness of my own, and no man should. My righteousness now is based only on faith in Jesus Christ.
- There are many enemies of Christ who will end up in hell. But we eagerly wait for Jesus to come down from heaven, to be under His rule.
- Remember that the Lord is coming soon, so in your prayers always thank God first for all He's done for you, then ask God for your needs.

- I have all I need now that Epaphroditus has brought me your gifts. God will supply all your needs too. To our God and Father be all the glory. We all send you our greetings. May the grace of Jesus Christ be with you.

Additional comments on the book of Philippians:

This letter from Paul covers many topics, but the recurring theme is one of joy and rejoicing. He gives them hope and encouragement to continue their good works even when times are difficult. His message to them is his message to us, that even through challenging times we should be happy because of our relationship with Jesus. We have this life on earth in our flesh bodies, but we'll also have a life with Christ in our spiritual bodies. So be joyful.

He acknowledges that peace and happiness can be difficult living in a society filled with pressures and expectations. We know that all too well. Once we give in to the heaviness of life we let loose of our thankfulness and joy and try to find it in material possessions and temporary fulfillments. We may find ourselves in meaningless quarrels and with bad attitudes, emotions that we've initiated that can't be blamed on others. We must control our feelings, strive to be fulfilled even in the worst of times, and anchor ourselves to the fact that there is joy in helping and serving others in the name of Jesus.

Yes, it's hard to stay positive and trust that everything will end up okay. We may have family, friends, health and adequate resources, but the greatest of Christian possessions is knowing we can ask God for peace and guidance. Paul offers us the following two versus in his letter to the Philippians, among many others, which gives us love and assurance.

Chapter 4:6-7. Do not be anxious about anything, but in everything, by prayer and petition, with thanksgiving, present your requests to God. And the peace of God, which transcends all understanding, will guard your hearts and your minds in Christ Jesus.

Chapter 4:13. I can do all things through Him who strengthens me.

Colossians

Paul's letter to the Christians in Colossae was written around 60-61 AD, and was one of the nine letters he wrote to regional churches during his lifetime. He'd never been to Colossae, in Asia Minor, but knew of their conversion from his colleague Epaphras who'd gone there and established a body of believers. Paul was still imprisoned in Rome, but he didn't let that prevent him from reaching out to those who were under pressure to follow the old Laws and Commandments given to their forefathers. Many in Colossae didn't believe that Jesus was really the Son of God.

Once Paul learned of the false teachers there, he knew he had to write them to prevent dissention within their ranks. Jewish legalism was all the people knew back then, even after Jesus had been crucified, so the small group that Epaphras had reshaped was under pressure to revert back to old beliefs. The message from Jesus that one could be saved and have eternal life, apart from just doing good works and following the commandments, was hard for societies to latch onto. Salvation by grace to those who believed was a total about-face transformation to anyone immersed in Old Testament mandates. Some challenged the deity of Jesus, so Paul needed to remind them that Jesus' death on the cross put an end to rituals such as circumcisions and other longstanding practices.

- From Paul and brother Timothy, may God give the people of Colossae peace and grace. We are praying for you with wisdom from the Spirit.
- Praise God for He has rescued us from the power of darkness and brought us into the kingdom of His Son, by whom we are set free.
- Jesus is the visible likeness of the invisible God, superior to all living things. God created the universe through Him, He who existed before all other things. In union with Him our sins are forgiven.
- He is the head of the church, which is His body. God made peace through His Son's sacrifice and death on the cross. At one time we were God's enemies, but with the death of Jesus we are now His friends.
- Paul was made a servant of the church. God's secrets were once hidden from all mankind but are now revealed. The secret is that Christ is within us. We can all share in the glory of God. God's secret was Jesus.
- Don't be deceived by the worthless means of human wisdom. It's been handed down for ages, and it's not from Christ. You were once spiritually dead due to your sins, and being Gentiles without knowledge of Jesus and the Law.
- God forgave our sins by nailing them to the cross. Keep your minds fixed on things in heaven and not on things of the earth. Your real life is with Christ, and when He appears we too will share in His glory.
- Get rid of your anger and hatred feelings. No insults or obscene talk shall come from your lips. There is no longer any distinction between Jews and Gentiles, because Christ is in all, and Christ is all.

- Be kind, gentle, and patient. Forgive one another just as the Lord has forgiven you. Everything you do or say shall be done in the name of the Lord. Give thanks through Him to God the Father.
- Parents shall not irritate your children or they'll become discouraged. Whatever you do, work at it with all your heart. Be persistent in prayer. Your speech should always be pleasant and interesting.
- Tychicus gave you all the news about me. He and others will tell you everything happening here. Finish your task in the Lord's service. Read this letter to all the church. May God's grace be with you.

Additional comments on the book of Colossians:

Paul made several bold statements to these new Christians in Colossae that they needed to understand first and foremost. He told them that Christ was not created, but that He existed before all of creation and is supreme over everything. He is not new to the earth, and that Jesus is God's authority and there in no gospel at all without Jesus and His work. He lives among us. He was seen, heard and touched. He served, He washed the feet of others, He died for our sins. He is alive, and wants to be your friend.

Jesus wants a relationship with us. When we pray to God, it is through Jesus that our needs and requests are filtered. When we say "in Jesus name we pray" at the end of our prayers, we're realizing that it's through Jesus that our Father will receive our words. He makes intercession for us. But before asking for anything, we should always praise and thank God first.

It's obvious by the words of Jesus and the letters from Paul that heaven keeps a loving protective eye on all the children in the world. In 3:21, fathers are told not to provoke their children to anger. The bible tells us to not let harm come to them, to keep them safe beneath our wings, and guard them. When we pray, pray for the children too. Pray for their faith, safety, health, and friendships. Ask God to give them peace and happiness, and good character. Ask God to protect them from the anger of impatient adults. Follow and abide by these following passages:

Isaiah 54:13 All your children shall be taught by the LORD, and great shall be the peace of your children.

Matthew 19:14 Jesus said, "Let the little children come to me and do not hinder them, for to such belongs the kingdom of heaven."

Matthew 18:6 Whoever offends one of these little ones, it is better to have a millstone hung around their neck and be drowned in the depth of the sea.

I Thessalonians

Pauls' epistle to the church in Thessalonica is probably the oldest of his letters to survive, written in or around 50 AD. Paul had established a church there, in this capital city in the Roman province of Macedonia, that was named after the half-sister of Alexander the Great. Paul had been there a few months earlier with Timothy and Silas during his second missionary journey, probably working at his trade and preaching to pagans at every opportunity. After moving on, he began to worry how these new converts were doing, so he sent Timothy back to check on them.

Paul wanted to make sure this new church was maturing in its faith, just as a new believer must mature and grow. In this letter he reminded them that a walk with God takes obedience. There would be little encouragement from those around them, so a faithful life would require them to have great endurance and will. He understood that living within the boundaries of pagan rules would give anyone there a sense of conformity, but fitting in with others is not always the way of a Christian. Paul told them to stay the course, and to begin planning for the Lord's return.

- To those in the church, we brought the Good News to you with the power of the Holy Spirit. You suffered much, but received our message with joy.
- Your faith in God has spread. People tell how you've turned away from idols to serve the living God. One day, His Son who He raised from the dead will come from heaven and rescue you from this sinful world.
- God has judged you worthy of His good news. Live a life that pleases Him. Always give Him thanks, for He is at work in those who believe.
- You will be persecuted just as Jesus was by His countrymen. The Jews who killed Jesus also killed many of His prophets.
- We wanted to visit you again but Satan kept interfering. We sent Timothy to strengthen you, and to measure your faith. He returned to report that you have much faith and love. Be holy in the presence of God.
- Please God in everything. Live with your wife in an honorable way. Treat others fairly or the Lord will punish you. You have His Holy Spirit, use it.
- Love one another, and do even more than you're doing. Nonbelievers will see you and respect you, and want the joy you have. Jesus died and rose again, so God will take all those who died believing in Him.
- Those alive when Jesus returns will not go ahead of those who have died. At the sound of God's trumpet and after the dead have risen, the living believers will be gathered among them in the clouds to meet the Lord in the air. The Lord will come as a thief in the night. Be thankful in all circumstances.

Additional comments on the book of I Thessalonians:

Paul focused much of this letter on praising the Thessalonians for keeping their faith, because he knew how easy it would be for them to become lackadaisical and drift away from his teachings. He asked them to do even more than they were doing; to recognize that all the goodness around them was a gift from God for them to share with others. He encouraged their deeper growth during times of uncertainty and to always give thanks to God in all things, resisting any temptation to defraud and seek revenge on others.

Paul had told them about the second coming of Jesus, something they believed but didn't quite understand. They understood His return could be any day and quickly approaching, so when church members died and Jesus hadn't appeared they became confused about the fate of dead believers. This prompted Paul to explain in more detail the impending rapture of believers and the following seven years of tribulation. Paul detailed it for their understanding in I Thessalonians 4:13-18:

"But I would not have you to be ignorant, brethren, concerning them that are asleep, that ye sorrow not, even as others which have no hope. For if we believe that Jesus died and rose again, even so them also which sleep in Jesus will God bring with Him. For this we say unto you by the word of the Lord, that we which are alive and remain unto the coming of the Lord shall not prevent them which are asleep. For the Lord Himself shall descend from heaven with a shout, with the voice of the archangel, and with the trump of God: and the dead in Christ shall rise first: Then we which are alive and remain shall be caught up together with them in the clouds, to meet the Lord in the air: and so we shall ever be with the Lord. Wherefore comfort one another with these words."

II Thessalonians

This second letter from Paul to the Thessalonians probably came around 51 AD, not long after his first letter to the new church there. He'd learned the unbelievers outside the church were continuing to persecute the new Christians who were still naïve and immature in their faith, and therefore easily misguided. Paul claimed that false teachers might be showing them letters that they said came from him, when they did not. He didn't want believers to be misled so easily. Some of new members had stopped working thinking that Jesus was about to return for them, so Paul had to tell them that the Second Advent may not be as imminent as they believed.

- We recognize the way you've endured through the persecutions you're experiencing. It makes you worthy of the Kingdom which is to come. God will punish those cruel unbelievers, and give you relief.
- You've been told by false teachers that the Day of the Lord has come and gone, but it has not. It won't occur until the Wicked One appears and claims to be God. He is destined to end up in hell.
- When Jesus does come for us, the Wicked One will be revealed and be killed. Until then, he'll perform false miracles and wonders to trick us.
- God chose you to be holy people, those who'll keep their faith in the truth. He will strengthen you to always do what is good. Believers will be guarded, and the Lord will protect them from the Evil One.
- Avoid those not following the instructions we've provided. Those not willing to work shouldn't be allowed to eat. Some only want to meddle in the affairs of others when they should be living diligent lives.
- May the Lord give you peace. Notice the way I (Paul) sign each of my letters, so you can recognize letters coming from false teachers.

Additional comments on the book of II Thessalonians:

The Christians in Thessalonia had been lied to and told that Jesus had already returned, so Paul wanted to discredit that statement and give them further instructions while they waited for the Lord. He repeats some preaching from the prophet Daniel, giving the signs and times that must be in place before the trumpet sounds and Jesus comes again.

These new believers discovered that the greater their faith, the more they were tested. Just as in nature, the higher you ascend the stronger the wind. The resistance to our faith can blow us off course, but we must hang on, pray, and persevere. Paul wanted them to know they'd be challenged, and to prepare for the lies and negativity coming from false teachers around them. But they'd be okay; God had them by the hand.

I Timothy

Timothy was in Asia Minor when Paul met him and saw the depth of his faith and conviction, so he invited Timothy to accompany him on his second missionary journey. Paul needed another companion and helper since he and Barnabus had split up earlier over a disagreement on whether to add John Mark to their team. When Paul left for Macedonia, he left Timothy in Ephesus to combat the continued battle with false teachers and to provide guidance to the believers there. These two Jewish Christians made a good team.

Hearing of Timothy's work in Ephesus, Paul wrote this first letter to him around 63 AD. He knew Timothy might need help keeping the church there organized and functioning, so he provided him information on what should be taught and how the body of the church should operate. He encouraged Timothy to have a firm agenda, and in 6:12 to "fight the good fight of faith" to keep believers there on the straight and narrow path toward eternal life.

- To Tomothy, my true son of faith. From Paul, apostle to Jesus Christ.
- The Law is good when used as it should be. But it must be remembered that the Law was not made for good people but for criminals.
- Jesus came into this world to save sinners, and I was the worst of them. God had mercy on me, but some men don't listen to their conscience and have ruined their faith. God wants everyone to be saved, and that's why I was sent to be an apostle to the Gentiles.
- In church services, every man should pray and women should be modest. Everyone should dress properly and have humility.
- A church leader must be a leader without fault, and be self-controlled and orderly. He must not love money, and be respected by others.
- Helpers within the church should have good character, along with their spouses. They should not gossip, but be honest in everything.
- Some people will abandon their faith over time and may speak badly of the church. But everything that God created is good.
- Train yourself for a Godly life. Physical exercise is good, but spiritual exercise is valuable in every way. Be an example for the believers there.
- Don't rebuke older men, and show respect for widows who may live alone. Let the congregation know to take care of their relatives and their own family. If they don't they are worse than an unbeliever.
- Keep yourself pure. Good deeds are plainly seen. Show no favor to any one person. Drink water but take a little wine to help your digestion.
- Anyone teaching a different doctrine than the true words that came from Jesus Christ is swollen with pride, and knows nothing. If we have food and clothes we have enough. Some want money, a source of all evil.
- Strive for righteousness, godliness and endurance. God is with you.

Additional comments on the book of I Timothy:

If you're in a church that seems a little unstable, the information in this book could be invaluable in correcting the problem. Paul provides to Timothy exactly how a church's leadership and organization should be structured. He gives his young assistant complete instructions on what appropriate conduct should look like within the church, what the qualifications of the leaders should be, and even how the women should dress and act. He made a point to emphasize one of Jesus' many roles in the church and His many roles in the world. In 2:5, Paul wrote "For there is one God, and one mediator between God and men, the man Jesus Christ". This book touches on some of the challenges facing churches today.

What qualities would you look for a church? You might want to read the church's doctrine and determine if it meets your beliefs. If it states they don't believe or preach that there's a Holy Spirit, but you firmly believe there is, then that church may not be right for you. Scripture can be interpreted very differently which causes some churches to split and become two separate denominations, but all churches should adhere to core Christianity beliefs. A church should align with your biblical understanding and convictions. If their doctrine is within your beliefs, you might attend there for a few months to see how you feel, and how you fit in.

One main purpose of a church is to edify you; to guide you in a manner that improves you morally. Determine if your church is doing that. A second element would be to determine if the church's purpose is to worship God. Churches have varying worship styles and varying music programs, to name only a few of the many differences. Does the church music worship God or simply entertain the congregation? Is there too much socializing going on and not enough devotion? More importantly may be a third factor; whether the preacher's message is from the Bible and straight from the word of God as written. You should be fed from the sermon you hear, and be uplifted by it. Yes, finding the right church is really that important.

Christians realize that the Bible is the supreme holy book, the word of God written by chosen believers with guidance and direction from the Holy Spirit. We accept the belief that justification and salvation comes by faith and not solely by following the Commandments and performing good works and deeds. We acknowledge that Jesus is God in human form who came to us as the Son of God, that He died on the cross for our sins, and that He was buried but then resurrected and ascended into heaven. Anyone who accepts Him and confesses their sins can be saved and have eternal life. We're forgiven for our sins due to God's grace, not for anything we've done. There's God the Father, God the Son, and God the Holy Spirit, as explained in **Appendix F**. Jesus is alive today for you to accept into your heart and soul. Church members are the children of God, and Jesus is the head of the church.

II Timothy

Three or four years after Paul first wrote to his protégé Tomothy, he writes him this second letter. It was written from within a murky prison cell, telling Timothy to continue preaching the word of God in Ephesus even if Paul wouldn't be around to support him. They'd been a team for ten years by now, but Paul felt this imprisonment might be his last. He mentioned in his letter many of those who'd supported him through the years but also some who had stood in his way. He wanted Timothy to know who he could rely on if he wasn't there. Some of Paul's letters will appear later in the New Testament, but this was probably the last letter he wrote before his death.

Paul had been imprisoned then released in Rome five years earlier, but this time the emperor Nero was in charge and trying to rebuild his charred city among accusations that he'd killed most of his family. His bitterness and paranoia in part made him turn against the Christians there, including Paul, seeking others as scapegoats for his failures. Before Nero ended his own life at the age of 30, Roman officials began killing the Christians. Sadly, Paul was beheaded within a year of writing this letter to Timothy.

- From Paul to Timothy, my dear son. I know the faith you have, just as your mother and grandmother had. God has given us His Spirit, which has filled us with power, love, and self-control.
- Don't be ashamed to witness for the Lord. He has saved us and called us for this purpose. Through Jesus, He has ended the power of death. His Spirit is within us, so do the good things He's entrusted to you.
- Most of my friends have deserted me. Take the teachings you've heard me proclaim and share them with dependable people. Be a soldier of Jesus, a descendant of David. Just as we'll die for Him, we'll also live with Him.
- The Lord knows those who are His people. They must turn away from all wrongdoing and strive for righteousness, faith, love and peace.
- Keep away from foolish arguments. Servants of the Lord should not quarrel. Be kind and gentle as you correct your opponents. In the last days people will be selfish and greedy. Keep away from such people.
- There are people opposed to the truth, even opposed to Moses. They are failures in the faith. Everyone will see how stupid those people are.
- You know all that's happened to me. Every godly person will be persecuted. The evil will go on deceiving others, and worsening.
- As you know, all scripture is inspired by God and is useful for teaching the truth and giving instructions for living right. Serve God, and do right.
- Teach that God and Jesus will judge the living and the dead. Jesus will rule the world. Sadly, most people only listen to what they want to hear.
- The hour has come for me to be sacrificed. No one stood with me, but I want God to forgive them. I'm going to God's heavenly kingdom. Amen.

Additional comments on the book of II Timothy:

Paul knew how easy it was for anyone to veer off course when trying to live the good life of a Christian, and it's even harder for us today in a world full of distractions and temptations. Being with other believers helps one sidestep negative patterns throughout life, while encouraging one another to avoid anything unbiblical or anything giving the appearance of being unbiblical. Understanding what the character of a Christian must be and look like is the first step in knowing right from wrong when we face those critical decisions.

Reading II Timothy and the words of Paul lets us measure how we would act if we knew our days on earth might soon come to an end. He turned his attention away from himself and onto Timothy, instructing him to keep fighting for the gospel and the righteousness of those in the Ephesus church. As we age and the hour hand of time seems to spin faster and faster, we hope we can keep our focus on the new life that awaits us in heaven just as Paul did. No one wants to leave family and friends behind, but the bible tells us there'll be family and friends in heaven too that we haven't seen in a while. A song says they'll be waiting near the far side banks of Jordan, just sitting drawing pictures in the sand. And when they see us coming they will rise up with a shout, and coming running through the shallow waters reaching for our hand.

Paul said it perfectly in this letter to Timothy. Beginning in 4:7 he wrote: "I have fought the good fight, I have finished the course, I have kept the faith; in the future there is laid up for me the crown of righteousness, which the Lord, the righteous Judge, will award to me on that day; and not only to me, but also to all who has loved His appearing." That crown of righteousness fits all sizes, and we pray there's one for us too.

To earn a crown doesn't require us to sing in the choir or never miss bible school. We don't have to preach on a street corner or ever be a church leader. The only requirement is to have faith, period. Faith to truly believe that Jesus is the Son of God, that He died for our sins, that he was buried but rose again, and that now He sits in heaven at the right hand of God awaiting His return to set up His Kingdom. If we believe that and admit that we're a sinner, and pray to God for His forgiving and saving grace, and turn our lives over to Him with a true repentant heart, then He will save us and give us eternal life. Then the Holy Spirit will guide you to a place of worship, even if it's in your recliner, and help you live the life God wants for all His children. You must walk with Him the rest of your life, asking for His forgiveness for any sinful things you'd done during times of weakness. As Paul said, fight the good fight until the end. If we do, one day we'll be looking in amazement at the omnipotent face of Jesus.

Titus

Much like Timothy, Titus was a friend and supporter of Paul who traveled with him on his third missionary journey. A Greek believer, Titus was left on the island of Crete to organize and oversee the new churches there while Paul traveled on to set up churches in other areas. Paul wanted Titus to establish the duties of church elders and explain what the roles of the members should be, even the slaves. From Nicopolis, in modern day Greece, Paul wrote this letter to Titus around 65 AD.

The resistance from Jews and native inhabitants in Crete would make Titus' mission more difficult. Paul warned him that many there still believed in the rituals of the old Laws, including their demands that Titus be circumcised. Paul wanted Titus to resist their demands in order to show that his belief and faith in Jesus alone released him from any and all requirements put in place during the days of Moses and the Old Testament prophets.

- From Paul to Titus, my true son in faith. You are there to appoint church leaders, making sure they are reputable and without fault. They must be upright and self-controlled, not arrogant and quick-tempered.
- Some there will try to deceive the new believers. Rebuke them and tell them to let go of old Jewish rituals and commandments.
- You must be a fine example of good behavior. Be serious when you preach. The grace we've received from God makes us give up worldly needs and passions. Let no one there try to look down on you.
- There are rulers and authorities there that you must obey. Have a gentle attitude toward everyone. We have God's Holy Spirit abundantly within us, so offer eternal life to all who believe through faith in Jesus Christ.
- Spend your time helping with real needs. God's grace be with you.

Additional comments on the book of Titus:

The instructions that Paul gave to both Titus and Timothy at their respective locations made them and himself available to spread the Good News in three different areas at once. Paul taught the path to salvation needed to be shared with anyone and everyone seeking peace, love and eternal life. The set of beliefs taught and given to us through Jesus wasn't meant to be reserved and stored away, but used to bring others to Christ.

The free gift of salvation was beginning to be understood by the Gentiles and old-school Jews around this time, although many still held onto the Laws and Commandments given to Moses. Paul knew that being saved was to have faith and belief in Jesus, nothing more. So he told Titus in 3:9 to avoid foolish arguments about the Law, because they are useless.

Philemon

This letter from Paul, written around 61 AD, was to his friend Philemon who had served with him in the past. While in Asia Minor, Paul was visited by a man named Onesimus who had been a slave to Philemon before running away. Paul was able to save Onesimus through his preaching. In this letter he told Philemon that he was sending his slave back to him. He asked Philemon to pardon and show leniency on his slave, to receive him with love as a Christian should do, and to move forward together in harmony. Paul was in a Rome prison when he wrote this letter.

- From Paul and Timothy to our friend Philemon. God gives you peace.
- You have brought me great joy and encouragement. Therefore, I ask you to do what needs to be done. I have become a spiritual father to Onesimus, and I'm sending him back to you. He'll be useful to us.
- I'd like to keep him here with me but I'm in prison. He is no longer just a slave, but a dear brother in Christ. He means a lot to me, and to you he'll be your slave and also a believer in the Lord.
- Welcome him back as your partner, just as you view me as your partner. If he owes you anything just charge it to my account. I will pay you back. Remember all I've done for you, so do things for him.
- Others with me here in prison send you their love. May the grace of the Lord Jesus Christ be with you all.

Additional comments on the book of Philemon:

Although this is the shortest of all letters written by Paul, there are many life lessons and lots of education embedded in his words. He felt confident that his friend Philemon would receive his slave back without incident, since he was a brother in Christ and knew the significance of helping and being there for other Christians. But the big word in this epistle is the word forgiveness. A word easy to say, but hard to do.

God holds each of us accountable for the way we treat others. A slave back in the days of Jesus was not someone you'd normally think of as your equal. The relationship was one from a master to a subordinate, between someone with a lot to someone with very little. Paul wanted Philemon to know that his slave was an equal, a child of God like all other believers, one who deserved the Christian love and forgiveness afforded everyone. But even today, we feel how difficult it is to forgive someone. In God's eyes, getting our feelings hurt isn't a reason to be hostile and contrary to the ways of a Christian. From the cross, remember that Jesus asked His Father to forgive those torturing Him. He doesn't want us to have grudges toward others.

Hebrews

Reading through this book leads us to conclude it was written by a Christian Hebrew to other Hebrew believers, asking them to resist falling back into the practice of Judaism although they're being persecuted for their new-found Christian beliefs. Some of the structure and use of terms in this book are in the style of Paul's writings, but it could have been written by other Jews or even a collection of Jewish believers. There's no mention of the Roman conquest of Jerusalem or their destruction of the second Temple in 70 AD, so this book can be dated in or around 65 AD.

We're reminded once again in Hebrews that the ways and perceived benefits of the old Jewish Laws and Commandments had been replaced by the life and ministry of Jesus Christ, His death and His blood. New believers are told not to abandon their Christian faith during tough times but to rely of Jesus, who knows all about temptation and suffering for the way He lived. And He's still alive today, filtering our lives and actions so that we are presentable to God the Father. The sacrificial blood of Jesus did away with the sacrificial blood of animals for cleansing, giving everyone who believes through faith the cleansing and opportunity for communion and unification with God.

- God used to speak to us through prophets, but now He speaks to us through His Son. Through Jesus, God created the universe. Jesus achieved forgiveness for man's sins. He's much greater than angels.
- Jesus was crowned with glory and honor because of the death He suffered. He's the One who leads us to salvation. He shared man's human nature and knows the temptations and traps we must avoid.
- Jesus is faithful and the Son in charge of God's house. Just as Moses was chosen, Christ was chosen and does God's work.
- We're told to help one another. We have heard the Good News and accepted it in faith. We're all partners in Christ and with Christ.
- The word of God is sharper than a double-edged sword. It sees where our soul and spirit meet. Everything we do is exposed to God, nothing is hidden. To Him we must all give an account of ourselves.
- The Son of God was tempted in every way but did not sin. God made Him a high priest forever, in the order of Melchizedek.
- New believers are not ready for solid food. They must drink milk just as a child does until they grow and mature in God's word and be able to recognize good from evil. They must turn away from useless works.
- Those in God's light have tasted the gifts from heaven and received the Holy Spirit. If they abandon God's faith they can't return to repent a second time because they'd be placing Jesus on the cross once again to be crucified. They'd be exposing Jesus to public shame.
- God will never change His purpose and promises. His word is an anchor in our lives. The Laws given to Moses cannot make anything perfect, so they've been set

aside. A better hope has been provided. Jesus is the guarantee of a better covenant with God.

- Jesus lives on forever and His work doesn't pass off to someone else. He saves those who come to God through Him, and pleads for them.
- We have a High Priest sitting at the right hand of God. A priest gives sacrifices and offerings to God. Jesus gave His blood.
- If there was nothing wrong with the first covenant between God and His people, then there would have been no need for a second one. God has made the first covenant old, and old things soon disappear.
- Early worship had a tent or Holy Place with specific rules and a place for every item inside. The priest had a daily ritual, then once a year he would go behind a second curtain to offer a blood sacrifice.
- When Jesus entered the Holy Place He didn't take animal blood for a sacrifice, He took His own blood and obtained eternal salvation. Because of that, Jesus is the One who arranged a new covenant.
- In the past sins were forgiven only if blood was shed. Everyone dies once, and is then judged by God. When Jesus comes again it isn't to deal with sin. He'll be here to save and gather those who're waiting for him.
- The Jewish Law wasn't a perfect model of real things, buy only an outline of things to come. God did away with the old sacrifice requirements, then sacrificed Jesus only one time to replace it.
- The Holy Spirit tells us that God will put His Laws in our hearts and write them on our minds. He won't remember the sins of believers any longer. Once Jesus died and arose, a sacrifice was no longer needed.
- A fierce fire awaits those opposed to God. The Lord will judge His people. It could be terrifying to fall into His hands for judgement if you haven't followed Him.
- It was by faith that those in ancient times won God's approval. Having faith is to be sure of the things hoped for and of things unseen.
- Anyone coming to God must have faith that God exists. He'll reward those who seek Him. It was faith that kept Enoch from dying, and it was faith that made Noah hear things from God that were to come in the future, things he couldn't see with his own eyes.
- It was faith that made Abraham enter into foreign lands promised to him, and it was faith that gave him and Sarah a child in their old age.
- It was faith that made Moses' parents hide him for 3 months after his birth, and for Moses to leave Egypt without fear from the king.
- It was faith that led the Israelites across dry land at the Red Sea, and faith that made the walls of Jerico fall after seven days of marching.
- We should rid ourselves of sins that hold onto us so tightly. We must keep our eyes fixed on Jesus. He went through so much for us because He loves us. When our parents punish us so we can learn, we respect them. How much more should we submit to our spiritual Father.

- Keep walking a straight path. Live a peaceful holy life, because no one will see the Lord unless they follow Him. Love one another as Christian brothers. Remember those who suffer, as though you were suffering.
- Be satisfied with what you have, and don't chase after money. With the Lord as our Helper, how could anything really hurt us?
- Christ is the same yesterday, today, and forever. Our cities here are temporary, so look for the city which is to come. To please God we must do good and help one another. God is pleased when we do.
- God raised our Lord Jesus from death. He is the Great Shepard of the sheep by which the eternal covenant is sealed. I beg you to listen patiently to all these messages. May God's grace be with us all.

Additional comments on the book of Hebrews:

The past few books preceding this letter were letters that Paul wrote to believing Gentiles scattered throughout the region, but this letter was written to the Hebrews. It contains several references to the saving blood of Jesus and how His death saved the world. It also tells us how Jesus filled the gap between His Father in heaven and all who'll ever live on earth, ushering in a new covenant to replace the old. But the main theme of Hebrews is faith. So much that many refer to Hebrews Chapter 11 as the "faith chapter" in the Bible.

Faith means we're certain about the things we cannot see or touch, and that we're sure that all the things the Bible says did happen or will occur. It was faith that drove Noah to work on the ark year after year and then get on board when no one else but his family believed the rains were coming. It was faith that made Abraham leave his home and move from place to place waiting for the things God had promised him. It was faith that made the Israelites cross the Red Sea on dry land and not worry that the divided waters would crash down upon them.

But with faith we're told to be doers as well, to help others so that our works demonstrate God's love toward them so they'll want to learn more about Him. The bible tells us in James 1:22, "Be doers of the word and not hearers only, deceiving ourselves." We're to help others, knowing in faith that we'll be rewarded on judgement day for our good deeds. And as stated in Hebrews 9:27, everyone will be judged. A Christian must be kind and humble while always loving and helping others. Having faith means having the good works and deeds to prove it.

James

This letter was written to the 12 Jewish tribes who had scattered from their homeland after learning that Saul of Tarsus was on a mission to hunt down Christian believers and persecute them. Yes, it's the same Saul who would later be called the Apostle Paul after a voice from heaven struck him down and asked why he was tyrannizing and victimizing God's people. This letter and those through the letter from Jude were written specifically to Jewish people, who were still under Jewish Law and knew nothing of Paul's message to the Gentiles. However, some did believe that Jesus was the Son of God.

James was a half-brother of Jesus and not the James who was one of the 12 disciples. It was probably only after Jesus' resurrection that he became a believer, and grew to be a leader in the Jerusalem church. He wrote this letter in or around 46 AD to convince those who had converted from Judaism to keep their faith. He tells them to remain faithful during trials and temptations, to let their actions speak of their faith, and to speak without boasting or judging. After serving as a figurehead in the church for years, it's believed he died in 60 AD after being thrown from the Temple and severely stoned and clubbed.

- From James, a servant of God, to God's people scattered throughout the entire world. I want to tell you about wisdom and faith.
- When trials come your way, you have the faith to face them and endure. When you pray, pray with no doubts at all. You must believe in your prayers without doubt or you'll receive nothing from the Lord.
- Happy is the person who remains faithful under pressure. God will reward those who love him. Temptations and evil desires will lead to sin.
- Be quick to listen and slow to speak. Get rid of filthy habits and bad conduct. For blessings, listen to God's word then put it into action.
- Control your tongue or your religion is worthless. God considers pure religion to be taking care of orphans and widows, with no corruption.
- Don't treat people differently because of their outward appearance. If you do, your judgement of them is based on evil motives. Obey the Law of the Kingdom and love your neighbor. If you break one Law you've broken them all.
- God will show no mercy to the person who has not been merciful. Your actions should prove you have faith in God for others to see.
- Many Old Testament characters and prophets were put right with God because of their faith. Faith without actions is dead.
- Teachers will be judged more strictly than others. The smallest error can lead to terrible things. A tiny flame can ruin a whole forest. Watch what you say. If man can tame wild animals he should be able to tame his tongue. Use it to thank the Lord. Don't use it to speak goodness then evilness.
- Where there is jealousy and selfishness there is evil. Don't fight and quarrel. If you want something, ask God for it instead of quarreling about it. A friend to the world

makes himself an enemy to God. Be humble. Don't swear. Say yes when you mean yes and say no when you mean no.

- Do not criticize or judge a Christian brother. God is the only lawgiver and judge. We should always do the good we all know we should do. We must be patient and keep our hopes high until the Lord returns. When in trouble we should pray. The prayer of a good person has a profound effect.

Additional comments on the book of James:

This book is not only full of great advice for Christians, but it's full of basic behaviors and wisdom for anyone and everyone striving to be a better person. James tells us not to gossip, watch what we say about others, avoid temptations, don't judge other people, help those less fortunate, don't boast, have patience, and to follow God's counseling. Those who follow those guidelines from James while maintaining or developing a close and personal relationship with God through belief in Jesus Christ will be rewarded. Christian people are good people; people you can go to and count on when any need arises.

James tells us that if we're Christians and we truly believe and follow God's word, no one around us should doubt our faith. He says it'd be very obvious to others because only a believer could have such a caring and loving spirit for their fellow man. We're to act correspondingly to our faith. When we do our deeds and works, our actions will show our faith.

Remember that song we were taught as children? "If you're happy and you know it clap your hands, and if you're happy and you know it stomp your feet." That song teaches children to express how they feel, and if they're exhibiting feelings of contentment and joy it should be easy for others to distinguish their mood and see the happiness in their lives. That's how James describes the ways and characteristics of a Christian, because others should be able to see the joy and contentment in our lives. All of us would rather be around people who are humble and kind rather than those who are deceitful, boastful and selfish. His message to us is that a believer should act like a believer, in hopes that those who see the love and calmness within us will want it in their lives too.

James 1:19 tells us to be swift to hear, slow to speak, and slow to wrath. James 1:26 says if a man seems religious but can't bridle his tongue, his religion is in vain. James 3:10-11 says that out of the same mouth can come both a blessings and cursing. That should never happen, in the same way that a single water fountain cannot give both sweet water and bitter water. James 4:10 promises that if you humble yourself in sight of the Lord, He will lift you up. (Prayer) With a humble and loving spirit, help us to follow the Christian behaviors given in the book of James. Amen.

I Peter

This letter, much like the earlier letter from James, was written to Christians scattered throughout Asia Minor. By this time there were probably both Jew and Gentile believers, and Peter wanted them to know that following the ways of Jesus and proclaiming to be a Christian could bring them pain and suffering. He would know, because he'd been beaten and jailed for preaching God's Word. He warned of persecutions, referring to believers as aliens living and existing among those who refused to turn away from Judaism or believe anything that wasn't based on the traditions given in the Old Testament.

Peter was probably in Rome when he wrote this letter in or around 63 AD. More than any other book in the bible it seriously warns Christians of the suffering they'll have to endure in order to keep their faith. He knew firsthand because he'd walked with Jesus for three years and seen how He'd been persecuted by those who believed differently than they did. Sadly, when we read the world news of today and witness the things happening in our own communities, the bullying, oppression and killing of those who contradict the beliefs of others, it still exists and has even worsened since the time of Christ.

- Let us give thanks to God who gave us new life when He raised Jesus from death. We look forward to the blessings He has for us.
- You may have to suffer to prove your faith is real. Faith has to be tested to show that it will endure. When Jesus is revealed, you'll be rewarded.
- We must love God and believe in Him although we've never seen Him. We've been called to live a holy life, so be obedient to God. Spend your time on earth praising Him, and removing all evil from your life.
- Jesus was scorned by men but accepted by God. The Jews are the chosen race, a holy nation, but they rejected God's plan for them.
- Don't give in to your bodily passions which are at odds against you soul. Silence the talk of foolish people by your examples of doing good deeds. Respect everyone and love your fellow believers as we all honor God.
- Be very conscious of God's will. When Christ was insulted He did not answer back with an insult. Jesus carried our sins in His body when He went to the cross. Because of His wounds and death we are healed.
- Don't use outward aids to beautify ourselves. Our beauty should be our true inward self and our gentle quiet spirit because those things have greater value in God's eyes. Don't let disrespect interfere with your prayer requests or get in the way of God's gift of life for you.
- Do not pay back evil with evil. Have reverence for Christ in your heart.
- It is God's will that it's better for us to suffer for doing good than for doing evil. When Jesus died and was made alive spiritually, He went and preached to the imprisoned spirits who hadn't obeyed Him back in Noah's time. He wants everyone

to accept Him and have eternal life, even by giving us additional opportunities to become His children.

- We've sinned enough. Live the rest of our lives controlled by God's will. The end of all things is near. Share your love because love covers over many sins. Use your special gifts that God gave you to help others.

- We share Christ's sufferings when we're insulted and mistreated for being a believer in Him. Don't be ashamed, just thank God that you have Christ in your heart. Serve Him; be an example to His flock.

- Be alert and be humble. The devil roams around like a lion looking for someone to devour. Be firm in your faith, for throughout the world others are suffering for their faith. God will give us firmness and a strong solid foundation. To Him be all the power forever.

Additional comments on the book of I Peter:

In America, the most negativity we usually receive for being a Christian is an occasional snide remark. Sadly, in other parts of the world Christians are still suffering and being killed for their beliefs. In this book, Peter tells both Jew and Gentile to expect mistreatment and imprisonment from those priding themselves on persecuting anyone who doesn't worship what they worship or believe. He tells them to be proud and thankful that they're not suffering for being evil, but for honoring God.

From all the significant and timeless messages given to us in I Peter, let's look closer at two of them. In 3:18-20, the Bible tells us after Jesus died on the cross, by the Holy Spirit He went and preached to the spirits in prison (disobedient sinners). It goes on to say that He's referring to those sinners back in the days of Noah who probably stood there watching him build the Ark for 120 years but were not brought aboard due to their corruption. It's very clear that God wants no person left behind on judgement day. He will try and try again to preach to sinners through Himself, the Holy Spirit, or by any act or means that causes man to accept Jesus as their Lord and Savior.

The second message to highlight is given in 4:10, telling us that every person has received a gift from God to be used to minister to others. Your special gift may be to serve, or to preach Sunday school, or it may be something as simple as gathering people together, or your ability to cook well. You may be a musician wondering why you were able to master your instrument so quickly. Was it because it's your special gift from God? Your gift could be anything, and you need to know what it is. Are you where God wants you to be today? Are you sharing your special gift? With prayer, we should all be able to understand how God wants to use us. Whatever gift you have, remember it was specifically given to you to advance the Kingdom of God.

II Peter

This second letter from Peter was written to the same groups of new believers who'd received his first letter. He was still in Rome and probably still imprisoned during the reign of Nero, so scholars have dated this letter in or around 66 AD. Peter had learned of the false teachers within the Asia Minor churches and the dissention it was causing among the rank and file. He pleads for them not to believe any false interpretations of God's word by knowing unmistakably who God is. No matter how many times Christians had been warned of deceitful teachers, it was still easy for man to give into temptation and what might be considered an easier path through life. Peter knew, just like we know, that being a Christian in a sinful society isn't easy.

- From Simon Peter, who through the love of God and our savior Jesus Christ has been given a faith as precious as ours.
- God's divine power has given us all we need to live a religious life. Do all you can to add goodness, knowledge and endurance to your faith. Be active and effective in your knowledge of Lord Jesus.
- Do not believe false stories and teachings about Jesus. We were there when He preached, and when the voice from heaven told us He was God's Son and how God was pleased with Him.
- Be confident in the messages given to us by the prophets. All they told us came from God through the power and control of the Holy Spirit.
- Now false prophets are appearing among you. When they deny the Master they are bringing destruction upon themselves. They will try to profit from their distorted and deceitful stories. Don't follow them.
- God didn't spare the fallen angels, and he didn't spare the ancient world. He flooded earth to bring an end to godless people who disliked His authority. He saved Noah and his family. He will rescue Godly people.
- False teachers act by instinct like wild animals who are born to be captured and killed. They are under God's curse so they'll be destroyed.
- It's better to have never known righteousness than to have it then throw it away. Even a pig who has been washed and cleaned will go straight back to roll in the mud. Once you have God's blessings, fight to keep them.
- Remember all the words spoken long ago by the holy prophets. In the last days, people will appear who are controlled by their own lusts. They will ask where your God is, and why He promised to come again but has never appeared. They forget it was He who created heaven and earth.
- The heaven and earth of today is being preserved by God to be destroyed by fire. That's when godless people will be judged and also destroyed.
- Don't forget this. There's no difference in God's sight between one day and a thousand years. To Him the two are the same.
- The Day of the Lord has not happened because He is patient with us. He doesn't want anyone to be destroyed, so He gives us every chance to turn away from sin.

But He will one day come like a thief. The heavens will disappear and the earth will vanish with everything in it.

- We are waiting for what God has promised. We await a new heaven and earth where the righteous will be at home. Wait for the Day of God and do all you can to make it come soon.
- As you wait, be pure and faultless in God's eyes. Love Him as much as He loves you. His patience gives everyone a chance to be saved.
- Paul wrote of these things using the wisdom God gave him. Some things he wrote about were difficult to understand, so the false teachers twist his words just like they do with words in the old scriptures.
- So please be on guard. Don't be led astray by people who don't know God or His message to us. Until He comes again please continue to grow in the love and grace of our Lord and Savior Jesus Christ. Amen.

Additional comments on the book of II Peter:

Peter was one of the best witnesses to Jesus' earthly ministry because he was there, he spoke with Him, and they traveled and ate together. So when it came to the false witnesses and the things they'd erroneously preached to anyone who'd listen, Peter was the man who could set the record straight. It wasn't always easy because the parables and Old Testament ways were difficult for early believers to dissect and understand, just like they are for many of us today. We must rely on the power of the Holy Spirit within us to guide us and keep us on the path of righteousness and rectitude.

What is it that makes us fight internally and doubt the truth? Back in the days of the Native Americans, it wasn't the early settlers and calvaries that caused most of their deaths, it was the internal battles and killings among the different tribes. Some men fight over resources or to settle long-standing disputes, but many fights are caused by one group wanting other groups to believe the same things they believe. The truth is that the largest threat to believers and children of God often comes from other believers and children of God, or those who think they are. That was Peter's concern, and he spent most of this letter addressing that issue.

Through the years many Christians have predicted when Jesus would return to earth to set up His Kingdom and put an end to all these wars and the destruction of His creation, but no one knows when He'll come. Peter reminds us that God is patient, and doesn't want anyone to be punished for the way they've lived. Sinful people are living extended days in order to turn to God for salvation. God will wait and wait for just one more lost soul to repent and love Him. After all, He has all the time in the world.

I John

The writer of this letter does not identify himself, but his references to being present during the life of Jesus and his other testimonies made the early scholars link it to John, the same apostle who wrote the gospel of John given to us as the fourth book in the New Testament. Jesus stated His love for John many times throughout His life, and in John 19:26-27 He asked the disciple He loved (John) to behold His mother after His death on the cross. So John moved Mary into his home in or around Jerusalem to care for her. It's believed he lived there until after Jerusalem fell in 70 AD, then moved to Ephesus. This letter is dated approximately 90 AD, around the same period when John wrote all the books attributed to him.

This letter was probably sent to the seven churches that John mentions in the book of Revelation. He was concerned about the many false prophets and how their lies and sinful messages might be discouraging the believers there. He feared the passion and devotion that Christians had for God had weakened, so he told them to stay strong and committed to their faith because it would bring them eternal life. He knew that a belief based on faith often brought doubt and dissension among the weak, but that the Holy Spirit within them would provide all the love and strength they'd need to endure.

- I write to you about the Word of life, which has always been there. Join with us and the love we have for God the Father and His son Jesus.
- God is light with no darkness within Him, and those who follow Him will see the light. If you're living in darkness you're not a follower of Jesus. We all have sinned but the blood of Jesus purifies us from those sins.
- Jesus pleads with His Father on our behalf when we stumble and fall short. Christ is the means by which all sins are forgiven. To know Christ is to obey His commands. Strive to live just as Jesus did.
- Whoever loves his brother lives in the light, so nothing in him would cause someone to sin. Do not love the world or anything that belongs in it. Loving the world means you don't love the Father. Everything in the world you're proud of came from the world; it didn't come from God.
- The end of times are getting closer because many enemies of Christ have already appeared. It will all pass away, but he who does the will of God will live forever. You know the truth because you've been given the Holy Spirit.
- Anyone who says that Jesus is not the Messiah is an enemy of God. Whoever accepts or rejects God or Jesus accepts or rejects them both.
- I am writing because there are those who'll deceive you. Let the Holy Spirit within you teach you what to believe and what is true. Obey the Spirit.
- Remain in union with God and you won't need to hide when He comes.
- We are called God's children, so in fact we are. When God appears we will be like Him. We'll see Him as He really is. If you're like him you will not sin. If one continues

to sin he belongs to the devil. The Son of God came for that very reason, to destroy the damage and sin the devil had caused.

- Christ gave His life for us, so we should give our lives for our brothers. Don't believe all who claim to have the Spirit. There are many false prophets, but the Spirit within you is more powerful than those belonging to the world. God is love, so if you don't know God you don't know love.
- No one has seen God but He lives in every believer. If you love the Father then you love the Son. Our faith will make us victorious over the world.
- Jesus came from the water of His baptism and the blood of His death. His Spirit, water and blood give the same testimony. Jesus is the source of the eternal life that God gave us. If we have the Son then we have eternal life.
- Be sure that God hears you when you ask for anything that's according to His will. If your brothers commit a sin that doesn't cause a death, pray to God and He'll give them life. Children, keep away from false gods and false prophets. Know your true God.

Additional comments on the book of I John:

John gave both encouragements and warnings in this letter. False teachers were saying that Jesus wasn't the true Messiah, so John spent a good part of this letter telling believers that God will integrate them into the very image of Jesus if they'd just trust and believe in Him. His message told the early church followers that if they stayed true to God and looked upon Him as their Father, then they'd have the affection in their hearts to love one another and to keep His commandments. To love and believe in God meant to love and believe in Jesus. He made that point very clear.

Since God is love, God expects us to love one another regardless of our differences. All of us carry burdens, and at times they become so heavy that we can't manage the loads by ourselves. In Galatians, we learn that helping one another actually fulfills a law given to us by Christ. When we pray we need to remember those who need intervention and guidance from God, and that includes ourselves.

In I Corinthians 13, we learn that charity and love is patience and kindness. Love does not envy or boast, and it's not arrogant and rude nor irritable and resentful. We may all define love differently. The parents of a newborn know and understand love, and the care an adult gives their aging parent knows love, but no matter how it's expressed it all comes from one source. From I John 4:7, "Beloved, let us love one another: for love is of God; and everyone that loveth is born of God and knows God." So, not loving is not knowing God since He is love. A big takeaway from reading I John is realizing the awesome power of God's love.

II John

John's second letter was probably sent to the same churches that received his first letter. He addressed it to the "elect lady and her children", presumed to be his metaphor for the churches and believers who worshiped there. There was so much persecution going on, he may have felt the need to address the early churches and followers more discretely. Where his first letter focused on having love for one another, this one pinpoints the need for believers to maintain their fellowship against those spreading false precepts and doctrines which could cause believers to question their faith. John wants Christians to show their love, but only on a level equivalent to the truth they're hearing. This letter was composed just after his earlier correspondence, around 90 to 95 AD.

- To the dear lady and her children. May our Father and His Son give us grace and mercy, our source of love and the truth that remains forever.
- Love and truth is not a new commandment, it has been with us from the beginning. We must all live in obedience to God's commands.
- Many deceivers have told us that Christ did not come to us as a human being. Those people are enemies of ours and an enemy of Christ. Be careful not to give up hope on all we've accomplished.
- Do not speak or show any kindness to those who lie and twist the truth. Don't welcome them into your home. We have the Father and Son in us.
- I have so many things to tell you but I'd rather speak with you in person. It would make me happy if I'm able to meet with you soon. The church I belong to here sends you their greetings and love.

Additional comments on the book of II John:

John realized how the trusting nature of Christians often makes them accept and trust anyone entering their lives, even strangers they really know nothing about. Believers are loving people who want to believe what others say, often without any basis or foundation of their knowledge. He pointed out that we must be on guard, knowing when to filter and separate what we're told into which statements are true and which ones to reject. Being fair-minded is a virtue, but being susceptible and too impressionable can damage any church being fed false information. Believers want the truth.

One of the weapons Satan uses to sidetrack us is deceit, a weapon he's become very proficient at. That makes it super important for us to know what the bible says, so we can prove or disprove suspicious teachings. Once again, we are back on the subject of truth. Our belief in the truth of the bible and all it says is the common bond between Christians around the world. Let's study our Bibles so we can recognize Satan's deceit when we hear it.

III John

John's third epistle continued the warnings he'd sent out to Christians in his first two letters. He'd asked them to love one another, to know the truth of God when they hear it, and now he was addressing false teachers just as so many others had done before him. It's the shortest book in the bible, and oddly never mentions the words Jesus or Christ. It was written around 95 to 99 AD, probably from the island of Patmos where he was exiled.

He wrote this to his friend Gaius, and it indirectly tells Gaius that there's a man among them named Diotrephes who is causing division in their church and that maybe they should turn to Demetrius to guide them. John had earlier addressed the problem with Diotrephes, who had risen into a leadership position, but Diotrephes refused to change his ungodly ways. John was an old man by this time, but continued to send out both encouragement and warnings to believers.

- To Gaius, my dear friend. I pray that everything is going well. I was so happy to learn how faithful you've been to the truth. Christians must help other people so we can all share the truth in our works.
- I wrote a letter to Diotrephes but he paid no attention to it. He talks about us and tells lies. He does not welcome our Christian brothers when they arrive there. Don't imitate the dreadful things he does.
- Those who do good belong to God. Those who do bad things don't know God. You have Demetrius there, and everyone speaks well of him. I have so much to tell you when we speak face to face. We send our greetings.

Additional comments on the book of III John:

Having faith is not easy. It's believing with all your heart that something or someone is real and having total confidence in it without proof. Early Christians often doubted their faith in God, especially when they were being punished for their beliefs and were being told to take a different and much easier path. True Christians understand that God has given them a path to follow, and although other paths may be simpler they could never be as rewarding. No path made by man could ever upgrade God's path for us.

False teachers like Diotrephes tell us to follow their paths to righteousness and we'll be rewarded with riches and fame, enough to convince some people to place other things ahead of their faith and belief in God. But true Christians know that what the world views as valuable is worthless to God. Be on guard against temptations, and know the truth of our Creator. III John 1:4 tells us we should "have no greater joy than to hear our children are walking in the truth."

Jude

There are several men in the Bible named Jude and Judas, but it's believed this Jude was the half-brother of Jesus and brother to James as mentioned in Matthew 13:55 and again in Luke 6:16. He identified himself as a servant of Jesus, possibly a late follower who wrote this epistle sometime between 65 to 70 AD. It was probably sent to the early Jewish churches and believers.

- To those called by God who live under His protection. I encourage you to fight for the faith God has given you. Do not distort His message as some have just to feed their immoral ways.
- Remember Sodom and Gomorrah, and those who suffered punishment as a warning to all. They despised God's authority and paid the price.
- The false teachers have followed the ways of Cain. They rebelled, and only took care of themselves. Their trees will never bear fruit. For their shameful deeds, God reserved a place for them in the darkest place.
- Enoch prophesied long ago that the Lord and His angels will come and bring judgement on the godless sinners. They follow their own paths.
- Always remember what the apostles preached, that during the last days others will make fun of you and cause divisions among the followers of Jesus. They do not have the Spirit that you have.
- Keep yourselves in the love of God, and pray using the power of the Holy Spirit within you. Our merciful Lord will give you eternal life.
- Show mercy to those who have doubts and pull as many as you can from the fire. Our Savior and Lord has glory, might and authority, and all the power and dominion both now and forever. Amen, and amen.

Additional comments on the book of Jude:

The words of Jude give an appropriate introduction to the final book in the Bible, the book of Revelation. It's a warning that uses Old Testament references to make us realize that perilous times are ahead for sinners when thousands and thousands of the Lord's saints come to usher in God's Kingdom. Those who have been self-serving, disobedient, unholy, false witnesses, and enemies to the children and elderly cannot hide. All sins will be shown, and we'll each be judged by our life's work whether good or bad. There is no escape.

The devil does not have red skin, horns, and a long tail. He takes many forms to tempt you with things you desire, knowing your weakness for worldly treasures is an easy way to infiltrate your better judgement. The Bible tells us there'll come a time when everyone experiences hardships and suffering before Jesus returns to earth to gather His children. Are you a Christian, waiting to be caught up in the air with Him? His return is getting nearer each day.

Revelation

The visions of future events described in the book of Revelation were revealed by Jesus and His angels to the apostle John around 95 AD after he'd been exiled to Patmos, a small Greek island in the Aegean Sea. John would receive these sacred insights in the form of imaginative representations and prophecies, presented primarily in a symbolic language which made it difficult to understand. God wanted John to record what was revealed and send it to seven specific churches in Asia Minor, or what is present day Turkey. Revelation is a term in the Greek language meaning apocalypse or the uncovering and divulging of divine truths and mysteries unknown to man.

This book provides many details about the persecution of unbelievers and the forces of good versus evil that'll continue on earth until Christ intervenes. Many of these events were mentioned earlier in the books of Daniel, Ezekiel and others. We'll learn about the Rapture or wholesale transfer of believers from earth into heaven, and the seven-year tribulation with its suffering and hardships. The nefarious actions of Satan and the Antichrist, the second coming of Christ, the Millenium, the final judgment of all people, and the new heaven and earth are all described in this book. For a condensed summary of Revelation in an easy-to-understand format, see **Appendix E**.

- God gave Jesus a revelation of coming events for Him to pass along to His servants. Jesus gave John the following messages and truths.
- John was in Patmos, sent there as punishment for proclaiming God's word when he was told not to. In the Spirit on the Lord's Day, John heard a loud voice speaking to him. He was told to write down what he'd see and hear, and send it to seven specific churches in Asia.
- John saw a glorious figure and seven gold lampstands. The figure held seven stars in his hand and had a two-edged sword coming from His mouth. He told John the seven lampstands represented those seven churches and the stars represented the angels of those churches.
- The church in Ephesus knows what they've done. They've suffered for My sake, but they no longer love Me. They've fallen away.
- To the church in Smyrna, false teachers have spoken against you but don't be afraid. You'll suffer but stay faithful to Me and you'll have life.
- To the church in Pergamum, from the One with the two-edged sword. You have followers of Balaam and Balak among you who love false idols. You must turn away from your sins.
- To the church in Thyatira. I know you tolerated Jezebel who claimed to be a messenger of God. Each of you will be repaid for the sins you've committed. For those following Me, you'll have victory and authority.

- To the church in Sardis, wake up and be strong before you completely die. Before you know it, I will come upon you like a thief in the night. But those who'd kept clean will have their names in the Book of Life.
- To the church in Philadelphia, this message is from the One who is holy. You've been faithful to me, so I'll make those following Satan bow at your feet. You'll be safe from troubles, and will belong to the new Jerusalem coming from heaven. Let no one rob you of your victory.
- To the church in Laodicea, from the origin of all that God created. You are lukewarm; neither hot nor cold, so I'll expel you. You're naked and blind but don't know it. I'll knock, and if you follow me I'll enter and eat.
- John saw a door open in heaven, and a voice sounding like a trumpet. Someone sat on a throne, surrounded by a rainbow of colors. Twenty-four elders wearing gold crowns sat on thrones, plus there were other thrones. Seven torches were lit, representing the seven Spirits of God.
- Four living creatures surrounded the throne. One looked like a lion, another like a bull. A third one had a man's face, and another looked like an eagle. Each were covered with eyes, and each had six wings.
- They sang, then the elders worshiped the one sitting on the throne who held a scroll covered with seven seals. An angel asked who was worthy to open the scroll. A Lamb appeared, looking as if it'd been killed, with seven horns and seven eyes which are the seven Spirits of God.
- The Lamb took the scroll. John heard millions of angels praising the Lamb. The Lamb opened the first seal and the tribulation began. A rider with a crown sat on a white horse, as though destined to conquer.
- The second seal was opened and a red horse appeared. The rider was given a sword and the power to bring war upon the earth. A black horse came from the third seal, with the rider holding a pair of scales.
- From the fourth seal came a pale-colored horse with a rider named Death, given authority over one-fourth of the earth to kill by any means.
- The Lamb opened the fifth seal. The souls of those beneath the alter shouted loudly, asking when the Lord would punish those who killed them. They were told to rest a little longer, since others must die first.
- The sixth seal was broken. The sun turned black and there was an earthquake. Stars fell to earth, and all mountains and islands moved. Everyone hid from the Lamb's anger and from the one on the throne.
- Four angels stood at the earth's four corners, holding back the wind. An angel came with the seal of God, telling the others not to harm anything on earth until 144,000 of God's servants, twelve thousand from each tribe of Israel, had His seal on their foreheads.
- An enormous crowd gathered dressed in white robes and holding palm branches. They all fell at the throne and worshipped God. An elder stated that these people were the ones who survived the persecutions.

- God will protect this enormous crowd and the Lamb will be their Shepherd. They'll never be hungry or thirsty, and will always have life-giving water. God will wipe away every tear from their eyes.
- When the Lamb opened the seventh seal there was silence in heaven. Seven angels stood with trumpets. Incense burned, and God's people prayed. Fire was thrown on earth causing thunder and earthquakes.
- The first angel blew his trumpet. Fire and blood poured out burning a third of the earth. The second angel's trumpet threw fire into the sea, turning it to blood. A third of the sea creatures and ships were destroyed.
- The third angel blew his trumpet and a large burning star fell on a third of the rivers, making them bitter. Many died from drinking bitter water. The fourth trumpet's sound caused the sun and all heavenly bodies to lose a third of their brightness.
- An eagle warned of the horrors that would come from the other three trumpets. The fifth trumpet blew and the abyss in the depths of earth was opened. Locusts were given power for five months to torture those people without God's seal on their foreheads, but they couldn't kill them.
- These locusts looked like horses but with faces of men, with a king ruling over them. In Greek, the king's name meant Destroyer.
- The sixth angel blew his trumpet and a voice said to release the four angels who were bound near the Euphrates River. There were two million mounted troops who destroyed a third of all mankind. Those not killed still didn't turn away from sin or repent of their sinful ways.
- An angel wrapped in a cloud came from heaven, with a face like the sun. He put his right foot on the sea and his left foot on land. He roared, and seven roars answered. A voice from heaven told John to keep secret what the roars had told him, and not to write it down.
- The angel standing on land and sea took a vow to God, and said there would be no more delays. When the seventh trumpet blows, God will reveal His secret plan. John was told to take the scroll the angel held.
- The angel told John to eat the scroll, which tasted like honey. He then proclaimed God's message to all, then measured God's temple and altar.
- The witnesses are the two lamps and olive trees. They have authority over water, and can order plagues on the earth. A beast from the abyss will kill them but their bodies will not be buried. After three and a half days they'll come alive and go up to heaven. Then strong storms came.
- The seventh angel blew his trumpet. A voice said the Lord will now rule the world forever, so everyone worshipped God. God's temple in heaven was opened and the holy Covenant Box was visible.
- A woman appeared in the sky about to give birth, with 12 stars on her head. A red dragon then appeared, throwing a third of the stars to the ground. The baby was taken into heaven, and the woman fled to the desert. God would protect her there for three and a half years.

- There was a war in heaven. Michael and his angels fought the dragon and threw him out. A loud voice announced that God's salvation had come. Be happy, but fear the dragon who was now on earth.
- The woman who'd given birth was given wings to fly to safety for three and a half years. A beast that looked like a leopard arose from the sea, and the people worshipped him. He'd have power for three and a half years.
- Everyone on earth would worship this beast except those whose names were in the Lamb's book. A beast arose from earth and did miracles to deceive everyone. It forced all people to be marked with the number 666 (which may have stood for a person's name or an unknown code).
- John saw the Lamb standing on Mount Zion, along with 144,000 people who had God's name on their foreheads. These people were the only ones who'd kept themselves pure, who'd only worshipped the Lamb.
- An angel shouted that it was time for God to judge all mankind. Another angel announced that Babylon had fallen. All who worshipped the beast would be tormented. All believers would rejoice and be happy.
- John saw someone sitting on a cloud. An angel announced it was time to harvest the earth with a sickle, so it was done. John saw those who'd had victory over the beast singing the songs of Moses and the Lamb.
- Angels were told to pour out the seven bowls of God's anger onto the earth. Those marked by the beast suffered, all sea creatures died, the sun burned people, but the people would not turn away from their sins.
- Another angel poured his bowl on the Euphrates River and it dried up. Kings were gathered in a place called Armageddon and an earthquake came. Great cities in all countries were destroyed, including Babylon.
- An angel showed John how the famous prostitute would be punished. In the desert, the woman sat on a red beast. On her forehead was a name that had a secret meaning. They were dead but would reappear.
- The beast's seven heads stood for seven kings and hills. A few still ruled, and would fight the Lamb but the Lamb would win. The woman stood for the great city that rules over all kings of the earth.
- An angel said Babylon had fallen. The sinful kings all wept. All who contributed to her sins watched from far away. Babylon was punished because the blood of God's people was there. The twenty-four elders and four living creatures fell down and worshipped God.
- A large crowd praised God. The time had come for the wedding, when the bride becomes one with the Lamb. Heaven opened and out came a white horse with a rider called Faithful and True. His name was the Word of God. On His robe was written "King of Kings, Lord of Lords."
- The kings of earth and the beast gathered to fight the Rider. The beast and false prophet were thrown into a lake of fire. An angel grabbed the dragon, also called the devil, serpent, and Satan, and bound him for a thousand years. After that, he'd be set free for a short time.

- John saw all God's people who'd died. They came back to life to rule with the Lord for a thousand years. Others who'd died would come alive after the thousand years. These were the first to be raised.

- When Satan is let loose, he'll try to deceive all nations of the world. He'll battle God's people until a fire comes down from heaven and destroys him. He'll be thrown into the lake of fire to remain there forever.

- The Lord sat on the great white throne and the dead stood before Him. Books were opened, and the dead were judged according to what they'd done during their lives. Those from the sea and all others who were dead received their judgement. All those without their names recorded in the Book of Life were thrown into the lake of fire.

- John saw the old heaven and earth disappear, and new ones appear. The new Jerusalem came down from heaven. It had high walls and twelve gates, each with the names of the twelve tribes of Israel. The city was square, and God's new home would now be with mankind.

- The streets were of pure gold. There was no temple in the city, and no sun or moon in the sky. God is the temple, and His Glory provides all the light. Only those names in the Lamb's book could enter the city. Those remaining outside the gates were immortal.

- Jesus said He was coming soon, so happy are those who'd obeyed what's been written in this book (the bible). Jesus will bring His rewards with Him and give them out according to what each person has done. Come and accept the waters of life, to whoever wants it.

- John warns mankind not to add or take away from the words of the bible or God will punish and take away from them. So be it. Come, Lord Jesus. May the grace of Jesus be with all.

Additional comments on the book of Revelation:

Once you've read Revelation, and our **Appendix E** if needed, you should understand God's ultimate plan for humanity. Imagine a life without sin or evil, without pain or sorrow, and being reunited with loved ones who'd gone on before. Imagine living forever in the love and grace of God which has no end.

The last words from Jesus as told in the Bible are "I Jesus have sent mine angel to testify unto you these things in the churches. I am the root and offspring of David, and the bright and morning star. Surely, I come quickly."

Introduction to the Appendices

First and foremost, the Bible is not an easy book to understand. The following appendices will explain in more detail some parts of the Bible that many find are difficult to grasp onto and interpret. Each conclusion will be based on what the Bible says and not on popular opinion. As you go through these Appendices, read the referenced chapters and verses so you'll know exactly what the Bible says about each topic. Always pray to God for understanding.

Appendix A: <u>Jesus and the Initial Purpose of His Earthly Ministry.</u> The contents may surprise you.

Appendix B: <u>Is Salvation through God's Laws or by Faith in Jesus?</u> This compares the path to salvation as taught in the Old Testament before Jesus' earthly ministry, to the path to salvation given to us through the blood of Jesus as taught to us by Jesus and the apostle Paul in the New Testament.

Appendix C: <u>Paul's Ministry to Gentiles, and the Mysteries of God</u>. Paul's role in God's overall plan of salvation was extremely important and often underrated. His letters and messages were filled with the Holy Spirit.

Appendix D: Is <u>"Once Saved Always Saved" really true?</u> Jesus will always love us, but do believers fall from grace when they give up on Jesus and revert back to a life of sin after being saved?

Appendix E: <u>Revelation, a Simpler Overview of these Future Events</u>. This provides a comprehensive summary of this book without all the symbols, objects and representations. A simple three-page explanation.

Appendix F: <u>The Godhead Trinity: Father, Son, and Holy Spirit</u>. All three are one and one is all three, and it says so in your Bible.

Appendix G: <u>Who Did Adam and Eve's Children Marry? Who was there?</u> A question often asked, with an answer that'll seem obvious once you read it.

Appendix H: <u>It's Our Choice if We End Up in Hell, so Quit Blaming God!</u> We alone decide if we're headed to heaven or hell after death. God gave us the free will to do as we please, so we shouldn't blame others for the choices we've made.

Appendix I: <u>When God added Gentiles to His Salvation Plan.</u> There was a time when only the Jewish Nation was offered salvation. But what happened on the road to Damacus changed everything!

Appendix J: <u>Faith Facts and Interesting Biblical Tidbits</u>. A brief collection of often overlooked statements and occurrences as told in the Bible, both interesting and significant. Plus a few questions and answers.

Appendix A

Jesus and the Initial Purpose of His Earthly Ministry

When Jesus first began His earthly ministry, His initial purpose was to save Israel to fulfill God's earlier promises to them. Here's what the Bible says:

- Matthew 10:5-7. These twelve (apostles) Jesus sent forth and commanded them, saying "**Go not into the way of the Gentiles**, and into any city of the Samaritans enter ye not" (the Samaritans were part Jewish and part Gentile, who followed a form of Judaism). "**But go rather to the lost sheep of the house of Israel.** And as ye go, preach, saying the kingdom of heaven is at hand."
- Matthew 15:22-26. "And, behold, a woman of Canaan (a Gentile) came out of the same coasts and cried to Him, saying, Have mercy on me, O Lord, thou Son of David; my daughter is grievously vexed with a devil. But He answered her not a word. And His disciples came and besought Him, saying, Send her away; for she crieth after us. But He answered and said, **I am not sent but unto the lost sheep of the house of Israel.**" Then Jesus said, **"It is not meet** (good) **to take the children's bread, and to cast it to dogs."** Yes, He was referring to those outside of Israel (Gentiles) as little dogs, a term used by Greeks.

That's very straightforward. In Jesus' own words (paraphrasing the above) "Go not to the Gentiles (the non-Jewish people), but rather go to the lost sheep of Israel." Then He said, "I was sent here only for those who are lost in Israel." It seems clear that at first Jesus came to earth only to save Israel. Why was that?

Well, God loved the nation of Israel and He stated it many times. In Jeremiah 31:1 it says, "they shall be My people". God had made a covenant promise to Abraham nearly 2,000 years earlier that in addition to land and many descendants, the Jewish people would have His promise of a Redeemer for the atoning and deliverance from their sins. In Luke 1:72-73, it says, "remember His Holy covenant, the oath He swore to our father Abraham." To keep that promise, God sent His son Jesus to be that Redeemer to fulfill His promise to the Jewish nation. Micah 5:2 says He'd come from Bethlehem, and Isaiah 9:6 says He'd be called The Mighty God and The Prince of Peace. It's obvious they were referring to the arrival of Jesus.

During Old Testament times, the Israeli Nation had struggled trying to keep God's Laws and the Ten Commandments, which they had to do to keep their part of the bargain in their covenant agreement with God. That was the only way they had to please God and gain their salvation. But they failed miserably, over and over again, so there had to be a better way for God to save His people from their sinful nature. So a new and second covenant was introduced into the world through Jesus, not one which required animal sacrifices and the Temple worships of old, but one based on the unmerited grace of our Lord. When Jesus died on the cross, His blood washed away all the sins of those who would follow and believe in Him through faith.

As we learned reading the four gospels Matthew through John, many of the Jews rejected Jesus' earthly ministry and He was eventually beaten and handed over to the Gentiles who had Him crucified. The new covenant superseded the older version which in the end could never bring a person to their salvation. In Hebrews 8:7-8, it says that if the first covenant had been faultless, then a second covenant wouldn't have been needed. So the second covenant, made initially with Israel and Judah, was here to stay.

The new covenant promise from God is based on faith, simply believing that Jesus died, was buried, and that He rose again and ascended into Heaven. Plus it's no longer only for the Jewish, it's freely offered to both the Jew and Gentile and to the whole world. So when we read in John 3:16 "For God so loved the world that He gave His only begotten Son, that whoever believeth in Him should not perish but have everlasting life," we understand that Jesus gave that to us through His death and resurrection. But it wasn't that way during the Old Testament times because the begotten Son hadn't even been born yet.

So Jesus came to fulfill God's promise that He'd made to the Jewish nation thousands of years earlier, that they'd have a King and Redeemer. That was the initial focus of Jesus' earthly ministry, as Jesus Himself stated when He said that He was sent here for the lost people of Israel. God kept His word so now we have the Redeemer, and the entire world has access to Jesus and His blessings.

In the end we see that Jesus came first to the Jews, then to the Cross, and then to us. From the very beginning of time, God so loved the Jewish people that He'd never forsake them. The Bible says that He wanted them to receive Him and become His priests to all nations. It's written in Exodus 19:6, where it reads "And ye shall be unto Me a kingdom of priests, and a holy nation." Ezekiel 11:20 says "They may walk in My statues, and keep mine ordinances and do them; and they shall be My people, and I will be their God."

God knows all, so it was all foreplaned. God loved Israel and its people so much that He sent them Jesus. That needs repeating... God loved Israel and its people so much that He sent them Jesus. Can we ever imagine how much love that would take? So through Jesus and His crucified blood all the people throughout the world are now able and worthy to receive the glorious gift of salvation and everlasting life. But first, you must believe and accept Jesus.

Appendix B

Is Salvation Through God's Laws or by Faith in Jesus?

The simple answer is that true salvation requires both. The path to righteousness is keeping God's moral, worship and civil laws plus keeping His Commandments and believing in Jesus. When God dealt with Moses 3,500 years ago, He gave him His Laws and told him to share them with Israel so they'd know what He expected of them. He wanted them to be obedient, and to follow all of His instructions. He promised, and made a binding covenant promise with them, that He'd bless them if they'd refrain from sin. But those Laws were difficult and even impossible to live by, therefore practically no one was receiving redemption and salvation. Plus, nowhere in the Bible does it say that if you simply follow God's Ten Commandments that you'll be saved.

We must keep in mind that before God gave us His Laws, sin was undefined. If a man wanted to covet his neighbor's wife and kill his sheep, there was nothing to tell him it was wrong. God's Commandments told us what was right (righteous behavior), therefore we could deduce that not following His Commandments and Laws was wrong (sinful behavior). We all know that God is sovereign and that He knows what'll happen before it occurs. He knew that defining righteousness to the Jews gave them an ethical direction to follow, but He also knew they'd fail. But it was a great way to keep them in a relationship with Him until Jesus gave us a brand new covenant based on faith and belief.

Approximately 1,500 years later God initiated His second covenant with Israel to replace the first one, seeing that the sinful nature of man would never allow them to keep the Laws He'd given them through Moses. Furthermore, biblical research tells us there are now more than 1,000 total commands given to us in the bible on how to live right. Man's nature could never be that disciplined. If God hadn't offered something different, like a new path to earn eternal life in heaven, man would never receive true salvation. This new covenant was easier to follow, and even provided a path for a sinful person to truly repent and earn their way into heaven. But His Laws and Commandments still had to be followed.

Following the rules given to us in the Old Testament could only lead us to an unpardoned death, but God's new covenant based on faith and belief in Jesus gives us life. Paul's preaching tells us that if we repent of our sins and believe in our hearts that Jesus died, was buried and then resurrected, that we are saved and will be with Jesus in the Kingdom of Heaven. That promise is not because of anything we've done to earn it, but because of God's grace and His unmerited love and mercy given to us through Jesus. That's all that's required. Scripture explains how the Law was replaced, requiring us to believe and have faith in God's grace. Only through faith and the grace of God can we be saved. Let's see what the bible says about all that:

Following the Law was not the path to salvation, but could lead to death:

- Romans 6:14. For sin shall not have dominion over you: for ye are not under the law, but under grace.
- Romans 7:10. And the commandment, which was ordained to life, I found to be unto death.
- Romans 3:20. Therefore by the deeds of the law there shall no flesh be justified (declared righteous) in his sight: for by the law is the knowledge of sin.
- Romans 7:6. But now we are delivered from the law, that being dead wherein we were held; that we should serve in newness of spirit, and not in the oldness of the letter.
- James 2:10. For whoever shall keep the whole law, and yet offend in one point, he is guilty of all.
- II Corinthians 3:3. Forasmuch as ye are manifestly (clearly) declared to be the epistle (letter) of Christ ministered by us, written not in ink but with the Spirit (Holy Spirit) of the living God; not in tables of stone (the Ten Commandments), but in the fleshly tables of the heart.

It's by faith and belief in Jesus' death and resurrection that we are saved:

- Ephesians 2:8. For by grace are ye saved through faith; and that not of yourselves: it is the gift of God.
- Galatians 3:26. For ye are all the children of God by faith in Jesus Christ.
- Romans 3:28. Therefore we conclude that a man is justified (made righteous) by faith without the deeds of the law.
- Galatians 3:11 & 13. But that no man is justified by the law in the sight of God, it is evident. For; The just shall live by faith. Christ hath redeemed us from the curse of the law, being made a curse for us: for it is written, Cursed is every one that hangeth on a tree.
- Galatians 5:17-18. For the flesh lusteth against the Spirit (Holy Spirit), and the Spirit against the flesh: and these are contrary the one to the other: so that ye cannot do the things that ye would. But if ye be led by the Spirit, ye are not under the law.
- Romans 6:23. For the wages of sin is death; but the gift of God is eternal life through Jesus Christ our Lord.
- Galatians 2:21. Don't frustrate (nullify) God's Grace. If righteousness came by the Law, then Jesus died for no purpose (in vain).
- Colossians 2:14-17. (Jesus) blotted out the ordinances (Laws) against us and nailed it to His cross. Let no man judge you in meat (what you eat), or drink, or observance of holy days, or new moons, or the sabbath days. (These were all the earlier Jewish rules and outdated requirements for salvation).
- Galatians 1:6-9. Don't remove yourself from the gospel and grace of God into another gospel. If we, or an angel, or any man preach any other gospel to you, let him be accursed.

God gave us a new covenant, since mankind could not follow His Laws:

- Hebrews 8:13. In that he saith, A new covenant, he hath made the first old. Now that which decayeth and waxeth old vanishes away.
- Hebrews 8:6-7. But now hath he ordained a more excellent ministry, by how much also he is the mediator of a better covenant, which was established upon better promises. For if that first covenant had been faultless, then should no place have been sought for the second.

So are we supposed to throw out God's Commandments and Laws, now that we know the path to heaven is through our faith and belief in Jesus? Of course not. Everyone knows, especially Christians, not to steal and murder. A Christian could never do those things, and the Holy Spirit placed by God into the hearts of the saved would never lead a person into doing anything that was prohibited by His Laws. We're all still under God's Law, we're just no longer under the penalty of those Laws. Everything God did and will do has a purpose. He gave us His Laws to be followed. Even the non-believer must follow them, most of which were adopted and used as the foundation for our present day laws. The Ten Commandment stones are holy, and were placed in the Ark of the Covenant for a reason. They still apply, because Jesus was still quoting them in the New Testament. They define the rights and wrongs in civilization.

God's Commandments and Laws must still to be followed today:

- Ecclesiastes 12:13. Let us hear the conclusion of the whole matter: Fear God, and keep his commandments: for this is the whole duty of man.
- Matthew 5:19. (Jesus speaking) Whosoever therefore shall break one of these least commandments, and shall teach men so, he shall be called the least in the kingdom of heaven: but whosoever shall do and teach them, the same shall be called great in the kingdom of heaven.
- I Timothy 1:8. But we know that the law is good, if a man use it lawfully;

So from scripture we read that God gave the Jewish nation His Laws, and through a covenant He promised to bless them if they'd follow them. But the sinful nature within us, which began in the Garden of Eden, made it impossible for man to comply with God's Laws and His covenant requirements. But we must still follow His commandments. In Matthew 19:17, Jesus was asked what good thing will bring eternal life. This was before His death and before our faith and belief in Him would give us eternal life, so He answered by saying "keep the commandments."

But in the New Testament after Jesus died for our sins, through His grace we had a new covenant and a better way to be saved and achieve righteousness. If we'll confess our sins, cleanse our hearts, and believe in Jesus' death, burial and resurrection, then we're saved. A child of God must be full of faith and belief, and still follow God's commandments. If we want eternal life, Jesus has made what was once very difficult to do into something exceedingly uncomplicated and manageable.

Appendix C

Paul's Ministry to Gentiles, and the Mysteries of God

The Old Testament is full of many instances where God blessed the Jewish people of Israel over and over again only to see them deny him and turn their backs in unbelief. Acts 28:27-28 tells us their ears were dull of hearing and their eyes were closed. Jesus used a parable in Luke 13:6-9 to say a fig tree that doesn't produce fruit must eventually be cut down. So in 70 AD, the Roman army invaded Jerusalem, destroyed the city and it's temple, and scattered the Jewish residents throughout the region.

Of course God still loved the Jewish nation, but they would not change their ways so He could restore and heal them. So going forward, God would send His love and grace that was rejected by the Jews to all the world so that anyone and everyone could hear and embrace it. This act of God to include the Gentiles in His plans instead of only the Jewish people meant that all of mankind, through the work of Jesus, would help to restore the world to what God meant for it to be. This act ushed in the Gospel of Grace, or Age of Grace.

Saul of Tarsus, better known as the apostle Paul, was chosen by Jesus in Acts 9:1-20 to bring this good news to the world, built around the belief in the life, death, burial and resurrection of Jesus Christ. God had kept this a secret since His creation of heaven and earth, withheld from the knowledge of man until He'd determined the time was right to reveal it. Throughout the Bible God's secrets and mysteries are mentioned many times but not explained in detail, but in Romans 16:25-27 and in Ephesians 3:1-11 they are revealed, mostly to Paul. They're comprised of several events.

The first mystery known only by God was that He'd eventually reveal Himself to man in human form, when Jesus told Philip in John 14:9 that "he who hath seen me hath seen the Father." The second mystery or secret was that His Holy Spirit would descend and live within believers, mentioned in Galatians 2:20. Thirdly, unknown for thousands of years, was that both Jews and Gentiles could share the promises that God made through Jesus, told by Paul in Ephesians 3:3-6. Another secret, not realized by the Jewish nation, was that Jesus was with them to fulfill the covenant promise God had made to Abraham. After His many miracles, they still never realized He was their Savior.

Possibly the greatest of all secrets withheld from mankind was revealed when Paul told those in Corinth, in I Corinthians 15:50-54, that all deceased followers of Christ would be raised to be immortal and live forever. Another, told in Romans 12:25-32, was that God would save Israel as a race even after their rejection of Jesus and the scattering of Jews throughout the world.

Another secret revealed, told in II Thessalonians 2:3-10, was that a wicked one would come before the end of time to deceive and lead many away from the real Christ. But God would prevail and His will shall be done when He gathers all believers, Ephesians 1:9-10, to overturn our sins and establish Christ as the Head of the Church, Ephesians 5:23. The Church is the body of Christ, reaching throughout the world so that all believers can be a part of it to make up what will become the Kingdom of Heaven. By His saving blood we'll all be cleansed of unrighteousness and renewed with the purity of a virgin, Ephesians 4:23-32, worthy of being in the body of Christ.

God revealed all these mysteries to Paul and called him to preach them to the world. Paul's work should never be understated, as he worked tirelessly establishing many new churches in the name of Jesus while being beaten, shipwrecked, snakebit, flogged, and spending over five years imprisoned or held in custody. He was the sole minister of Jesus to the Gentiles, and until Jesus called him to preach to them they had no hope and were without God, stated in Ephesians 2:11-12. Paul was given his mission and he worked diligently the rest of his life to carry it out until his death around 68 AD.

Paul had helpers along the way, among them Timothy and Titus, helping him preach the newly revealed gospel of Jesus Christ. He embraced his purpose, saying in Romans 11:13 that he was the apostle of the Gentiles, and in Romans 2:16 he said that God shall judge the secrets of men by Jesus Christ according to my gospel. He owned his calling, and since he knew some of God's secrets and mysteries he began referring to his preaching as his own.

Inevitably, there came a time when Paul's preaching of faith clashed with the apostles and Jewish elders who still preached circumcision and the Laws of Moses, so a meeting was held to eliminate the confusion. At this point, the Gospel of Christ was the only true message, and it was being offered to both Jews and Gentiles. Paul had moved people away from Old Testament beliefs (the Gospel of Law) and into the gospel of Jesus (the Gospel of Grace), but false teachers were telling their listeners that their salvation still depended on whether they'd been circumcised and whether they followed the Commandments. As told in Galatians 2:7-10 and in Acts 15:1-9, and approximately twenty years after Jesus' resurrection, Paul with Barnabus and Titus met with others in Jerusalem to discuss the problem. When the Jewish leaders saw that the gospel to Gentiles was committed unto Paul, and the gospel to the Jews fell to them and the apostles, the leaders gave to Paul and Barnabus the right hands of fellowship (shook hands) that they should continue their work with the heathen (the Gentiles). But now, they'd all preach the message and saving grace of Jesus.

So the mysteries that were withheld for thousands of years were given mostly to Paul, who spent the remaining years of his life spreading the Good News. Before Jesus came, people were kept under the Law and unaware of what God would reveal (Galatians 3:23-26). The Law was their schoolmaster that led them unto Christ. Now we're all children of God by our faith in Jesus.

Appendix D

Is "Once Saved Always Saved" really true?

There are basic results in life that we've come to expect. One is that good people will be rewarded for their decency and goodwill while the bad people will be punished. That seems fair, but it doesn't always happen. Another expectation is that those who follow Jesus and are saved will behave and live according to their Christian beliefs. That doesn't always happen either. So what happens to a person who is saved when they purposely turn away from God and live the rest of their life in sin? Are they still due an eternal life with Jesus after death? Are their names still recorded in God's record book of life?

The answers to those questions are normally withheld until an article like this is completed and all the justifications are explained in a closing summary at the end. But those questions are so important that we need to give the most rational and wisest conclusions now. If a Christian in full knowledge has an apostasy and totally departs from their salvation for the remainder of their life believing that the statement "once saved is always saved" will shield them, they'd better understand the consequences. What if they're wrong? Why would anyone gamble their soul that their purposeful sinful life until death after once being saved wouldn't matter to God? Plainly stated, the risk is just too large for a saved but lifetime backslider to believe "once saved always saved" is the correct biblical interpretation. The final verdict on their life hangs on whether that statement is true or false.

Therefore, the purpose of this article is to convince Christians to continue their walk with Jesus without having a willing defiance and resistance to the gifts He gave us from His death on the cross. We all have a sinful nature, so we will all commit sins. Christians can repent from those sins and God will forgive them. This article isn't about that. It's about those who intentionally defy God and totally desert Him for the rest of their lives after receiving His gift of salvation, but still believing everything is okay with Him. But is it really? Many churches are split on this issue, so let's see what the bible says about what is often called the doctrine of "eternal security".

First of all, we know of some who were in the family of God before they willfully turned away from their salvation forever. How about Lucifer, the angel who willfully chose to depart from grace in order to corrupt God's perfect creation. Lucifer was not "once saved always saved" because we learn in Revelation that he'll be cast into hell. How about Judas, a man who walked with Jesus as His disciple. When he turned against Jesus, was he still "once saved always saved?" In Revelation 22:19, it says that anyone who takes away from God's word, God will take away his part out of the book of life. And in Revelation 3:5, Jesus is speaking when He tells us that he that overcomes (the temptations of sin) shall be clothed in white, and his name will not be blotted from the book of life. In both of those verses, it tells us that the names of saved people can go into the book of life, but they can also be removed.

John 3:16 says "For God so loved the world, that he gave his only begotten Son, that whoever believeth in him should not perish, but have everlasting life". Do you think that applies to those who only believed in Him for a month, or maybe five years, or does it apply only to those who believe in Him from salvation until death? Well, the bible tells us in Hebrews 3:14 "For we are made partakers of Christ, **IF** we hold the beginning of our confidence stedfast unto the end". That tells us that we must worship Christ until the end, until we die. How about Mark 13:13, where Jesus is speaking, "and ye shall be hated of all men for My name's sake; but he that shall endure unto the end, the same shall be saved." He doesn't tell us to only endure for a year, but until the end.

In John 15:1-6, Jesus speaks and tells us that He is like a vine that is rooted and stable and we are His branches. He says if we abide in one another, then we will bear fruit. But if we don't abide in Jesus, we are withered and therefore gathered and cast into the fire to be burned. He wants us to abide in Him, which is accepting and acting in accordance with His teachings, so we can grow, spread and be fruitful. If we don't, we're gathered and cast away. Jesus clearly makes that point. Furthermore, what if a saved believer does the unpardonable sin and expresses blasphemy against the Holy Ghost, as Jesus speaks of in Matthew 12:31-32? Jesus says that person shall not be forgiven neither in this world or neither in the world to come.

The bottom line is what's written in Hebrews 6:4-6. "For it is impossible for those who were once enlightened, and have tasted of the heavenly gift, and were made partakers of the Holy Ghost, and have tasted the good word of God, and the powers of the world to come, if they shall fall away, to renew them again unto repentance; seeing they crucify to themselves the Son of God afresh, and put Him to an open shame." So for those who are saved and have received God's love and Holy Spirit within them, and have received His blessings and promises of the heaven to come, for them to totally turn away from God would be like asking Jesus to shamefully die on the cross a second time just for them, to wash away their sins and restore them once again. Isn't that like saying that Jesus' death for us on the cross wasn't enough?

The requirements to maintain a lifelong walk with Christ is to accept Him as your savior and continue in your faith throughout your life, repenting when necessary to defeat sin and retain your spirituality. For a believer to apostatize and deliberately terminate his love for Jesus confirms that he never really had Christian convictions to begin with. In II Peter 2:21, it states that it's better for a person to never have known righteousness than to have had it, then turn away from it. How could that be stated any clearer? So again, is the phrase "once saved always saved" really true? Hopefully, this article will prevent Christians from betting their lives that it's true beyond doubt. If they're wrong, the consequences are simply too great. If you accept Jesus and worship Him until death, you won't hear Him say "I never knew you" as mentioned in Matthew 7:21-23. Instead, He might look at you and say "I know you. You never turned away from Me or My love for you. Welcome to Heaven."

Appendix E

Revelation, a Simpler Overview of these Future Events

In its simplest form, Revelation tells of a future time when there'll be a rapture of both the dead and living who were saved by accepting Jesus into their lives, and a Tribulation Period when there'll be many horrible deaths and devastations upon earth. Then after this seven year Tribulation, Jesus returns to earth to defeat Satan and be with His followers for a thousand years. There'll be a final judgement day to see who's name has been recorded in God's Record Book of Life based on their deeds and works during their lifetime. Unbelievers will be cast away but believers will live with Jesus for eternity in the new Jerusalem.

If that's too brief of a summary, more details and further explanations are given below. Keep in mind that the bible doesn't tell us exactly when everything will happen in the future, so there's some uncertainty about any timeline and the exact sequence of events. Although beliefs can vary significantly, most of the following is based on widely held interpretations of this book.

The book of Revelation is full of symbols and therefore very difficult to fully understand. For example, it uses many animals and objects to represent other things. This appendix does not attempt to explain what each animal and object stands for, but instead it focuses on the events that will occur between now and the end times as told in the Bible. If it's important for you to understand that a lampstand stands for a church, that a lighted torch represents the spirit of God, and that a black horse symbolizes famine, then this summary may not provide the information you seek. But to better understand the core message of Revelation and what it tells us about the future, the following summary will help.

Ever since Jesus died, ascended into heaven and the Holy Spirit filled His believers (the day of Pentecost), mankind has been living in the Church Age or the Age of Grace. That'll continue until the rapture occurs (the word rapture, meaning seized or taken suddenly, does not actually appear in the English Bible). The rapture is the day that all Christians, first the dead and then the living, are raised to meet Jesus in the clouds (I Thessalonians 4:16-17).

At the beginning of Revelation, John is shown future events through visions and is told to record them to send to seven specific churches located in Asia. Jesus knew the good and evil within each church, so the churches in Smyrna and Philadelphia were the only two He praised. His knowledge of the good and evil within each church also represents the good and evil within each of us. Our deeds reflect our faith, and each is recorded. Everything we do, good or bad, will be used when Jesus judges all of mankind one person at a time.

A slain Lamb, representing Jesus, held a book sealed with seven seals. Each seal represented a future event which would occur on earth before the book would be opened. Then tribulation began, a seven year period of oppression and suffering that exposed all those who'd oppressed Israel and refused to accept Jesus as their Messiah. To protect those who'd preached and died for the word of God, Jesus raptured them away from earth and out of harm's way before or during this Tribulation. The first seal Jesus opened revealed a conqueror riding a white horse and wearing a crown. At first that description might appear to be Jesus, but it's Antichrist the imposter. Each subsequent seal Jesus opened caused an event to occur on earth, some very tragic. The first four seals, each involving a horse, are often referred to as the Four Horsemen of the Apocalypse. They represent conquest, war, famine and death. During this time the Antichrist acts as Israel's friend and wants to rebuild their Temple, giving them a false hope of peace. He sets up Babylon as his capital city, one that represents wickedness and the opposition to God by Rome and other nations. The fifth seal was opened to show the souls of persecuted Christians and martyrs waiting to be avenged. Then Satan and his army fight heaven's angels but lose, and are cast out onto earth.

The carnage on unbelievers and the destruction on earth gets much worse during The "Great" Tribulation period, which is the final three and a half years of this seven year event. The sixth seal brought earthquakes, but God's angels held back the destruction until 144,000 of God's people were sealed as servants of God in their foreheads. The Antichrist then violates his peace treaty with the middle east, exposing his true sinful nature. The seventh seal was opened and seven angels were given seven trumpets. The first four trumpets brought plagues and even more devastations upon earth including the darkening of heavenly bodies. The fifth trumpet opened a bottomless pit where locusts were released to torment all those without the seal of God in their foreheads. The sixth trumpet caused four avenging angels in the Euphrates River to kill a third of all mankind. God's two witnesses prophesy (these witnesses are thought to be Elijah and Moses). The beast on land (the false prophet) uses the mark of the beast, the number 666, to mark the right hand or forehead of those following the Antichrist. God's two witnesses are killed and ascend up into heaven. The seventh trumpet sounded and the temple of God opened in heaven and His Kingdom is announced.

Seven vials or bowls full of God's wrath are poured on earth. The first four brought sores and fires, and turned water into blood. The fifth vial was poured on the beast. His kingdom turned to darkness but he still didn't repent. The sixth vial was poured on the river Euphrates, and the devil's spirit gathered sinners for the great battle at Armageddon. A beast appeared carrying a mysterious woman with Babylon written on her forehead. Jesus and His angels bring God's fury upon those who follow Satan. Babylon, Satan and the beasts are defeated. A voice from heaven said, "It is done." The horrors brought on by Satan, the Antichrist and false prophet have ended. Seven years of Tribulation is over, and those who are for God have been clearly distinguished from those who are against God. God's wrath has ended.

Jesus has returned, and it's the Day of The Lord! Heaven applauded and praised God for His judgement on Babylon. The marriage of the Lamb (Jesus) to His Church took place (His Church are all those who've accepted Jesus and been born again). A white horse came from heaven, ridden by the One who is Faithful and True, the Word of God. Written on Him was King of Kings, and Lord of Lords. The beast and his kings are cast into the lake of fire. Satan is bound and chained for a thousand years and put in a bottomless pit, but will return later for a brief time. The souls of those who'd stayed true to God lived and reigned with Him for the millennium, a thousand years. Then Satan was released and gathered his army for battle, but fire came down from God in heaven that killed them. The devil, Antichrist and false prophet would be tortured forever in the lake of fire. This portion of scripture tells of two indescribable events. Jesus has taken His believers and followers to reign with Him, and all those under the demonic rule and leadership who battled the forces of God have been extinguished once and forever. Judgement day is here.

The Great White Throne Judgement will be for those who never accepted Christ as their savior. Christians will also be judged, but through Jesus they've been saved without condemnation as told in John 3:18. Those whose names were not in the book of life are judged and sentenced according to their actions here on earth, then they're cast into the lake of fire as their second death (Revelation 21:8). This is not a judgment to determine the salvation of Christians, for they've been saved. They'll be judged only to determine their rewards for any deeds and works they'd performed on earth in Jesus' behalf.

The heaven and earth that existed is gone, and a new heaven and earth appear. A new Jerusalem comes down from heaven onto earth. There's no more crying, death or sorrow since all former things have passed away. The new Jerusalem, with streets of gold, has walls and fountains containing the names of the twelve tribes and the twelve apostles. There's no Temple and no sun above since God and the Lamb will provide the truth and light. The time is at hand. Jesus is the Alpha and Omega, the offspring of David and the morning star. Let no man add or remove what's in God's book. Jesus will come quickly, and His grace will be with us all. These final versus remind us that we'll all be judged just like the seven churches were at the very beginning of Revelation. We want our actions here on earth to earn our names being in God's Book of Life. Don't let Jesus' review of your life cast you into fire.

Let us pray: Lord, come quickly. We want to see the new Jerusalem here on earth, and with reverence and humbleness we want to look into the eyes of almighty God. What a glorious day that will be. Amen.

Appendix F

The Godhead Trinity: Father, Son, and Holy Spirit

Some things in the Bible are not for our understanding. Humans are incapable of absorbing the sovereignty and preeminence of God and how He works. One blessing of the Bible is that it teaches us about the Trinity of God, Jesus, and the Holy Spirit, and all they offer us if we'll accept them and believe. Those three are the same holy entity, synonymously interchangeable while maintaining the mission and presence of one. Just the thought of it is momentous, and too important and powerful for us to comprehend.

Let's see what the Bible says about it. In I John 5:7, it says "For there are three that bear record in heaven, the Father, the Word, and the Holy Ghost: and these three are one." Of course the Word is in reference to Jesus, confirmed in John1:14 where it reads "And the Word was made flesh, and dwelt among us, and we beheld his glory, the glory as of the only begotten of the Father, full of grace and truth." This is backed up in another verse, in Revelation19:13, when heaven opened up and Jesus sat upon a white horse. It reads, "And he was clothed with a vesture dipped in blood: and his name is called The Word of God." So the bible confirms that these three are one.

To learn more about God the Father we'll turn to John 4:24, where Jesus says, "God is a Spirit: and they that worship him must worship him in spirit and in truth." This is confirmed in John 1:18, where John tells us, "No man hath seen God at any time." But throughout the Old Testament we read where God was seen and spoke to people. Was it really God who was there or was it Jesus, the human-form existence of God? That's answered in Colossians 1:15 when the apostle Paul tells us that Jesus is the image of the invisible God, the firstborn of every creature. So, God is a Spirit and has therefore never been seen, and Jesus is the image of our invisible God. The Bible tells us that.

To learn more of what the Bible says about Jesus, let's begin by understanding all that He is. When He was on earth, there were times when He would speak and call out to His Father like most sons would do, in order to know the will of His Father. One of many examples was when He was being baptized and praying in Luke 3:21. Another was in Mark 1:35, when He prayed after a night of healing and casting out demons. And we all know that He spoke to His Father from the cross, asking God to forgive those crucifying Him because they know not what they do, as in Luke 23:34. He was in human form all those times, and prayed to God just like the rest of us do.

However, there were just as many times in the bible when He didn't pray to God because He was God. In John 2:1-11, He turned the water into wine without asking if it was God's will. Often, He would forgive and heal sinners without having to pray for their forgiveness. In Matthew 15:28, He healed a woman's daughter because of her great faith. Then on the Mount of Olives in John 8:1-11, an adulterous woman was brought to Him and He forgave her. During those times and so many others He didn't need to pray and ask for their forgiveness, He just forgave them. Since Jesus is the human form of God, He already had the authority.

In I Timothy 3:16, it reads, "And without controversy great is the mystery of Godliness: God was manifest (clearly revealed) in the flesh, justified in the Spirit, seen of angels, preached unto the Gentiles, Believed on in the world, received up into glory." Yes, Jesus was God revealed in a flesh body.

So where there is God there is Jesus, and where there is Jesus there is God, and where they are so is the Holy Spirit being freely given to every believer. Two verses verify that. Paul writes of Jesus in Colossians 2:9-10 and says, "For in him (Jesus) dwelleth all the fullness of the Godhead bodily." Then in John 14:9 Jesus tells Philip, "he that hath seen me hath seen the Father." That's very clear. The three are one, and where there is one there are three.

Even from the very beginning, in the book of Genesis, it tells us that God created the heaven and the earth. In the original writings, the Hebrew word Elohim was used for the word God. It's a plural noun for God, and it comes from the word Eloah. It's plural as in God, Jesus, and the Spirit. So was Jesus there when the world was created? Again, let's see what the Bible says. In Colossians 1:16-17 where Paul is writing about Jesus, it says "For by Him (Jesus) were all things created, that are in heaven, and that are in earth, visible and invisible, whether they be thrones, or dominions, or principalities, or powers: all things were created by him, and for him: And he is before all things, and by him all things consist." If that's not convincing enough, read in Genesis 1:26 during the creation, where it says, "Let **us** make man in our image". Who would **us** be when man wasn't created yet? **Us** is not a single entity. It was the trinity, all three. Yes, Jesus was there from the very beginning.

We know the bible tells us it was God who gave Moses the Commandments etched in stone tablets, as told in Exodus and in Deuteronomy. But in John 14:15, Jesus says "If ye love me, keep My commandments." They were His commandments too. Again, the Bible is telling us what God does, Jesus also does. As we documented earlier from I John 5:7, there are three that bear record in heaven, and these three are one. They cannot be separated. So what does the Bible tell us about the third member, the Holy Ghost or Holy Spirit?

The Holy Spirit is easier to understand. Galatians 5:22 tells us "But the fruit of the Spirit is love, joy, peace, longsuffering, gentleness, goodness, faith, meekness, temperance." It's given from God to every believer to direct us, teach us, empower us, and to intercede for us. In the Bible the Holy Spirit is often referred to as the Dove, the Advocate, the presence of God, and in John 14:26 Jesus says He's our Comforter. In John 14:16, all the Godhead are mentioned in one statement from Jesus when He says, "And I **(Jesus)** will pray the **Father,** and He shall give you another **Comforter**, that He may abide with you forever." So the Holy Spirit is masculine, referred to as He again in John 15:26 and in John 16:7-8. A sinful body with a sinful spirit would not receive the Holy Spirit. But once a person accepts Jesus as their Savior they receive the greatest of gifts, including the presence of the Lord, the forgiveness of their sins, the promise of eternal life, and the indwelling of the Holy Spirit.

In summary, the Bible tells us that God is holy and incredibly perfect but has never been seen, and that He, Jesus and the Holy Spirit are as one and together they make up the Trinity or Godhead. **They're all God, so there's God the Father, God the Son, and God the Holy Spirit.** One of them is all three and all three of them are one, and it's been that way even before creation.

Appendix G

Who Did Adam & Eve's Children Marry? Who was there?

One of the many questions people will ask when they begin reading the Bible is about Adam and Eve, and Cain and Abel. Specifically, they wonder if there were people living on earth before Adam and Eve, and if not, then who would their children marry, especially Cain? First of all, there are people and events in the Bible that God chose to briefly mention and others that He emphasized and explained. The questions about earlier humans and the marriage of Cain have little to do with God's primary message and purpose of the Old Testament, which was to introduce the Jewish nation through the use of their descendants, leaders, prophets, and Laws to their coming Savior, His Son Jesus Christ. Through faith, we must believe every word in the Bible although some stories are difficult to comprehend. If we begin questioning one event, would we then begin to question whether Jesus died for our sins? Christians believe what the Bible says, understanding that many narratives outside the storyline of Jesus just weren't important enough for elaboration.

However, to briefly expand on the questions above, we know through modern science and geological dating methods that there were animals and humans on earth long before approximately 6,000 years ago when Adam and Eve were created. Museums are full of dinosaur bones and fossils from millions of years ago to prove that. God didn't create other beings after creating Adam and Eve, because Acts 17:26 tells us that God made all nations of one blood. And in Genesis 3:20, it states that Eve was the mother of all the living. We don't know exactly when God created everything that's ever lived, and it's not information we absolutely need to know. Again, the focus of the bible is on Jesus Christ and the saving of souls.

Determining where Cain's wife came from will require more explanation. As always, let's see what the Bible says. We learn in Genesis 5:4-5 that after the birth of Cain and Abel, their brother Seth was born when Adam was around 130 years old. It tells us that Adam and Eve had even more sons and daughters before Adam died at the age of 930. Contrary to today's laws, there was nothing during the time of Cain that prohibited marriages within the same family or bloodline. Adam and Eve were perfectly created because everything God created was good, as told in Genesis 1:31. There were no diseases, inferior gene pools, or genetic disturbances to corrupt the health of their offspring. They were pure. When Eve was created from Adam's rib, told in Genesis 2:21-22, they obviously had the same DNA but would go on to have many perfectly normal children. In Genesis 20:2 and 20:12, Abraham married his half-sister. In Genesis 29:12 and the following verses, Jacob married two of his cousins. After the great flood, Noah's people would've married within the family because everyone else had died. It was commonplace back then. There were no other options.

That leads us back to Cain. Adam and Eve had more sons and daughters (Genesis 5:4) over hundreds of years until Adam died. God told Eve in Genesis 3:16 that He would greatly multiply her conceptions and He did. So Cain would've had sisters, cousins, and nieces. Then we're told in Genesis 4:16-17 that Cain married and his wife bore a child. His wife had to be a family member because there were no other females on earth at that time to marry. After Cain had killed Abel and traveled to Nod, there could've been dozens or even hundreds of women living in the area, all descendants and blood relatives of Adam and Eve. In early Hebrew texts, Cain's wife was called Awan and was sometimes referred to as his sister although the Bible doesn't confirm that. It was not until we read in Leviticus 18:6-17 that God prohibited marriages within the same family, knowing that over time the gene pools of mankind had been contaminated and compromised which could cause both physical and psychological issues to any children.

Appendix H

It's Our Choice if We End Up in Hell, so Quit Blaming God!

We must never think that God sends people to hell, because it's our choices and actions that determines our fate after death. We can choose to either accept and follow Jesus into eternal life, or reject His love and accept that we will end up in hell. It will be one or the other, there is no middle ground. It clearly states in John 3:16 "that whosoever believeth in Him should not perish (will not go to hell), but have everlasting life." How could that possibly be stated any clearer? If we don't believe in Him and live a Christian life, then when we perish we will not have an everlasting life with God in heaven because we will be in hell, period.

God made us and gave us and His angels the free will to make choices in life, to either love Him or not love Him. Sure, He could have created us to love Him and follow His every command, but we all know that forced love is no love at all. God wants every last person on earth to follow Him, but if we choose not to then we must accept that we have determined that we'll end up in hell. God wants no soul left behind, and is saddened by the pain and cruelty He sees being perpetrated by the sinners in the world.

Consider this; even before a child is born parents realize their child could grow up to be a blessing to them, or the child could be so full of sin that their life is filled with bitter disappointment, disgrace, heartbreak and pain. Regardless, they'll still want the child, and will risk all the heart-wrenching pain they might suffer from the actions of that child for the chance that the child will love them. Life is so precious that parents will always take that risk, and so it is with God. We're born, and God loves us although our free will may give God tremendous pain and disappointment. He allows us to set our own path. Sadly, when we abuse our free will and use it in unrighteous sinful ways, God is heartbroken.

There'll come a day when God will take away our free will that we've abused, failed miserably to manage, and is being used by most of mankind to send them to hell. God loves us too much to see our sins continue on and on. Most of life ended when the dinosaurs were wiped out. Most of life ended again when sin became so rampant that God flooded the world. And it'll end again before we ruin everything God created, and that's when Jesus comes for His followers. There's still time for sinners to repent and ask Jesus into their lives, but the signs are telling us the time is near. So people get ready, because there's a train a comin'.

Appendix I

When God added Gentiles to His Salvation Plan

Very early in the Old Testament we read and learn that the Jews are God's chosen people. He continuously watched over them, protected them, and forgave them when they strayed from His path. He made it perfectly clear in Jeremiah 31:1 when "saith the Lord, will I be the God of all the families of Israel, and they shall be my people." God's covenant with them included His promise of land, many descendants, and the promise of a redeemer. But all through the Old Testament we read where most Jews turned away and defied God, so their need for the coming redeemer became their main hope for atonement.

Over thousands of years the Jewish nation anxiously awaited for the One who had been forecasted to come. But when Jesus did arrive to begin His earthly ministry they rejected Him as their Savior, unwilling to accept Him partially because they knew He'd arrived through the earthly lineage of Mary and Joseph. Unaware that they were in the presence of God the Son, they thought Jesus was narcissistic to claim He was someone sent to fulfill God's covenant and to save them. Their anger led to the horrific treatment He received, culminating in His crucifixion. God was extremely disappointed with the Jews, but as stated in Isaiah 55:8-9, His thoughts and ways were not of the Jews because His plans were so much higher than theirs. They didn't fully realize what they'd done by rejecting Jesus, but God did, so He stopped the Jewish timeline leading to the long-awaited appearance of their redeemer and instead ushered in a redemption plan for the Gentiles. But even then, God kept a remnant of His chosen people. Even after their holy temple was destroyed again in 70 AD and they scattered, God didn't give up on them.

So on the road to Damascus around 40 AD, as told in Acts 9:1-16, God chose the Christian's worst persecutor and most unlikely Jew to preach and bear His name before the Gentiles. He wanted the Gentiles, who were viewed by Jews as immoral heathens, to know they were now included in His grace, His forgiveness, and salvation plan. God had kept these secrets and mysteries hidden from mankind until the time was right to reveal them (learn more in **Appendix C**). It was difficult for the Jews to embrace that change or even believe it came from God. But it did, and Paul became what could be called the thirteenth apostle, preaching to the Gentiles while Jesus' twelve apostles continued preaching to the Jews. This change opened the door for any and all of mankind to be included in God's ultimate plan when the Day of the Lord comes and Jesus returns to earth to set up His kingdom. The gospel, which is the good news of salvation offered to us by faith through the death and resurrection of Jesus, spread to all people worldwide. Now anyone anywhere who accepts and follows Jesus can become a member in the Body of Christ, made up of any and all believers of any race, color or creed.

Appendix J

Faith Facts and Interesting Biblical Tidbits

The Bible contains so much information that it's easy to read past some events that deserve more attention and discussion. Here are just a few:

1. The King of Salem, Melchizedek, was introduced in Genesis 14:18 as the priest of the most high God. Who was this man who Abraham tithed and gave a tenth of all he had as told in Hebrews chapter 7? He was without father and mother, having neither the beginning of days nor the end of life, and was made like unto the Son of God. Obviously he was an extremely holy priest. But the highest priest is Jesus, with a priesthood superior to all others, and with His ultimate authority He'd introduce a better covenant to all mankind. Melchizedek was a significant divine individual, although somewhat mysterious.

2. In Genesis 18:1-16, the Lord and two others visited Abraham where they sat and ate beneath a tree. Yes, the Lord had a meal as Abraham stood by Him (surely in amazement). Afterwards, He told Abraham and Sarah they'd have a son, although they were both old and stricken in age. Sarah laughed thinking the Lord was joking. Later they had a son named Isaac.

3. In John 1:18 and again in I John 4:12, it is written that no man has seen God at any time. In John 5:37, Jesus tells us that we have not heard God's voice at any time or seen his shape. Then in John 4:24, Jesus tells us that God is a Spirit. So, then who was it that appeared to Adam and Eve walking through the garden (Genesis 3:8), or appeared to Abraham (Genesis 17:1), or had many conversations with Moses and used His finger to write the Ten Commandments (Exodus 31:18)? It was Jesus who did all those things, the image of the invisible God (Colossians 1:15). In Revelation 19:13 when Jesus appeared in John's vision riding a white horse, His name is called The Word of God. He was made flesh and dwelt among us (John 1:14). In John 1:1-3, it tells us the Word (Jesus) was with God and the Word was God (God the Son), and that all things were created by Him. Jesus, who is the Son of God and Word of God, is the One who mediates and represents God in human form. Jesus has been with us from the very beginning, way before His birth in Bethlehem, and as Christians waiting to be raptured we'll be with Him until the very end.

4. Did you know that Jacob physically wrestled with a man that he knew as God and neither one came out ahead? Jacob said he wouldn't stop wrestling until he was given a blessing. It is told in Genesis 32:24-30. Was it really God, or an angel, or was God making Jacob wrestle with himself internally to make him face the guilt of his past and put it behind him? We all wrestle with God over things we shouldn't have said or done, but unlike Jacob we can win if we'll stop wrestling with it and just turn it over to God. God gave Jacob a new name, and He'll give us a new peace if we'll believe in Him and ask Him for guidance and wisdom.

5.   We know from reading the Bible that Jesus initially came to earth to fulfill God's covenant with the Jewish people of Israel, with no mention early on that the Gentiles (non-Jewish people) were included in His plan (see **Appendix A** for a more thorough explanation). But there were 2 times during His earthly ministry among the Jews that He turned His attention to healing Gentiles. In Matthew 15:21-28, He healed a Gentiles' daughter after seeing the tremendous faith the mother had in Him. Then in Luke 7:1-10, Jesus healed the servant of a centurion (a Roman army officer) after hearing the centurion's faith when he said that whatever Jesus commands in a word always comes true and brings miraculous miracles.

6.   On the biblical timeline, approximately 2,500 years passed from when Adam was created until Moses was born. Since it was Moses who God gave the Ten Commandments, anyone who lived before Moses's time had no written record of what was right or what was wrong. Therefore, sin ran so rampant that God started all over with the flood and Noah's ark. The Commandments gave mankind rules to live by, but the sinful nature of man could not follow them. Therefore, as told in Romans 3:23, all have sinned and come short of the glory of God. That's why God gave us Jesus, so that through Him all mankind might find an easier path into heaven.

7.   What is hell really like? Well, there's an eye-opening description of hell given to us by Jesus in Luke 16:19-31, involving a beggar named Lazarus and a rich man. They both died, and the sinful rich man went to hell while the beggar who believed in Jesus went in death to be with Abraham. In hell, the sinner was being tormented by flames when he saw Abraham and Lazarus far away, and Lazarus wasn't being tormented. The sinner asked for water, and then asked that his surviving family be warned of the torment awaiting them if they didn't turn from their evil ways. Abraham told the sinner that in hell there's a fixed gulf between the sinners and those who followed Jesus, and no one can pass from one side of the gulf to the other. Abraham's point was that if his family had refused to listen to Moses, the prophets, and the thousands they've heard preach God's word, then they should know there may come a time when it's too late to repent and go to the other side. He's telling us we'd better accept the one who died for us and repent now, before it's too late.

8.   In II Corinthians 5:10, we're told that everyone will appear before the judgement seat of Christ, but Christians won't be there to be condemned as stated in John 3:18 because they've been promised eternal life if they'll faithfully worship Jesus until the end (Mark 13:13 and Hebrews 3:14). Christians understand that Christ has paid for their sins both past, present and future, so they'll only be there for Jesus to judge the true nature of their hearts. Jesus will review what each believer has done to advance His cause and His glory, because James 2:24-26 teaches us that our faith without our works and deeds is dead. One could surmise that a person without works is a person without faith. The acceptance of Jesus through faith will get you into heaven, but the works and deeds done on earth in His behalf will give you rewards beyond belief.

9.   Ever wonder what will become of earth? The world news reports that because of nuclear weapons and global warming, or due to a virus or shortage of safe drinking water, that earth may eventually be void of all life. That would be catastrophic, but let's see what the Bible says about it. We were all created from a single cell to develop into all we can be before returning to dust, and the Bible tells us a similar fate awaits planet earth. Anything created can return to where it all began, which was from God. Just as Noah and the great flood cleansed a world full of sin, the Bible tells us our world will be cleansed again following a period of horrific worldwide immorality and devastation. That's the future of planet earth, told in II Peter 3:10. When Tribulation and the Day of the Lord comes, the heavens will pass away and the elements will melt away, including earth. Then, according to Revelation 21:1-2, there'll be a new heaven and earth. A new Jerusalem will come down from God to the new earth, where all Christians will dwell with Him. So the future of earth has been foretold, and like everything else that's ever happened since time began, it's in the hands of God.

10.   There are three times in the Bible when Jesus wept. In Luke 19:41, Jesus wept over the city of Jerusalem and it's Temple because neither had fulfilled their purpose to Him. In John 11:33-35, Jesus wept after seeing Mary cry over the death of her brother Lazarus. In Hebrews 5:7-9, Jesus shed tears that God would save Him from death. He knew He'd die, but He wanted His resurrection to be proof that we can all "die but live again" if we accept Him as Savior and receive God's eternal salvation.

11.   We serve a God who always loves us, but we should keep in mind that God's love can be either unconditional or conditional. His unconditional love is willingly and bountifully given to us due to His compassion, mercy and grace. There's no strings attached and it's given even if we're unworthy to receive it. On the other hand, God's conditional love is exactly what it says because a condition or action is required of us before we can receive His gift, promise or reward. Those two terms are not expressly defined in the Bible, but He gives us many examples. The simplest conditional promise might be in John 14:14, when Jesus says "IF ye shall ask any thing in my name, I will do it." He's telling us that if we don't ask it in His name, then it may not happen. Then in Psalm 37:4, we're told IF we delight ourselves in the Lord He will give us our desires. In other words, if we want what we desire, then we'd better delight ourselves in the Lord. And even God's gift of salvation is conditional, because Jesus states in Mark 1:15 that IF we want to be in the Kingdom of God then we must repent and believe. So if we don't repent and believe, we won't be in God's Kingdom. We must know which gifts from God are conditional based on our actions and decisions. If Christians meet God's requirements and conditions they'll receive many gifts and blessings.

12.   Paul reminds us in Galatians 3:11-13 that we are not saved by following the law of the Ten Commandments. We are saved by believing through faith that Jesus died on the cross for us, and that He was buried but rose again to ascend into heaven to sit by His Father. If we don't accept Jesus as our Savior after He died for us then His death was all in vain, as told in Galatians 2:21. Without the

cross and the blood of Jesus, there is no path into heaven. We must follow the Commandments and accept Jesus into our lives.

13.   Christians must beware of anyone who boasts of talking to spirits or seeing into the future. Many Bible verses warn us of those persons and activities. Leviticus 19:31 tells us to turn away from medium or wizardry, and Revelation 21:8 states that sorcerers and idolaters will burn in the lake of fire. We're told in Matthew 24:24 that false prophets who claim they can see into the future will perform great signs and wonders to lead us astray. The only reliable source for our future is the Bible. James 1:5 says to ask God for wisdom and He'll give it liberally. It'll be given when God knows the time is right, which isn't always when you're expecting it. God knows what His children need and He'll always provide it.

14.   Life can be hard, and no one escapes the worry and strain of everyday challenges. We live in a sinful world with endless temptations. But in I Corinthians 10:13, Paul gives all Christians the ultimate comforting message. He reminds us of God's faithfulness and that God will ensure that we never struggle and suffer with a temptation more than we can stand, and that He'll always give us a way to escape our temptations and the pressures they bring. It is extremely impactful and uplifting to know that God has each of our backs now and forever more. And then when He calls us home, as written in Revelations 7:16-17, He'll lead us unto fountains of living waters and wipe away all of our tears.

15.   After Judas betrayed Jesus and died, only 11 apostles remained. A good trivia question is: who replaced Judas to bring their number back to 12. In Acts 1:22-26, both Joseph (also called Barsabas) and Matthias were considered. Lots were drawn and Matthias was chosen to become the newest and twelfth apostle.

16.   You don't hear much anymore about people speaking in tongues. The Bible tells us in I Corinthians 14:27-33 that if any man speaks in an unknown tongue, there should be at least one person there who can interpret what was spoken. If no one can, maybe it wasn't a message from God at all but a false teacher acting as though he or she has a direct link to God. Speaking in tongues is a spiritual gift that'll be understood by those who God intended to hear it. In Acts 2:1-8, it says speaking in tongues is a gift from the Holy Spirit that allows the word of God to be understood without any language barriers to prohibit it. God will speak to us if we'll just listen, and He'll make sure we understand Him.

17.   Everyone sins and must ask God for forgiveness, but be aware that there's one unpardonable sin that God will not forgive. Matthew 12:31-32 and Mark 3:29 warns that any blasphemy against the Holy Ghost will not be forgiven. God's Spirit is not an "it", He's masculine because He is God (John 16:7-8) and must not be repudiated because He is there to offer us a new life with Jesus. No one should ever refuse God's Spirit.

18.   Will our self-righteousness earn our way into heaven? Some will attend church regularly, donate to the poor, visit the afflicted and watch after the elderly. They'll sing in the church choir and honor their father and mother in hopes that it brings them salvation. Those actions won't bring salvation; they're the results of salvation. The only path into heaven is through the blood of Jesus. Once you

accept Him, you will do those things and more. The Holy Spirit inside you will see to it. The fruits of salvation are given in Galatians 5:22-26, and those around us will know when we have them.

19.   When we read the story of Jonah being swallowed by a whale and being vomited back up after three days, it's something we might think would be impossible. But once Jesus tells the same story Himself in Matthew 12:38-40, there remains no doubt about the validity of that biblical record as to what it means or represents to mankind. If it weren't true or an appropriate example of God's love, Jesus wouldn't have referenced it. Among other things, that story tells us that no matter how much we run from God and turn our backs to Him, He'll still love us and take us back as His own.

20.   The Bible tell us that Jesus can come at any time and rapture those who've been saved, first those who've died then those who are alive. Although no one really knows the exact day or hour that He'll come, most Bible scholars feel this will be prior to Tribulation. Jesus tells us in Matthew 24:36 and again in Matthew 24:42 that only God knows when that'll happen. Then Jesus tells us beginning in Matthew 24:3 that many will come to deceive mankind by saying they're the real Christ, and there'll be earthquakes and famines, and false prophets will rise up, and nations will rise against nations. After this Tribulation period is over, Jesus will pronounce judgement on each of us and also on Satan. We'll all be judged based on how we've lived our lives. Christians will be with Christ during a one thousand year reign. Then Jesus will return for a period of victory and restoration, His second coming, bringing a new heaven and earth with Him. We're told of these events in book of Revelation and in Daniel chapter 12. So no one knows when Jesus will come, but we need to be ready to meet our Lord and Savior.

21.   One of the main reasons Jesus came to earth was for restoration, to realign mankind for acceptance into the Kingdom of God if we'd accept Him and follow His teachings. The forgiveness of our sins and the restoring of our faith is more important to Him than the physical healings or other miracles He could perform. A great example of that is found in Mark 2:1-12, when a man was brought to Jesus by his friends to be healed of palsy. Jesus knew he was there to be healed, but that wasn't what He did. The first thing Jesus did was to forgive this man of his sins even before addressing his illness. Why was that, when the man was brought there only to be healed? Well, Jesus knew He could give this man perfect health, but what good would it do a person to be healed of their illness but not of their sins? A healthy sinner is on a path to hell. To enter the Kingdom of God we must be forgiven of our sins, and as always Jesus is more concerned with our souls than our health. When you pray, you should first praise and thank God for all He is and all He does for you. Then, with a true repentant heart, always ask Him to forgive your sins. Also pray for the things you need and for the needs of others, if it would be His will. Then ask for the courage you need to get through your day.

22.   When we accept Jesus into our life and become a Christian, we immediately receive His Holy Spirit. It gives us self-discipline and a deeper care for others, because when God seals His Spirit within us (II Corinthians 1:22), we are anointed

with a more spiritual nature. This transformation within us is instant, but the growth and understanding of what it means to be a Christian and knowing how to spread God's message of love is a process that takes time. Just as a newborn receives milk to begin their growth and nourishment, a new member into the body of Christ must grow and develop the same way. As we're told in I Peter 2:2, just as babes we should desire the sincere milk of the word that we may grow. Then in Hebrews 5:12, it says we need to be taught the principles of God as we continue to need milk for growth, since we're not yet ready for strong meat. The growth of a Christian is continuous, because the depth of power and energy coming from God to each believer through His Holy Spirit has no end. We grow by reading His word, developing friendships with other Christians, doing works and deeds in His name, and by praying for God to show us His plan in our lives.

23. In Luke 15:4-10, Jesus expresses the joy and jubilation of finding and saving just one more person who'll repent and join the Body of Christ. He explains it by saying that out of 100 sheep only 1 may be lost, but a shepherd will leave the 99 sheep to stray in the field while he searches for the one who's lost. These 99 sheep don't feel lost because they have someone to protect and guide them. They know they'll never be forgotten or abandoned by the one they trust and follow. But, the 1 sheep who's not with the others knows without a doubt that he's lost. He's hopelessly wandering and needing to be found, cared for and saved. So when he's found it's time for joy and celebration. And so it is with us. Jesus will save us once we realize we're lost, and with joy He'll add us to his flock. He's always searching and patiently waiting for another lost soul to bring into the Kingdom of God, and when He does we're saved. Not just once, because when we first accepted Him <u>we were saved</u>. Today, <u>we are saved</u>, and at final judgement when the sinners and Christians are separated, <u>we'll be saved</u> from torment. Until He comes we must spend our lives loving one another and helping those less fortunate. We should aways remember that **when we get to heaven and we're standing before Jesus, we won't be rewarded for what we've got and accumulated but for what we've given**. There are many things we can do in life to please God. Among them are giving to those less fortunate than ourselves.

www.ingramcontent.com/pod-product-compliance
Lightning Source LLC
Chambersburg PA
CBHW080531090426
42733CB00015B/2552